The Do-It-Yourself Handbook for Keyboard Playing

From the Editors of Sheet Music Magazine
and Keyboard Classics Magazine

Compiled & Edited by

Edward J. Shanaphy

Joseph L. Knowlton

Contributing Editors

Katie Basquin
David Berger
John Browning
Raphael Crystal
Debbie Culbertson
Robert Dumm
May Etts
Ruth Price Farrar
David Hegarty
Ronald Herder
Judy Hobbs
Bill Horn
Jeane Huls
Stuart Isacoff

Byron Janis
David Kopp
Ruth Laredo
Mark Laub
Fran Linhart
Marcia Menter
George Nixon
Santiago Rodriquez
Mary Rundell
Edward Shanaphy
John Steinway
Lesley Valdes
Anatole Zemlinsky

Library of Congress Catalog Card Number 82-60298

Table Of Contents

TECHNIQUE

RHYTHM

Continued on next page

Table Of Contents

THE CLASSICS

ORGAN TECHNIQUE AND STYLES

SPECIAL FEATURES

CHORDS, HARMONY & THEORY

SCALES, KEYS, AND INTERVALS

keyboard theory

by Raphael Crystal

Some of our readers have requested that we devote some space to a review of basic music theory. We hope that those of you for whom this is a bit too elementary will bear with us during this brief but important discussion of scales, keys, and intervals.

Let us begin by looking at the keyboard. You can see that the white notes are not spaced equally. In some cases there is a black note between two adjacent white notes; in others there is nothing separating them. The shortest distance, or "interval," between two notes is called a

"half step." This is the interval from C to C#, or from C# to D. There are two pairs of white notes that are only a half step apart: B-C and E-F. The next interval in size is the "whole step," which consists of two half steps. The interval from C to D is a whole step, since it is made up of the two half steps C-C# and C#-D. The other whole steps between white notes are D-E, F-G, G-A, and A-B. Notice that the note a whole step above E would be F#, and the note a whole step above B would be C#.

As you probably know, we can play the major scale on the white notes by beginning on any C and proceeding up to the C an octave higher. The sound of this scale is familiar to everyone, and you may have assumed that all of the notes are equidistant. From the discussion above, however, it is clear that the major scale has a particular pattern: if

we number the notes of the scale from 1 to 8, there are half steps between notes 3 and 4 and between notes 7 and 8. All of the other notes are a whole step apart. (In our example the letters "Wh" stand for a whole step, and "H" stands for a half step.)

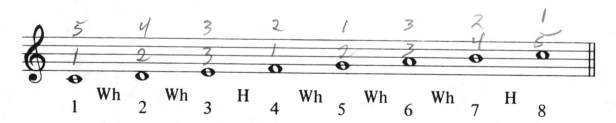

Suppose we want to start the major scale on the note G. If you play only white notes starting on G the scale will sound wrong. You will probably hear that the note which sounds "off" is the F, the seventh note of the scale. If we raise this note to F# the scale has its proper sound. Looking

at the intervals, we can see why this is so. The F# creates a half step between notes 7 and 8, which is required by the major scale pattern. It also creates the necessary whole step between notes 6 and 7.

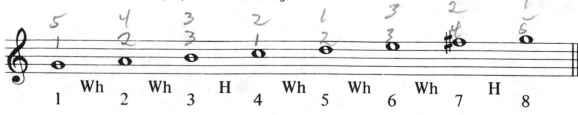

Now let us start the scale on the note F. Once again, your ear will probably tell you that the white notes alone do not produce the right sound. Here the "wrong" note is B, which must be lowered to B♭. This will produce the correct interval pattern: between notes 3 and 4 there will be a half step, A-B♭, and between notes 4 and 5 there will be a whole step, B♭-C.

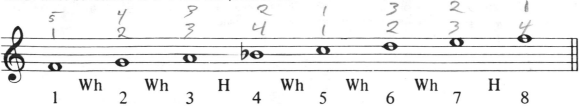

At this point you might well ask: what is the importance of the scale? It is not, after all, a piece of music itself. But the scale is a repertoire of notes, from which most of the tunes we know are drawn. When we say that a tune is in a certain "key" we mean that it makes use of the notes of that scale. A tune in C major would make use, primarily, of the notes of the C major scale.

In our next example, line a) shows the tune *Yankee Doodle* in the key of C. (You can tell the key of a tune by its final note: this is almost always the first note of the scale, or the "keynote." *Yankee Doodle* also begins on that note, but many tunes do not.) Notice that here only white notes are used, the notes of the C major scale. Line b) shows the same tune beginning and ending on the note G. Here it is necessary to use an F#. Try playing this line using only white notes, and you will see that the F natural sounds wrong. Line c) shows the tune in the key of F, and here a B♭ is necessary. In each case, the melody makes use of the appropriate major scale.

When we played *Yankee Doodle* in the key of G it was necessary to sharp the F each time it occurred. Ordinarily the sharps or flats used in a key are grouped into a "key signature" which is placed at the beginning of each line of music. These sharps or flats will apply throughout the piece, unless of course they are cancelled in a particular bar by a natural sign.

The example below shows the key signatures for all of the commonly used "sharp keys." We are already familiar with the key of G, where the seventh note of the scale is raised by using an F#. The key signatures are arranged so that in every case the last sharp in the signature — that is, the sharp on the right — is the seventh note of the scale. This makes it easy to find the key. If the last sharp is "7," the note above it will be "8," which is the keynote. For example, when there are two sharps in the signature the last sharp is C#; the note above this is D, which gives us the key. When there are three sharps the last sharp is G#; one note above we find the keynote, which is A.

G maj.   D maj.   A maj.   E maj.   B maj.   F# maj.   C# maj.

Continued on next page

The "flat keys" have a similar pattern. In the key of F, as we have seen, the fourth note of the scale is flatted, giving us a B♭ in the key signature. In every flat key the last flat of signature is the fourth note of the scale, There is, however, an easier way to find the key. When there is more than one flat in the signature, the next to last flat (that is, the second flat from the right) is itself the keynote. With two flats in the signature the second flat from the right is B♭, and the key is B♭ major. With three flats in the signature the second flat from the right is E♭, and the key is E♭ major.

F maj.   B♭ maj.   E♭ maj.   A♭ maj.   D♭ maj.   G♭ maj.   C♭ maj.

It is useful to be able to refer to all of the different intervals between notes by name. Let us first consider only the notes of the C major scale. In every case the name of the interval will be derived from the number of *letters* it involves. The interval from C to D is known as a "second" because it spans two letters — C and D. C to E is a "third" because three letters are involved — C, D, and E. C to F is a "fourth," C to G a "fifth," C to A a "sixth," C to B a "seventh," and C to C is an "octave."

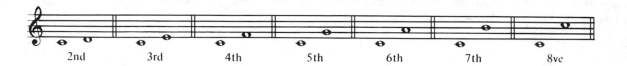

2nd   3rd   4th   5th   6th   7th   8ve

To fully describe the intervals, however, some additional information is needed, in order to take account of the flats and sharps. For this reason the interval C-D is called a "major second" and the smaller interval C-D♭ is called a "minor second." Likewise C-E is a "major third" and C-E♭ is a "minor third." C-F, for acoustical reasons, is called a "perfect fourth," while C-F# is an "augmented fourth." Similarly C-G is a "perfect fifth," while C-G♭ is a "diminished fifth" and C-G# is an "augmented fifth." C-A is a "major sixth" while C-A♭ is a "minor sixth," C-B is a "major seventh" while C-B♭ is a "minor seventh," and C-C is known as a "perfect octave."

min. 2nd   maj. 2nd   min. 3rd   maj. 3rd   perf. 4th   aug. 4th   dim. 5th

perf. 5th   aug. 5th   min. 6th   maj. 6th   min. 7th   maj. 7th   perf. 8ve

We can construct any interval starting on any note. One way to do this is by referring to the major scale. We know that the scale includes a major second, major third, perfect fourth, perfect fifth, major sixth, and major seventh. Suppose that you want to find the minor sixth above E♭. You would begin by thinking of the E♭ major scale. The sixth note of the scale is C; that would be the *major* sixth above E♭. To form a *minor* sixth the C should be lowered to C♭. (Not to B however. Remember the principle of counting by letter names! E♭-B would be an augmented fifth.)

E♭ maj. 1   2   3   4   5   6   7   8   maj. 6th   min. 6th

Sometimes it is easier to form the intervals by measuring them off by half steps. The major seventh is simple to construct because it is just one half step less than an octave. The minor seventh is two half steps less than octave. This method also works well for small intervals. The minor third consists of three half steps (e.g. C-C#, C#-D, and D-E$^\flat$) and the major third consists of four.

8ve   maj. 7th   8ve   min. 7th   min. 3rd   maj. 3rd

Thirds are particularly important because chords are built up in thirds. The simple major chord, for example, consists of a major third and, on top of that, a minor third. Thus, to construct a major chord on the note E we could count up four half steps and arrive at G#, the major third. Then we could count up another three half steps to B, in order to add a minor third on top. The resulting chord has the notes E, G#, and B.

maj. 3rd   +   min. 3rd   =   Emaj. chord

With the subject of chords we have come to the end of the "basics" and reached the beginning of the study of harmony. If you have understood and absorbed everything in this article you should be ready to embark on that study.

basic training

INTERVALS: THE RAW MATERIALS OF ALL CHORDS, Part One

by Ronald Herder

This is the first of a series of articles on the fundamentals of music. We'll be talking about intervals, triads, 7th and 9th chords, altered chords, progressions, and so on — all with the aim of making music a little more understandable, and making your playing and reading a lot more pleasurable!

Everything you're about to do will get you ready to find, play, and read all chords in all keys. To start, you first have to know a few basic *intervals*. An interval is the distance between two pitches. We'll take them one at a time so that you can build up your familiarity with their location on the keyboard and on the music staff. In Part One, we're going to cover the half-step, the whole-step, the minor 3rd, and the major 3rd. In Part Two, we'll go on to different kinds of 5ths and 7ths.

You can cut your learning time in half if you read this at the keyboard and take your time to play through each step.

Learn to find a HALF-STEP on the piano

1. A half-step is the distance between two neighboring piano (or organ) keys. The white keys E-F are neighbors; find them. The white keys B-C are neighbors; find them. All other neighbors consist of a white key and the black key just above it or just below it. For example, C-D♭ are white/black neighbors; find them. A-G# are white/black neighbors; find them.

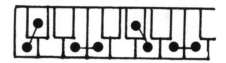

2. A half-step can also go *downward*. Find and play these downward half-steps: B♭-A   C#-C♮   E-E♭

3. Find and play other half-steps, both upward and downward. As you play each half-step, *say* the words "half-step." (This isn't as childish as it seems; it helps focus your concentration.)

Learn to find a WHOLE-STEP on the piano

1. A whole-step consists of *two* half-steps. For example, E-F# is a whole-step. It consists of the half-step E-F, then the half-step F-F#. Take the time to find these two half-steps that make up the whole-step E-F#.

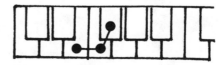

2. Play the whole-step G-A; say the words "whole-step" as you play these two keys. Play the whole-step G#-A#; say "whole-step" as you play.

3. A whole-step may also go downward. Play the downward whole-step E♭-D♭; say "whole-step" as you play.

4. Note that the letter names of the two keys of a whole-step follow the alphabet.

Learn to find a MINOR 3rd on the piano

1. A minor 3rd consists of *three* half-steps. For example, E-G is a minor 3rd. It consists of the half-step E-F, then the half-step F-F#, then the half-step F#-G. Take the time to find these three half-steps that make the minor 3rd E-G.

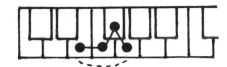

2. Play the minor 3rd F-A♭ . Say the words "minor 3rd" as you play these two keys. Play the minor 3rd C#-E; say "minor 3rd" as you play these two keys.

3. A minor 3rd may also go downward. Play the downward minor 3rd F#-D#. Find and play other downward minor 3rds.

4. Note that the letter names of the two keys of the minor 3rd *skip* a letter of the alphabet: E-(skip F)-G. . .F-(skip G)-A♭ ; and backwards, F#-(skip E)-D#.

Learn to find a MAJOR 3rd on the piano

1. A major 3rd consists of *four* half-steps (or two whole-steps). For example, E-G# is a major 3rd. It consists of the half-step E-F, then the half-step F-F#, then the half-step F#-G, then the half-step G-G#. Take the time to find these four half-steps that make up the major 3rd E-G#.

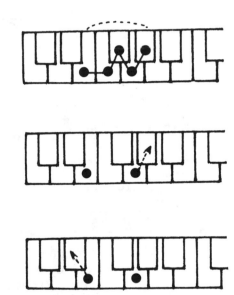

2. The major 3rd is a *half-step larger* than the minor 3rd. You can make the minor 3rd larger by either *raising the top note* or *lowering the bottom note* by one half-step.
   (a) Replay the minor 3rd E-G. Raise the top note, G, a half-step to G#. E-G# is a major 3rd.

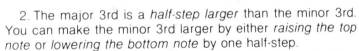

   (b) Replay the minor 3rd E-G. This time, lower the bottom note, E, a half-step to E♭ E♭-G is also a major 3rd.

3. Find and play these minor 3rd/major 3rd changes:
   D-F/D-F#   D-F/D♭-F   G-B♭/G-B   G-B♭/G♭-B♭
As you play these changes, say the words "minor 3rd/major 3rd."

4. A major 3rd may also go downward. Play the downward major 3rd A-F; say "major 3rd" as you play the two keys. Find and play other downward major 3rds.

5. Note that the letter names of the two keys of the major 3rd *skip* a letter of the alphabet: E-(skip F)-G#. . . D-(skip E)-F# . . . and backwards, B♭-(skip A)-G

Continued on next page

Learn to recognize the look of a 3rd on the music staff

A 3rd on the music staff is always written on two neighboring lines, or on two neighboring spaces. All of the following intervals are 3rds, *regardless of the accidentals in front of them.* (It is the accidentals that make them either major 3rds or minor 3rds.)

A

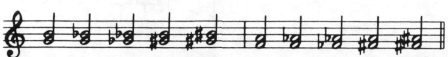

READING/PLAYING DRILLS

B 1. Read and play a series of minor 3rds:

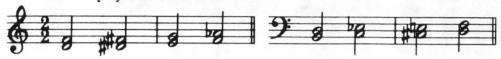

C 2. Read and play a series of major 3rds:

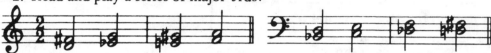

D 3. Go from a minor to a major 3rd:

E 4. Go from a major 3rd to a minor 3rd:

5. This series contains both minor and major 3rds. First play them. Then identify each one by marking either "m3" (minor 3rd) or "M3" (major 3rd) under the interval. Remember that "m3" will always consist of *three* half-steps; and "M3" will always consist of *four* half-steps.

F

HOW TO FINGER 3RDS

The following are traditional fingerings for 3rds that move in a scale-wise pattern.

G

12

INTERVALS: THE RAW MATERIALS OF ALL CHORDS, Part 2

Everything you're about to do will get you ready to find, play, and read all chords in all keys. If you missed Part One of this series, check it out as the first step of basic training. Its contents, plus this discussion of 5ths, will give you the raw materials you'll need to handle chords of all kinds.

Remember that you can cut your learning time in half if you read this at the piano, and take your time to play through each step.

Learn to find a PERFECT 5TH *on the piano*

1. A perfect 5th consists of *seven* half-steps between the bottom note and the top note of this interval. For example, C-G is a perfect 5th. It consists of these seven half-steps: C-C#, then C#-D, then D-D#, then D#E, then E-F, then F-F#, then F#-G. Take the time to find these seven half-steps that make the perfect 5th C-G:

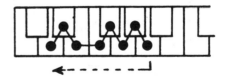

2. Find and play the perfect 5th E♭-B♭. Starting on the bottom note, E♭, count up the seven half-steps to the top note, B♭.

3. Find and play these and other perfect 5ths:

A-E   E-B   C#-G#

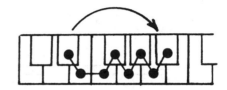

Use the same procedure of counting up seven half-steps from the bottom note. As you find and play each perfect 5th, say the words "perfect 5th." Saying the words is a device to help your concentration.

4. Note that the letter names of the two keys of the perfect 5th always *skip three letters* of the alphabet: C—(skip D, E, F)—G . . . E♭—(skip F, G, A)—B♭.

5. Also practice figuring out a perfect 5th *downward from the top note* of the interval. For example, play the downward perfect 5th A-D. This time count the seven half-steps downward from the top note A:

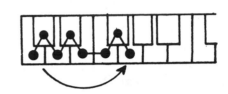

Learn to find a DIMINISHED 5TH *on the piano*

1. A diminished 5th is also called a "flatted 5th."
2. A diminished 5th consists of *six* half-steps between the bottom note and the top note of this interval. For example, C-G is a diminished 5th. It consists of these six half-steps: C-C#, then C#-D, then D-D#, then D#-E, then E-F, then F-G . Take the time to find these six half-steps that make the diminished 5th C-G♭:

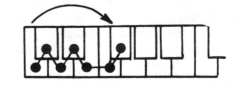

3. Find and play these and other diminished 5ths:

A-E♭   E-B♭   C#-G

Continued on next page

Use the same procedure of counting up six half-steps from the bottom note. As you find and play each diminished 5th, say the words "diminished 5th."

4. *This next item is important; read it carefully and play through the examples.* A diminished or flatted 5th is *a half-step smaller* than the perfect 5th. This means that you can change a perfect 5th into a diminished 5th by (a) *lowering the top note,* or (b) *raising the bottom note* by one half-step. Either way you are diminishing (reducing) the distance between the two notes of the interval.

(a) Replay the perfect 5th C-G. Lower the top note, G, a half-step to G♭. C-G♭ is a diminished 5th.

(b) Replay the perfect 5th C-G. This time raise the bottom note, C, a half-step to C#. C#-G is also a diminished 5th. Check this out by finding the six half-steps between C# and G.

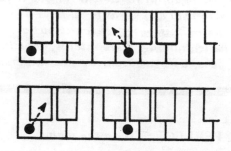

5. Find and play these and other perfect 5th/diminished 5th changes: D-A/D-A♭   D-A/D#-A   E♭-B♭/E♭-B♭♭   E♭-B♭/E-B♭ (B♭♭ is the same as the piano key A.) As you play these changes, say the words "perfect 5th/diminished 5th."

6. Note that the letter names of the two keys of the diminished 5th, like those of the perfect 5th, always *skip three letters* of the alphabet: C-(D, E, F)-G♭ . . . E-(F, G, A)-B♭.

7. Also practice figuring out a diminished 5th *downward from the top note* of the interval. For example, play the downward diminished 5th A♭-D. This time count the six half-steps downward from the top note A♭:

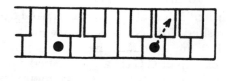

Learn to find an AUGMENTED 5TH *on the piano*

1. An augmented 5th is also called a "raised 5th."

2. An augmented 5th consists of *eight* half-steps between the bottom note and the top note of this interval. For example, C-G# is an augmented 5th. It consists of these eight half-steps: C-C#, then C#-D, then D-D#, then D#-E, then E-F, then F-F#, then F#-G, then G-G#. Take the time to find these eight half-steps that make the augmented 5th C-G#:

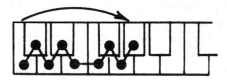

3. Find and play these and other augmented 5ths: D♭-A   F-C#   B♭-F#

4. *Important:* An augmented or raised 5th is *a half-step larger* than the perfect 5th. This means that you can change a perfect 5th into an augmented 5th by (a) *raising the top note,* or (b) *lowering the bottom note* by one half-step. Either way you are augmenting (increasing) the distance between the two notes of the interval.

(a) Replay the perfect 5th C-G. Raise the top note, G, a half-step to G#. C-G# is an augmented 5th.

(b) Replay the perfect 5th C-G. This time lower the bottom note, C, a half-step to C♭. C♭-G is also an augmented 5th. Check this out by finding the eight half-steps between C♭ and G.

Use the same procedure of counting up eight half-steps from the bottom note. As you find and play each augmented 5th, say the words "augmented 5th ."

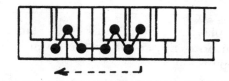

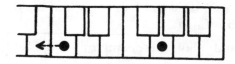

5. Find and play these and other perfect 5th/augmented 5th changes: D-A/D-A#   D-A/Db-A   G-D/G-D#   G-D/Gb-D

(Note that a sharp becomes a *double*-sharp when it is augmented: for example, the perfect 5th F#-C# augments to F#-C✗. C✗ is the same as the piano key D.) As you play these changes, say the words "perfect 5th/augmented 5th."

6. The letter names of the two keys of the augmented 5th — like those of both the perfect 5th and the diminished 5th — always skip three letters of the alphabet: C-(D, E, F)—G#, and so on.

7. Also practice figuring out an augmented 5th *downward from the top note* of the interval. For example, play the downward augmented 5th C#-F. This time count the eight half-steps downward from the top note C#:

Learn to recognize the look of a 5th on the music staff

A 5th on the music staff is always written on two lines with an empty line between, or on two spaces with an empty space between. All of the following are 5ths, *regardless of the accidentals in front of them.* (It is the accidentals that make them perfect, diminished, or augmented.)

Reading/Playing Drills

1. Read and play a series of perfect 5ths:

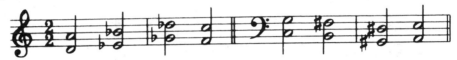

2. Read and play a series of diminished 5ths:

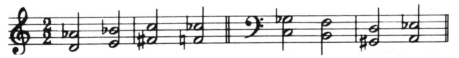

3. Read and play a series of augmented 5ths:

4. Go from a perfect 5th to a diminished 5th:

5. Go from a perfect 5th to an augmented 5th:

6. Read and play the series: dim.5/perf.5/aug.5:

LEARNING YOUR CHORDS

by Ed Shanaphy

The purpose of this article is to teach, from the very beginning, how chords are formed, how they are spelled, and how they are used in the performance of music.

If you are a very beginner to chord playing, or wouldn't even know a chord if it stared you in the face, this is primarily for you. It is important that you study this at a very slow pace, step by step. Do not try to rush through all the material and examples in a few short sittings. Rather, go slowly enough to let it all sink in. (You more advanced chord players can move along more rapidly through the basics, right on into the sections on added tones and voicings.)

THE BASIC CHORD DICTIONARY

As part of this article, we have created a basic chord dictionary (see page *18*), which has every three-note chord in every key. On top of each chord is a chord symbol such as "Am", "F#+", etc. Eventually, you will have to know all of these chords from memory; that is, when you are shown a symbol such as "Fm", you will know that this is an F minor chord, and you will be able to play it instantly.

The Basic Chord Dictionary starts with the key of A Major, and progresses through each key (read the very left column down vertically for all the key names.)

For each key we have supplied the simple major scale, numbering all the tones in the scale. In order to understand chords, you must have a working knowledge of scales. Therefore, we have them there as a point of reference. If you already know them, so much the better.

A chord is made up of a minimum of three notes. There are four-note chords, five- and six-note chords too. But the basic chord is three notes, called a *triad*. (A two-note chord is not theoretically a chord. It is an interval.) A triad (basic chord) is made up of the first, third and fifth tones of the scale. (See the brackets under the scales in our Basic Chord Dictionary. They point to the 1st, 3rd and 5th tones.) Therefore, to find an F chord, we go to the scale of F and select only the 1st note (F), the third note (A), and the fifth note (C) of that scale.

Those notes comprise a complete F major chord.

Exercise: Play each scale as written in our Basic Scale Dictionary. Find the 1st, 3rd and 5th tones of each scale. Be sure to do this in all twelve keys. Play all the major triads in the Basic Chord Dictionary (second column). Play them again with the left hand only.

MAJOR VS. MINOR

As we have seen, a major chord uses the scale tones exactly as they appear in the major scale. That is, the 1st, 3rd and 5th tones are lifted from the major scale with no altering. Once we alter any of those chord tones, that is make them sharper or flatter, we create a different *kind* of chord. For example, an A Major chord has a C# (the 3rd). If we alter that down to a C natural, we create an A minor chord. (Altering a tone downward by one-half step like this is called a flatted tone.)

RULE: To change a major chord to minor, use a flatted 3rd (or, lower the 3rd one half-tone.)

Exercise: Play column #2 again, but after you strike the major chord, lower the 3rd one half-tone to the very next note and strike the chord again as a minor triad. Repeat with the left hand separately.

NOTE: TRY TO MEMORIZE AS MUCH AS YOU CAN AS YOU GO ALONG.

At this point, we recommend that you not go on any further for a few days. Review on a daily basis what we have discussed and memorize all your major and minor chords in the order that they appear in the dictionary. Play them down vertically: A, D, G, C, F, etc. You will eventually know the next chord down because it is always a fifth below the one you are playing. For example, you are playing the C chord. A fifth below C, or five notes down, is F. That's your next chord. Learn them in the order they appear in the dictionary. This is a "cycle of fifths" progression which is going to become very important to you, especially for playing by ear.

* * * * *

THE DIMINISHED CHORD GOES TO THE MOVIES!

Years ago, during the era of silent movies, every movie theatre had a pianist who would improvise live music to accompany the action on the screen. Many great musicians earned their way through school doing this. Dmitri Shostakovich, the great Russian composer, for example, wore his fingers to the bone in the local movie houses providing music for the Russian versions of *The Perils Of Pauline*. The one chord, more than any other, which was used to distraction by these pianists was the diminished chord. When a diminished chord crashed down, you immediately knew that danger was imminent. And for the chase scenes, a series of diminished chords tremeloed by the right hand, while the left played ominous octaves, was the typical accompaniment.

You can go on endlessly, changing from one diminished chord to the next, until the chase scene is over.

Why do we bring you this piece of musical trivia, you may ask. Simple. It is a way of reminding you of what a diminished chord sounds like. As soon as you hear one, you'll remember Pauline's Perils and think...*aha! a diminished chord!* As you learn chords, you must also recognize their particular sound. And whatever "crutch" you need to help you recognize them is fine.

Take a look at our Basic Chord Dictionary. The third column titled **Diminished.** Can you analyze what has happened to our original major chord by way of alteration that gives us a diminished chord? For the minor chord we flatted the third. For the diminished we flat both the third and fifth. A dixieland musician was once asked to describe the difference between modern jazz and dixieland jazz. He said, "The modern jazz men flatten their fifths, we dixieland boys drink 'em!"

RULE: To play a diminished chord, flat both the 3rd and 5th of the basic major triad.

Exercise: Play each major chord in the Dictionary, starting from the top. Flat the third to create the minor chord and play the minor. Flat the 5th in addition to the third to create the diminished. Go on to each succeeding chord and do likewise. Try to commit whatever you can to memory, but do not get bogged down with memorizing.

THE AUGMENTED CHORD

Forming an augmented chord is simple. It is a major chord with a raised, or sharped, 5th. 99% of the time an augmented chord will lead to a chord whose root is a perfect fifth below. For example, a C augmented chord leads to an F chord. A G augmented chord leads to a C chord.

RULE: To form an augmented chord, simply raise the 5th of a major chord one half-tone.

Exercise: Play all the chords in the Basic Chord Dictionary, major, minor, diminished and augmented. Memorize the rules of forming them and try to play all the chords from memory.

At this point you should review and practice what you have learned for a few days. Let it all sink in. Play the chords with both hands separately and together.

* * * * *

RECOGNIZING CHORDS BY EAR

Now that you have a good working knowledge of chords, it's time to start training your ear to recognize each type: major, minor, diminished, augmented. The best way to do this is with a tape recorder. Turn on your tape recorder and record 10 different major chords from the chord dictionary. Pick them at random. Do the same for the minor, select 10 at random and record them. Same for diminished. Same for augmented.

Now record a random selection of about thirty chords, augmented, diminished, minor, major, etc. Mix them up well. You might even want to record more than thirty. After striking each chord, wait two seconds and then recite into the microphone what type it was: Major, minor, etc. In this way, when you play them back you will have time to guess the type of chord you just heard before the tape recorder tells you. Use your tape recording of these chords until you are absolutely certain that you can recognize all four types by sound. Now make another recording of random chords and see how you do. You should be batting 1.000 by now.

There is no doubt about it, you are now a chord musician who has a pretty good ear for chords. There is still much more to learn, but you are on your way to becoming someone who will be able to play by ear!

VOICING CHORDS AT THE KEYBOARD

To get a good sound from triads, (three-note chords), there are a few simple rules to follow. We will now ask you to refer to the examples called "Voicing Triads"

First of all, if a major or minor chord is in root position, that is a chord which has its root in the bass (a C chord with C in the bass, or a D chord with D in the bass, etc.), the left hand can voice three ways: it can play an octave; a 5th, or a 10th (if your hand can reach; if it can't reach you can "break" the 10th). Take a look at the examples #'s 1, 2, and 3.

Also, a good clean sound is achieved by not doubling the 3rd of a chord. For example, in a C chord, the 3rd, which is an E, should only appear once. Look at those examples again and notice that the third of the chord only appears one time in each chord.

The only exception to this rule is if the third is the melody note. Then you may double it. In fact, it sounds good if you double it. See example #4.

Please note that we have said that you use this rule to achieve a clean, open type of sound. For a big sound where each hand is crashing down on four notes or more, this doubling rule goes out the window.

Exercise: Pick out some major and minor chords and voice them for two hands in root position. Use the root of the chord in the melody, then the third in the melody, then the fifth. Obey the doubling rule, and use the three different left hand voicings we have discussed.

Why not record some of these voicings at random and see if you can recognize the majors from the minors? Also see if you can hear the top note (melody note). Is it the root, 3rd, or 5th?

When you use a chord tone in the bass which is not the root, you are inverting the chord, turning it upside down. When the third is in the bass it is called *1st inversion*, when the 5th is in the bass it is called *2nd inversion*. The best thing to do when voicing these inversions is to play an octave with the left hand. It sort of reinforces the inverted sound. But you may also use any other interval voicing for the left hand. The doubling rule for the 3rd still applies. (Playing an octave with the left hand does not qualify as a doubling.)

See the examples on inversions.

DRESSING UP YOUR CHORDS WITH ADDED TONES

Now that we have a basic working knowledge of triads, let's go on to getting a more 'pop' sound out of our major and minor chords. This is accomplished by adding tones to the basic three tones found in each chord.

The first tone we will add is the 6th. Go back to your scales in the Basic Chord Dictionary and find the 6th tone of the scale. That's the tone we will add to our major and minor chords. On page *20* we have created The 6th and 6/9 Chord Dictionary.

It shows you your major chord with 6th added, your minor chord with 6th added, and then shows you the major and minor chords with both 6th and 9th added.

The chord symbols used for each would look like this: C6, G6, Ab6, etc. (This means you play a basic major triad with an added 6th.) Cm6, Gm6, Abm6, etc. (The basic minor triad with an added 6th.) C6/9, G6/9, Ab6/9, etc. (This is the basic major triad with the 6th tone added PLUS the 9th scale tone added.)

Let us stop for a second. There's no 9th tone in our scales. Our scales stop at eight. But if there were a 9th tone what would you guess it would be? The answer is that it is actually the 2nd tone, renamed 9th. Rather than explain it, we will ask you to just accept it for now. The explanation will come later.

Exercise: Play all your major triads adding the 6th tone. Try to figure them out by using the scale method. Review the 6th chords in the 6 Chord Dictionary. Do the same with the minors. Play them with each hand separately. Now go on to the voicings on page *23*. Play them and notice how our same voicings rules apply to the left hand and to the doublings.

A 6/9 chord uses both the added 6th together with the added 9th. To find your added 9th for each chord, you refer back to your scales and find the 2nd tone of that scale. That's the 9th! By using these two tones together in a major or minor chord at appropriate times, you will be getting a true modern pop sound.

Continued on page 18

BASIC CHORD DICTIONARY

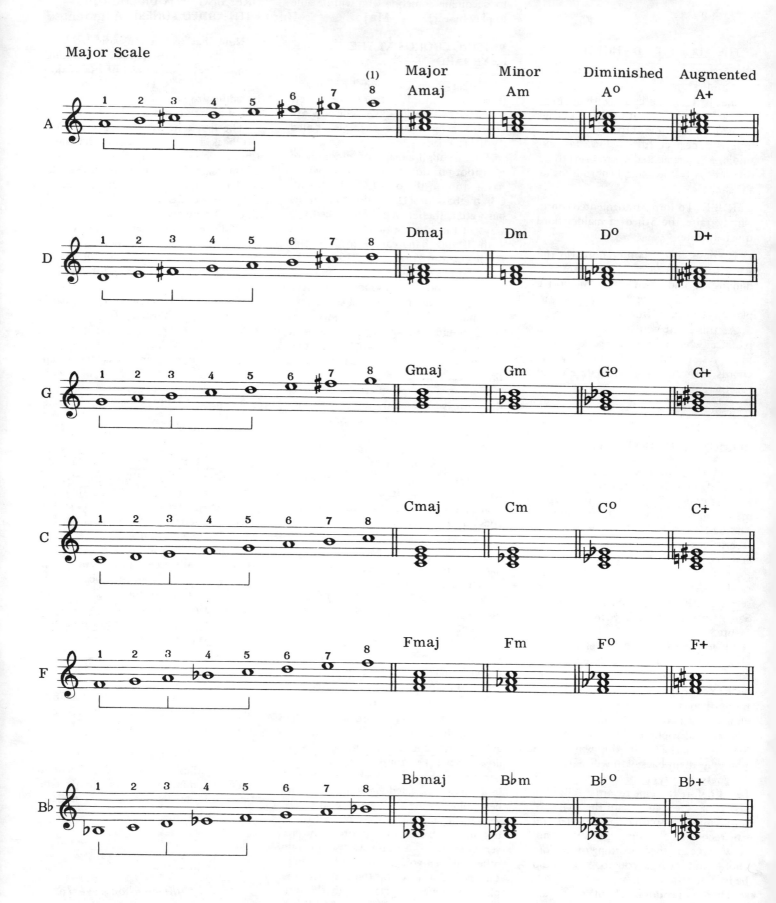

18

19

6th & 6/9 CHORD DICTIONARY

| Major | Minor | Major 6 | Minor 6 | Major 6/9 | Minor 6/9 |

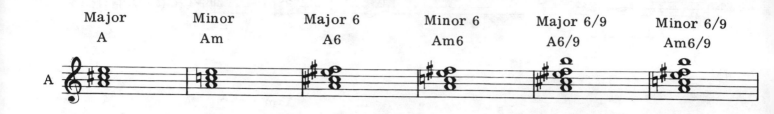

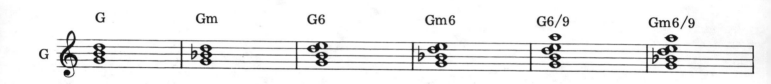

SILENT MOVIE SEQUENCE

"The villian enters"

"Chase scene" ♩ = 140 *(tremolo)*

"Hero getting close"

"Hero destroys villian!"

"Hero and heroine embrace in sunset!"
Slow

"The End"

VOICING CHORDS
VOICING TRIADS

Examples:
#1.   #2.   #3.   #4/

1st Inversion:
Fm   G   G   Bb   Cm   Cm

2nd Inversion:
D   Gm   Eb   Eb   Dm   F

VOICING 6th AND 6/9 CHORDS

Bb6   Bb6   Bb6   Bb6   G6   G6

Bb6/9   C6/9   Gm6/9   F6/9
(No 3rd)

Inversions (6 + 6/9)   Gm6   F6/9   Ab6/9   Fm6/9   C6/9
G6
(No Root)

basic training

by Ronald Herder

Triads: Four Recipes

A triad is a three-note chord. Traditional harmony (in classical, pop, jazz, and rock music) uses four kinds of triads, called <u>major</u>, <u>minor</u>, <u>augmented</u>, and <u>diminished</u>. Each kind of triad has its own ingredients. Once you memorize the ingredients and how to put them together (the recipe), you will be able to build any kind of triad with ease.

Preparation for everything

1. Review the way you locate a *half-step* on the keyboard. A half-step is the distance between any pitch and its closest neighbor. Practice locating the half-steps C-C#. . . E-F . . . and G#-A:

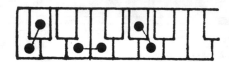

2. Review the way you locate a *minor 3rd* on the keyboard. A minor 3rd consists of *three* half-steps. E-to-G, for example, is a minor 3rd. Count the half-steps: E-F, F-F#, F#-G:

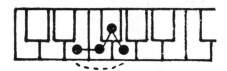

3. Review the way you locate a *major 3rd* on the keyboard. A major 3rd consists of *four* half-steps. E-to-G#, for example, is a major 3rd. Count the half-steps: E-F, F-F#, F#-G, G-G#:

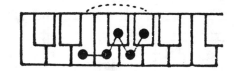

> *Important step:* Practice finding minor and major 3rds all over the keyboard. Begin some on white keys; begin some on black keys. Get used to the look, feel, and sound of minor and major 3rds.

Recipe 1: the MAJOR triad

1. Place your right thumb on middle C, your third finger on E, and your little finger on G. Play the three pitches together:

2. Look at your hand. Look at the *kinds* of 3rds you are playing. C-E is a major 3rd (four half-steps between). E-G is a minor 3rd (three half-steps between).

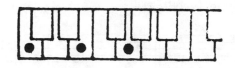

C

3. C-E-G is a **MAJOR** triad *because it contains a major 3rd on the bottom and a minor 3rd on top.*

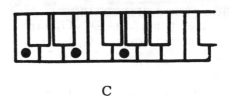

C

4. The abbreviation for this recipe is $\boxed{\begin{array}{l} \text{m3 (minor 3rd)} \\ \text{M3 (major 3rd)} \end{array}}$

5. Use the recipe $\boxed{\begin{array}{l} \text{m3} \\ \text{M3} \end{array}}$ to locate a major triad beginning on D . . .

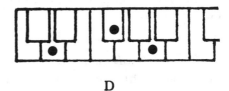

D

6. Use the recipe $\boxed{\begin{array}{l} \text{m3} \\ \text{M3} \end{array}}$ to find major triads built on other pitches.

Recipe 2: the MINOR triad

1. Place your right thumb on middle C, your third finger on E♭, and your little finger on G. Play the three pitches together:

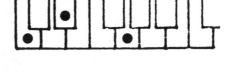

Cm

2. Look at your hand. Look at the kinds of 3rds you are playing. C-E♭ is a minor 3rd (three half-steps). E♭-G is a major 3rd (four half-steps).

3. C-E♭-G is a **MINOR** triad *because it contains a minor 3rd on the bottom and a major 3rd on top.*

4. The abbreviation for this recipe is $\boxed{\begin{array}{l} \text{M3 (major 3rd)} \\ \text{m3 (minor 3rd)} \end{array}}$

5. Use the recipe $\boxed{\begin{array}{l} \text{M3} \\ \text{m3} \end{array}}$ to locate a minor triad beginning on D . . .

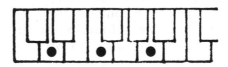

Dm

6. Use the recipe $\boxed{\begin{array}{l} \text{M3} \\ \text{m3} \end{array}}$ to find minor triads built on other pitches.

Recipe 3: the AUGMENTED triad

1. Place your right thumb on middle C, your 3rd finger on E, and your little finger on G#. Play the three pitches together:

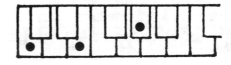

C+

2. Look at the kinds of 3rds you are playing. C-E is a major 3rd (four half-steps). E-G# is also a major 3rd (four half-steps).

3. C-E-G# is an AUGMENTED triad *because it contains a major 3rd on the bottom and another major 3rd on top.*

4. The abbreviation for this recipe is $\boxed{\begin{array}{c}\text{M3}\\\text{M3}\end{array}}$

5. Use the recipe $\boxed{\begin{array}{c}\text{M3}\\\text{M3}\end{array}}$ to locate an augmented triad beginning on D...

6. Use the recipe $\boxed{\begin{array}{c}\text{M3}\\\text{M3}\end{array}}$ to find augmented triads built on other pitches.

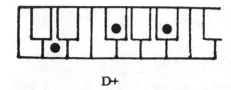

D+

Recipe 4: the DIMINISHED triad

1. Place your right thumb on middle C, your third finger on E♭, and your little finger on G♭. Play the three pitches together:

2. Look at the kinds of thirds you are playing. C-E♭ is a minor 3rd (three half-steps). E♭-G♭ is also a minor 3d (three half-steps).

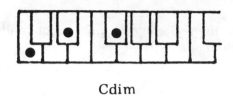

Cdim

3. C-E♭-G♭ is a DIMINISHED triad *because it contains a minor 3rd on the bottom and another minor 3rd on top.*

4. The abbreviation for this recipe is $\boxed{\begin{array}{c}\text{m3}\\\text{m3}\end{array}}$

5. Use the recipe $\boxed{\begin{array}{c}\text{m3}\\\text{m3}\end{array}}$ to locate a diminished triad on D...

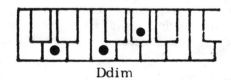

Ddim

Sheet-music symbols for the four kinds of triads

(a) A pitch letter by itself means: "Build a MAJOR triad on this pitch."

(b) A pitch letter followed by "m" means: "Build a MINOR triad on this pitch."

(c) A pitch letter followed by either "dim" or "o" means: "Build a DIMINISHED triad on this pitch."

(d) A pitch letter followed by either "aug" or "+" means: "Build an AUGMENTED triad on this pitch."

The four triads at a glance

$\boxed{\begin{array}{c}\text{m3}\\\text{M3}\end{array}}$	$\boxed{\begin{array}{c}\text{M3}\\\text{m3}\end{array}}$	$\boxed{\begin{array}{c}\text{M3}\\\text{M3}\end{array}}$	$\boxed{\begin{array}{c}\text{m3}\\\text{m3}\end{array}}$
major	minor	augmented	diminished

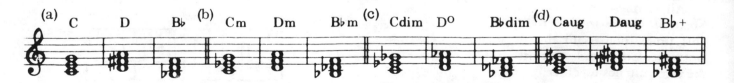

(Notice that all triads are written on three neighboring lines of the staff or on three neighboring spaces.)

Our next Basic Training article will talk about 7th chords. Since all 7th chords are built on triads, get ready by practicing today's lesson until the basic recipes come into your fingers quickly, easily, and without a second thought.

Building Blocks
(Inverting Triads)

by Ronald Herder

A triad is like a stack of building blocks, built from the ground up: a starting pitch on the bottom:

with a 3rd stacked above:

then with another 3rd stacked on top:

Depending on the *kinds* of 3rds we use — that is, whether they are *major* 3rds (M3) or *minor* 3rds (m3) — the resulting triad will be called "major," "minor," "augmented" or "diminished":

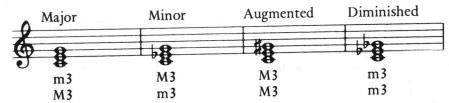

Major	Minor	Augmented	Diminished
m3	M3	M3	m3
M3	m3	M3	m3

If this is not clear, review our previous article (*"Triads: 4 Recipes"*).

Root position

All of these examples are said to be in "root position" because the starting pitch (middle C, this time) or "root" of the triad stays on the bottom of the stack. *But the triad does not have to stay in root position.* We can move the pitches around. We can play with these three building blocks, these three pitches. To do this, it is easier to re-name the blocks. It is, after all, a little clumsy to analyze the triad as "root . . . a 3rd above the root . . . then another 3rd above that."

Root-3rd-5th

The new names for the notes in a root-position triad will now be *root-3rd-5th*:

5th
3rd
Root

Continued on next page

This labeling simply identifies the triad's intervals *as they are numbered above the root:*

(a) the root, to begin:

(b) a 3rd above the root:

(c) and then a 5th above the root:

All triads have a root-3rd-5th stackup. What identifies a triad as major, minor, augmented, or diminished is the *kind* of 3rd (M3 or m3) and the *kind* of 5th: perfect (P5), augmented (aug 5), or diminished (dim 5).

Here are the four kinds of triads, labeled with their appropriate root-3rd-5th names:

Major	Minor	Aug.	Dim.
P5	P5	aug 5	dim 5
M3	m3	M3	m3
R	R	R	R

Inverting the triad

Inverting a triad simply means that we are turning it upside-down. We are restacking the blocks from this:

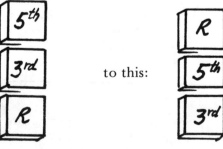

to this:

or this:

When the root block is pulled out and placed on top of the pile, the block marked "3rd" is now on the bottom of the stack:

On the music staff, this rearrangement looks like this . . .

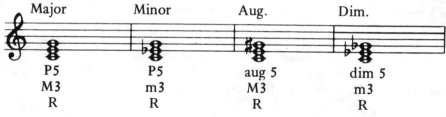

. . . and is called the *first inversion* of the triad.

But we can go one step further. We can pull out both the root and the 3rd and place them on top of the pile. Now the block marked "5th" is on the bottom of the stack:

On the music staff, this rearrangment looks like this . . .

. . . and is called the *second inversion* of the triad.

The following example manipulates the three pitches in triads built on the root D:

Practice these inversions in the next example.
(a) Play the given root-position triad.
(b) Write in its first inversion. Play it.
(c) Write in its second inversion. Play it.

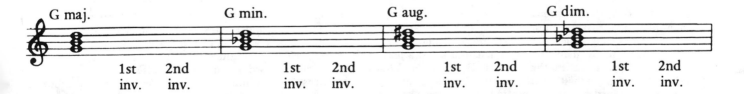

Finally, to really set this procedure in your mind and hands, practice the triad manipulation using various kinds of triads built on different pitches.

POP PIANO

by Raphael Crystal

A working knowledge of keyboard harmony is essential for your success as a popular pianist. You should understand the principles of chord construction, and the system for symbolizing chords. You should learn to recognize the sounds of different kinds of chords, and you will need to acquire facility in playing chords in various positions and keys. This can be done by practicing typical groups of chords, or "progressions."

Probably the most common kind of chord in popular music is the seventh chord. This is the "meat and potatoes" of popular harmony, to which you can later add more complicated and exotic structures. A seventh chord consists of four notes: the root, which gives the chord its name, and the notes that lie a third, fifth, and seventh above this root. Our example shows the C major seventh chord and its components:

Ex. 1

Cmaj7 = root + third + fifth + seventh

In popular music the root of the chord is usually, although not always, present in the bass. Above this the notes of the chord can be arranged in any number of ways. These arrangements are called "voicings." Here are the four basic voicings of the C major seventh chord, for the right hand and the left hand:

Ex. 2

The notes of a chord can be distributed between the two hands, as in (a) of our next example. This would be called an "open" voicing because there are large intervals between the notes of the chord. When a thicker sound is desired we use a "closed" voicing, and the notes of the chord are played by both hands (b). In stride piano and its derivatives the left hand plays the root of the chord in the low register and then leaps up to play a voicing in the middle register (c). In an arpeggio the notes of a chord will be repeated in many different registers. Notice that here the root is present only at the bottom of the chord — this makes for a lighter sound (d).

Ex. 3

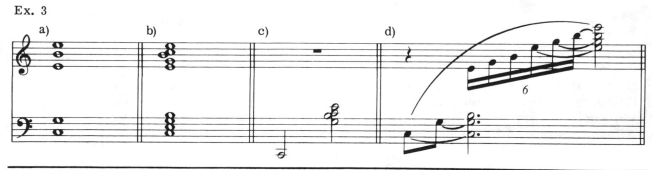

a)   b)   c)   d)

Let's look at the seventh chords to be found in the key of C major. We should point out that there are two ways of referring to chords: by their letter names (C, D, E, etc.), or by Roman numerals that indicate the positions of their roots in the scale (I, II, III, etc.). You should be familiar with both systems. The letter names are used on lead sheets and printed sheet music, and the pop pianist must be able to translate those symbols into notes. The Roman numerals permit us to generalize about the chords, and they are useful in transposing and playing by ear.

Notice that four different kinds of chords appear in our example. They are characterized by different interval structures, and each kind of chord has a distinctive sound. I and IV are major sevenths, consisting of a major third, perfect fifth and major seventh. The symbol for this kind of chord is maj7 or △7. II, III and VI are minor sevenths, with a minor third, perfect fifth and minor seventh. This chord is symbolized as m7 or −7. V is a dominant seventh, with a major third, perfect fifth and minor seventh. It is symbolized simply as 7. And VII is a "half-diminished" chord, with a minor third, diminished fifth and minor seventh. This is symbolized as m7-5 or ∅

Ex. 4

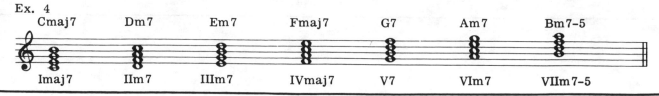

Cmaj7	Dm7	Em7	Fmaj7	G7	Am7	Bm7-5
Imaj7	IIm7	IIIm7	IVmaj7	V7	VIm7	VIIm7-5

Our next example shows a short passage in a jazz style that makes use of all the seventh chords found in C major. Here the chords appear in the left hand, accompanying a melody in the right hand. Notice that when the chords lie more than an octave below middle C they are opened up to avoid a muddy sound.

In minor keys the four kinds of seventh chords are distributed differently. I, IV and V are minor, II is half-diminished, III and VI are major, and VII is a dominant. The minor scale, however, is less stable than the major, and is subject to certain changes. Often the V chord becomes a dominant seventh, in order to provide a solid V7-I cadence. This necessitates raising the third of the chord (e.g. in C minor using a B♮).

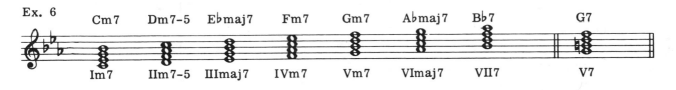

The following example illustrates all of the seventh chords in the key of C minor; it is a passage which might occur in a sentimental ballad. Here the harmony takes the form of broken chords in the left hand, together with some arpeggiated incomplete voicings in the right. Notice that in the third bar a B♮ is used to create a G7 chord.

For the sake of completeness we should mention several other seventh chords that are common in popular music but which do not occur naturally in the major or minor scales. These always require the use of accidentals, and are called "altered chords." Two of these chords involve altering the fifth of the dominant seventh chord. When the fifth of the chord is raised we get an "augmented seventh" chord. symbolized as +7. When the fifth is lowered we get a chord that is symbolized as 7-5. Two other altered chords result from the frequent use of the raised seventh degree in a minor key (e.g. the B♮ in C minor): these are the minor chord with a major seventh, symbolized as m(maj 7), and the diminished seventh chord, consisting of a minor third, diminished fifth and diminished seventh, and symbolized as dim7 or °7.

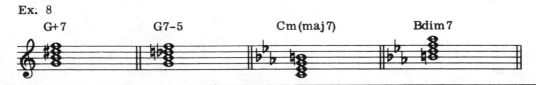

Continued on next page

To become fluent in the use of chords you will need to practice groups of chords, or "progressions," and you should understand how chords move from one to another. This movement is mainly governed by the relationship of the chord roots. The most common kind of chord progression is by a root movement of a descending fifth or ascending fourth, for example C-F or G-C:

A continuous movement by descending fifths is called a "circle of fifths" because it finally leads back to the starting point. If the movement remains within a single key it is called a "diatonic circle of fifths" (e.g. in the key of C, the progression C-F-B-E-A-D-G-C). You may have noticed that this is exactly the kind of progression that was used in examples 5 and 7 above.

Since the diatonic circle of fifths touches on all the chords in a given key, and since it includes many typical progressions within itself, it is very useful as a basis for exercises in keyboard harmony. The following circle-of-fifths exercise makes use of a partly open voicing in the right hand, with the chord roots in the left:

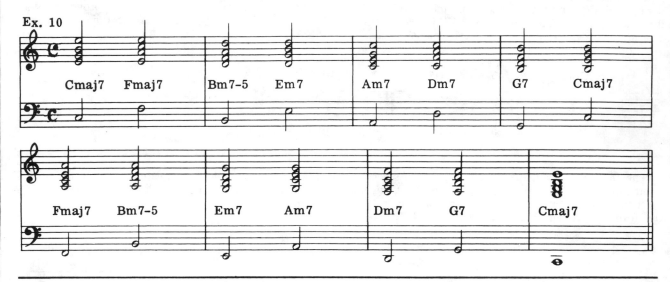

The above progression should also be practiced in minor. You can do this by simply adding a key signature of three flats. In the next to last bar, however, use a B to create a G7 chord.

The progression should be practiced in all keys. We suggest that you write out the transpositions, even if you can play them without doing so, in order to get used

to the look of the chords in different keys. Simply keep transposing up a half step for the keys of D♭, D, E♭, E, F, G♭ and G. When you reach A♭ it is desirable to use a slightly different form of the progression, in order to keep the right hand from going too high on the keyboard. This form of the exercise can be transposed up for the keys of A, B♭ and B.

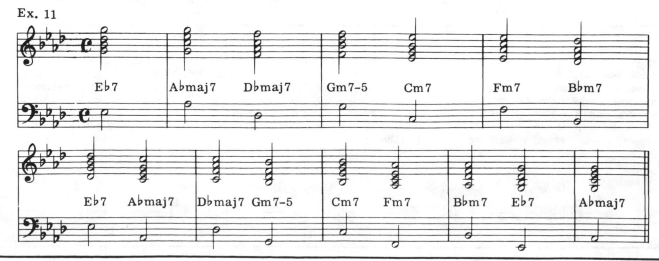

Progressions should always be practiced in a regular tempo — as if they were actual songs. You may want to apply various rhythmic patterns to the progression, such as the rock beat shown here:

Ex. 12

Cmaj7 Fmaj7 Bm7-5 Em7 etc.

It is also important to practice left hand voicings. Left hand chords should be confined to a middle register, from about the C below middle C up to the G above middle C. In the following exercise the chords are played in conjunction with roots in the low register. The right hand part is optional, but you may find that it actually makes the exercise easier to play, since the right hand establishes each chord before the left hand leaps up to it. This progression should be transposed up for the keys of Db, D, Eb and E.

Ex. 13

Cmaj7 Fmaj7 Bm7-5 Em7 Am7 Dm7 G7 Cmaj7

When we reach the key of F it is necessary to switch to another form, in order to keep the left hand chords in the proper range. This form of the progression can also be used for Gb, G, Ab and A.

Ex. 14

Fmaj7 Bbmaj7 Em7-5 Am7 Dm7 Gm7 C7 Fmaj7

For the keys of Bb and B you should return to the progression given in example 13, and transpose *down*.

By practicing these progressions you will learn to find your way around the keyboard. They are, in a sense, the harmonic equivalent of scales. In actual music, of course, the chords will usually not move in such regular, mechanical patterns, and the harmony will rarely be restricted just to seventh chords. But first things must come first. The seventh chords and circle-of-fifths progressions that have been discussed here are basic to popular harmony. When you can play these progressions fluently in all keys you will have taken a giant step forward in your development as a popular pianist.

How to build a 7th chord

by Ronald Herder

Step 1: Learn to find the interval of a major 7th above any pitch.

A major 7th is *one half-step* smaller than an octave:

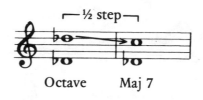

Step 2: Learn to find the interval of a minor 7th above any pitch.

A minor 7th is *one whole-step* smaller than the octave:

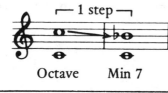
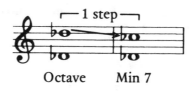
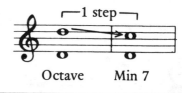

Step 3: Recognize how a 7th looks on the staff.

If the bottom note is a *line* note, such as middle C, the 7th above it will also be a line note. Note the two empty lines between these pitches.

If the bottom note is a *space* note, the 7th above it will also be a space note. Note the two empty spaces between these pitches.

Step 4: Locate other major and minor 7ths on the keyboard.

As you play these intervals, notice that a major 7th sounds more dissonant than a minor 7th. The minor 7th is "softer," a shade more gentle.

Step 5: Add major and minor 7ths to different kinds of triads

Once you are comfortable with the notation, keyboard "feel," and sound of major and minor 7ths, you will be ready to add them to various triads. This four-note construction — a root, 3rd, 5th, and 7th — creates the harmony called a 7th chord. The kind of 7th chord you build depends on the kind of triad you start with, plus the kind of 7th you add to the triad.

Chords that use the minor 7th

The dominant 7th chord: This chord consists of a *major triad* plus a minor 7th above the root. It is labeled by naming the root of the chord, then adding the number "7" — for example, C7, E♭7, F#7, and so on.

Practice building other dominant 7th chords by starting with any major triad, then adding a minor 7th above the root.

C maj. triad   min 7th   C7   E♭ maj. triad   min 7th   E♭7

The minor 7th chord: This chord consists of a *minor triad* plus a minor 7th above the root. Its label contains the name of the triad and the number "7" — for example, Cm7, E♭m7, F#m7, and so on.

Practice building minor 7th chords on other roots.

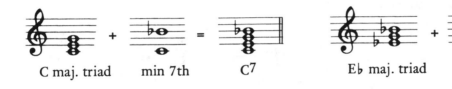

Cm   min 7th   Cm7   F#m   min 7th   F#m7

The half-diminished 7th chord: This chord consists of a *diminished triad* plus a minor 7th above the root. Its label has three symbols: the name of the root (C, for example), a small circle with a slash (Cø), and the number "7": Cø7.

Practice building half-diminished 7th chords on other roots.

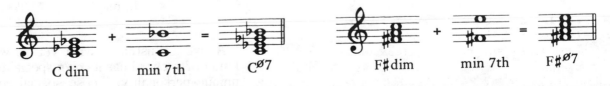

C dim   min 7th   Cø7   F#dim   min 7th   F#ø7

Continued on next page

basic training

Chords that use the major 7th

The major 7th chord: This chord consists of a *major triad* plus a major 7th above the root. It is labeled by naming the root of the chord, then adding the designation "maj 7" — for example, Cmaj7, E♭maj7, F#maj 7, and so on.

Practice building major 7th chords on other roots.

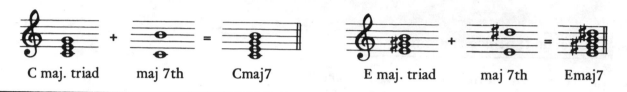

The minor/major 7th chord: This chord consists of a *minor* triad plus a major 7th above the root. Its label contains the name of the triad and the designation "maj 7" — for example, Cm maj7, Em maj 7, E♭m maj 7, and so on.

Summary

These five kinds of 7th chords are the ones most commonly used in popular sheet music. Once you get the hang of their constructions and labels, you should have a much easier time understanding and reading any commercial song arrangement or a simple lead sheet. To sum up what we've covered, here are the five chords, side by side, all built on the root D:

In a future article we will look at the equally popular diminished 7th chord, and review some infrequently used 7th chords. In the meantime, try out your new knowledge by writing out the following harmonies above the given roots:

Above all, listen to what you've written. Each kind of 7th chord has its own special tone color, its unique personality. Those special sounds are of course what the world of harmony is all about. ♩

basic training

Four New 7th Chords

by Ronald Herder

Step 1: *Review the way to find the intervals of a* **major 7th** *and a* **minor 7th** *above any pitch.* A major 7th is one *half-step* smaller than an octave. A minor 7th is one *whole-step* smaller than an octave.

Octave   Maj.7   Min.7   Octave   Maj.7   Min.7

Step 2: *Learn to find the interval of a* **diminished 7th** *above any pitch.*

A diminished 7th is *one-and-a-half steps* smaller than an octave.

Oct.   M7   m7   dim.7   Oct.   M7   m7   dim.7

(As you play these examples, note how the intervals "shrink," a half-step at a time, as you move from the octave to the diminished 7th.) In some instances the shrinking process forces the notation into double-flats as we reach the diminished 7th. Some writers prefer to simplify reading by changing a double-flat into its enharmonic equivalent on the keyboard: B♭♭ = A, E♭♭ = D, and so on:

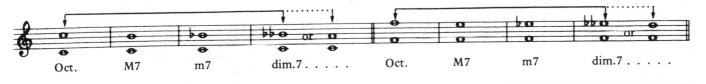

Oct.   M7   m7   dim.7 . . . . .   Oct.   M7   m7   dim.7 . . . . .

Step 3: *Learn to build a* **diminished 7th chord.**

The diminished 7th chord consists of a *diminished triad* plus a diminished 7th *interval* above the root of the chord. It is labeled by naming the root of the chord, then adding the symbols "°7"—for example, F#°7, A°7, C°7, and so on. (The tiny circle means "dim.")

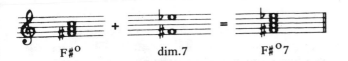

F#°   dim.7   F#°7

A°   dim.7   A°7

Continued on next page

The next two examples avoid the double-flat:

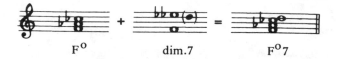

Step 4: Learn to build a **half-diminished 7th chord.**

The half-diminished 7th chord consists of a *diminished triad* plus a *minor 7th* above the root of the chord. Its label is identical to that of the so-called "fully" diminished 7th chord (the one we just looked at) except for a *slash* through the tiny circle: F#ø7, Aø7, Cø7, and so on.

Step 5: Learn how to handle altered 7th chords.

Two of the most popular 7th chords used in modern sheet music involve chromatic alterations of the 5th of the chord.

The major 7th chord with a raised 5th:

This harmony consists of a major 7th chord with the 5th above the root *raised one half-step*. Its label is the same as for a "normal" major 7th chord, but with the addition of the symbol "+5." ("+" means "augmented.")

An accurate but somewhat awkward label for the same chord is Caug^maj7, E♭aug^maj7, and so on. This focuses on the chord as an augmented triad plus a major 7th—a perfectly feasible, but rare, way to analyze the harmony.

The dominant 7th chord with a flatted 5th: This harmony consists of a dominant 7th chord with the 5th above the root *lowered one half-step*. Its label is the same as for a "normal" dominant 7th chord, but with the addition of the symbol "−5." ("−" means "flatted.")

basic training

Summary

The following is a complete roundup of the eight kinds of 7th chords we've covered in this and last month's articles. As you play through each set, pay special attention to the chromatic changes in every note except the root, and to the subtle shifts in harmonic color. Then apply what you've learned as you play through your favorite piece of sheet music.

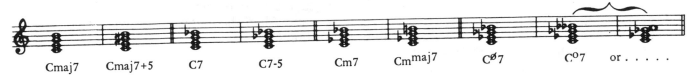

Cmaj7 Cmaj7+5 C7 C7-5 Cm7 Cm^maj7 Cø7 C°7 or . . . . .

Emaj7 Emaj7+5 E7 E7-5 Em7 Em^maj7 Eø7 E°7

It is true that this is a lot of information to fully absorb, but you can easily memorize the whole sequence of chords through *slow mastery*. In short, take your time. Then try your hand at completing the missing pitches in the following set:

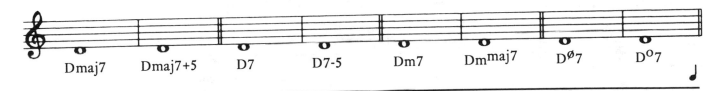

Dmaj7 Dmaj7+5 D7 D7-5 Dm7 Dm^maj7 Dø7 D°7

basic training

7th Chord Inversions and Voicings

by Ronald Herder

Most chord progressions in standard sheet music emphasize *root-position* voicings. ("Voicing" refers to the way the player distributes the notes of a chord between the two hands.) As long as the root of the chord appears as the *lowest* note, the chord is considered to be in root position; the other notes in the chord may be distributed in a variety of ways. All of the following are voicings of a root-position Cm7:

Voicings in the 1st inversion

If a note *other than the root* appears as the lowest note, then the chord is said to be *inverted.* If the 3rd of the chord is the lowest note, the chord is in its **1st inversion.** All of the following are voicings of a 1st-inversion Cm7:

Voicings in the 2nd inversion

If the **5th** of the chord is the lowest note, the chord is in its **2nd inversion:**

Voicings in the 3rd inversion

If the **7th** of the chord is the lowest note, the chord is in its **3rd inversion:**

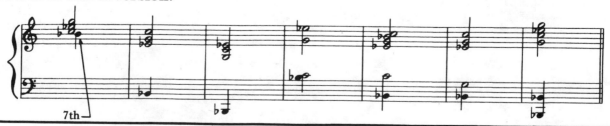

Inversion Exercises

Try your hand with the following inversions. First play the root-position chord, as shown, then fill in the missing chord tones in the inversion that follows it. As you work out different voicings above the given bass note, listen to the variety of sound that you achieve. Some voicings produce a rich sonority; some, a thinner, "open" sound; some, an unusual color.

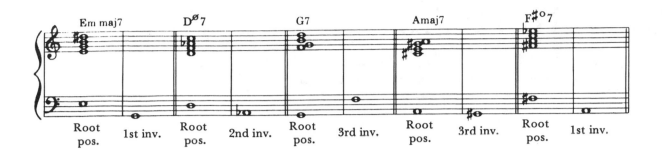

Voice-Leading

Just as "voicing" is the way chord tones are distributed *vertically* — that is, as a single harmonic structure — "voice-leading" is the way the chord tones of one harmony move *horizontally* to the chord tones of the next harmony. The whole idea of voice-leading becomes much clearer if you imagine that the chord you are playing is actually orchestrated for a small group of instruments. Imagine, for example, that the first chord in the inversion exercise, above, is being played by four trumpets and one trombone:

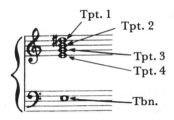

The next step is to imagine how each one of these instruments must move to get to a chord tone of the next harmony. If the next harmony is, say, an Am^7, a few possible voice-leadings may be. . .

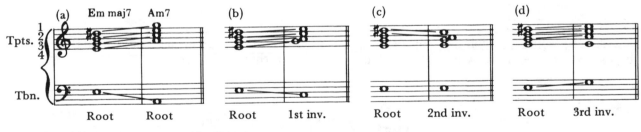

In (a), all instruments make a small jump. Voice-leading in (b) is a little smoother: Tpts.1 and 2 move only a half-step up; Tpt.3 moves a whole-step; Tpt.3 jumps a 3rd up; Tbn. jumps a 3rd down. Ex.(c) is smoother still, since Tpts.3 and 4, and the Tbn. do not move at all, remaining on chord tones that are the same in both harmonies. Ex.(d) mixes smooth voice-leading in Tpts.1,2, and 3 with a motionless Tpt.4 and a small jump in Tbn.

Although we will look at voice-leading in more detail in a future article, this short sampling will give you a good introduction to the use of chord inversions to create smooth movement from one harmony to the next. Remember to "orchestrate" your fingers as you practice moving through a chord progression. You will of course come to favor certain voice-leadings over others, simply because you like their sound. As long as you do not limit yourself through ignorance of other possibilities, there is no "right" or "wrong" way of passing from one chord to another. There is only your ear, your taste, and your style.

pop piano

Chord Voicing, Back To Basics

by Stuart Isacoff

First, any chord can be played in inumerable ways. Let's take a C maj7 chord to start with. Here are the notes:

Ex. 1

Now, here are some possibilities for playing those notes. Some seem to work better than others, but this depends a great deal on the context in which they are played.

Ex. 2

What we want to do in this workshop is to present some general, workable formulas for voicing chords. The best place to start with a basic solid voicing is in the middle range of your instrument — extremes are best saved for very special circumstances. We want to include all of the chord tones, and we want to spread those tones across a fairly wide expanse.

This would be a somewhat cramped way to play Cmaj7:

Ex. 3

So, let's try placing the root (1) and the fifth of the chord (5) in the left hand: **1-5**

Ex. 4

That's a good foundation. Now, add the third (3) and seventh (7) above, in the right hand: **1-5   3-7**

Ex. 5

Do we want to double any of the members of the chord? We would normally want to avoid doubling the *fifth* — doing so implies too much of the V chord quality. Doubling the *root* is OK, but this makes the chord more static (as opposed to dynamic) sounding. We can double the *third*, so that our formula becomes: **1-5   3-7-3**

Ex. 6

Or we can double the *seventh*. This formula is: **1-5   7-3-7**

Ex. 7

Try the voicings in the last two examples by using them to play all the chords in the key of C. (We can play the chords within the key in a *cycle of fifths:* I-IV-VII-III-VI-II-V-I).

Ex. 8

Next time, we'll look at how different voicings can be used to lead smoothly from one chord to the next.

43

pop piano

Chord Voicing, Pt. 2; Voice-Leading

by Stuart Isacoff

Last column, we looked at two common chord voicings: the first used 1 & 5 in the left hand, and 3,7,3 in the right; the second used 7,3,7 in the right hand.

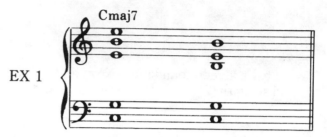

EX 1

In switching from one chord to another, we will frequently want to change voicings in order to avoid jumping all around the keyboard, the way we do in the next example.

EX 2

The reason we looked at these two voicings is that by changing from one to another we can limit the amount of motion the hands must go through. Here's the change from the C maj7 to F maj7 again, but this time, the F chord uses 7,3,7 in the right hand after we played the C chord with 3,7,3 in the right hand.

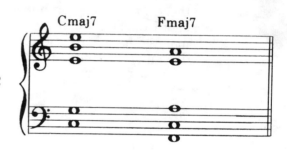

EX 3

We can play through a cycle of 5ths in the Key of C using this switching tactic, and the result is smooth and effortless.

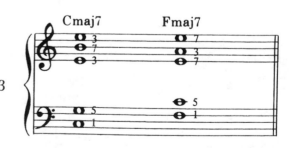

EX 4.

44

You can make up your own ways of moving from one chord to another by keeping in mind some simple rules:

● Whenever possible, hold a note that both chords share.

● Move each finger as short a distance as possible.

● Don't lose voices by suddenly changing from a five-note chord to one with only three notes; chances are, this will cause an "empty" feeling.

● If you begin with chords that use 7ths and 9ths, don't suddenly change to simple triads; try to maintain the sound *quality* evenly from chord to chord.

Here are three more examples of voicings that lead well into each other; these are more "jazzy" or "sophisticated," to give you an idea of the wide range of possibilities available.

pop piano

Chord Voicing, Pt. 3; Spaced-Out Sounds

by Stuart Isacoff

These sounds are very jazzy, and will not be appropriate for use in all the music you play. But it's interesting to see how they're built and it's good to have these voicings to add to your pallette of harmonic colors.

Chords which are suspended or have 11ths (the 4th and 11th are the same note, an octave apart), *do not contain the major third.* To voice a suspended chord in fourths, start on the 5th of the chord:

Ex 1

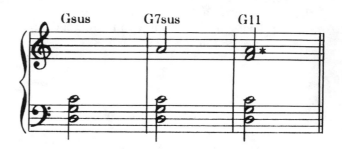

* The A is found a fourth below the bottom note, D, but we've moved it up for a less muddy effect.

You may notice from the last example that we can produce an 11th sound by hitting the root of our chord in the left hand, and playing the major triad which lies a whole step below in our right.

Ex 2

Dominant sounds can be voiced by starting on the dominant seventh. Here, the right hand does not play a string of perfect fourths; the distance between the seventh and the third of the chord is an *augmented fourth.*

Ex. 3

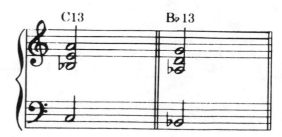

We can extend the dominant voicing by piling up more fourths above it. The result is that we add the ninth and the fifth of the chord.

Ex 4

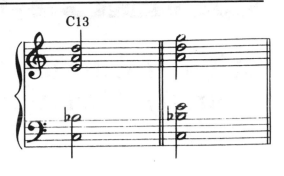

At times, we may even want to extend it further by placing the root of the chord *on top;* here, the bottom note in the left hand is the seventh of the chord.

Ex. 5

Going back to our dominant voicing (example 3), we can see that by beginning on the 3rd of the chord instead of on the 7th, we end up with a new sound: the augmented 9th. This sound is popular in rock and jazz.

Ex. 6

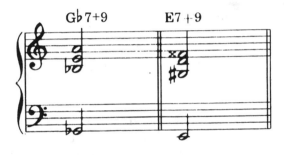

Switching back and fourth between the 13th sound and the augmented 9th sound allows us to play a V- I progression by simply moving the right hand down one half step:

Ex 7

In fact, we can play the whole circle of fifths with this voicing by continually moving the right hand down in half steps. Isn't that amazing? ♩

Ex 8

Altered Chords (Part 1): Variations on II⁷

by Ronald Herder

The II⁷ is a favorite and familiar chord in jazz, pop, and folk pieces. We find it by locating the 7th chord *built on the second degree* (II) of a conventional scale — for example:

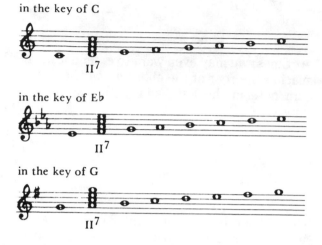

in the key of C

II⁷

in the key of Eb

II⁷

in the key of G

II⁷

In this form, in any major key, the II⁷ is classified as a **minor 7th chord** — consisting of a *root*, a *minor 3rd* above the root, a *perfect 5th* above the root, and a *minor 7th* above the root:

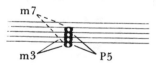

m7

m3   P5

1st alteration: Raise the 3rd

This alteration — very common in both popular and classical music — consists of raising the 3rd of the chord by one half-step. This changes the minor 3rd to a major 3rd, and converts the chord from a *minor-7th* type to a *dominant-7th* type. In practice, the change propels the chord progression more powerfully to the V chord of the key:

Dm7   D7   G   Fm7   F7   Bb   Am7   A7   D

2nd alteration: Flat the 5th

Flatting the 5th by one half-step creates a standard jazz harmony, also known by the name "half-diminished 7th." The alteration of the original minor 7th chord is marked by the symbol (b5) or (−5) next to the chord name. This half-step change adds a touch of harmonic color to the bland minor 7th, at the same time lending a stronger *downward* motion to the 5th of the chord:

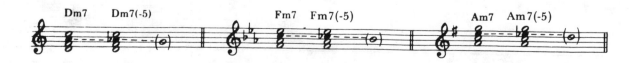

Dm7   Dm7(-5)   Fm7   Fm7(-5)   Am7   Am7(-5)

3rd alteration: Raise the 3rd and flat the 5th at the same time

A combination of the two previous alterations. Its chord symbol names the dominant 7th chord, plus the indication (♭5) or (−5).

In practice, the upward-moving 3rd and the downward-moving 5th create a powerful inward flow to the pitch caught right between the two altered notes:

4th alteration: Flat both the root and the 5th

This double alteration — lowering both the root and 5th of the chord by one half-step — creates an extremely strong downward motion of the chord to the tonic of the key. For this reason, it is a frequent jazz substitution for the standard V-I progression.

The symbol for this "chord of the flatted 2nd" ("2nd meaning "II") is based on the pitch of the lowered root, with the double alteration converting the original *minor* 7th chord into a new *major* 7th chord.

Exercises: Do-it-yourself variations on the II⁷ chord

All of the previous alterations can be found in standard sheet music. Prepare yourself for their appearances by consolidating what you've now read, in the form of the following exercises. These will give you an opportunity to apply what you know in various keys.

Fill in the missing chord tones, following the given chord symbols based on the raised 3rd:

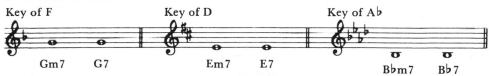

Fill in the missing chord tones, based on the alteration of the flatted 5th.

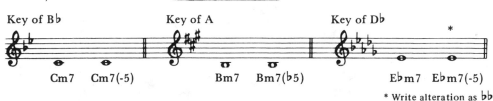

* Write alteration as ♭♭

Fill in the missing chord tones, based on raised-3rd/flatted-5th alterations:

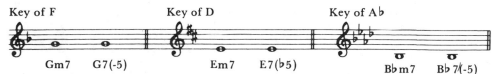

Fill in the missing chord tones, based on "chords of the flatted 2nd":

basic training

Altered Chords (Part 2): Games with Rubik's Cube

by Ronald Herder

The standard progression II-V-I is used throughout music of the Western world to establish a firm sense of key or tonality. The II chord (supertonic) sets up the arrival of the V chord (dominant) which, in turn, creates a drive toward final resolution to the I chord (tonic)—the "home" tonality, or final resting point, of a key.

In classical and folk music, both II and V generally appear as either a triad or a 7th chord; the tonic chord, almost always as a triad:

In popular music and jazz, however, the plain triad is invariably avoided because it is too bland in context. This means that the II chord will generally appear as a II^7, straight or altered; the V chord, as V^7, V^9, straight or altered; and the I chord, as I^7, I^9, or with an added tone (usually the added 6th above the root). In any of these forms, the basic II-V-I progression becomes more colorful, richer, sometimes spicy.

To show you how to manipulate the II-V-I progression to your taste, I've set up a kind of simplified "Rubik's Cube" of the more colorful versions of these three harmonies. Play them first as separate chords in order to get their individual sounds in your ear. Then read the explanations below.

(all in the key of F major)

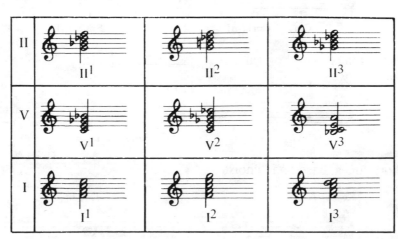

Top row: Alterations of II⁷

The unaltered II⁷ in the key of F is
Alteration II^1 flats the 5th. Alteration II^2 raises the 3rd and flats the 5th. Alteration II^3 flats both the root and the 5th.

Middle row: Alterations of V⁷

The unaltered V⁷ in the key of F is
Alteration V^1 flats the 5th. Alteration V^2 flats the 5th and adds a minor 9th. Alteration V^3 adds a 6th above the root "C." (The added "A" can also be analyzed as the top of a V^{13}.)

Bottom row: Alterations of I

The unaltered I in the key of F is
Alteration I^1 adds a major 7th above the root, changing the triad into a major 7th chord. Alteration I^2 adds both a major 7th and a major 9th above the root, changing the triad into a major 9th chord. Alteration I^3 is a major 7th chord with an added 6th ("D").

The point of the "Rubik's Cube" setup—and the fun of the experiment—is to give you a simple *visual* device for *interchanging* different chords in different ways. Only a few of the many combinations are written out below, notated for two hands.

These examples play with various voicings of the chords, rearranging the top notes while still keeping each harmony in *root* position. (Note that the root progression G-C-F is always in the bass—standard procedure in most pop and jazz keyboard styling.)

Before you play each progression first notice which alterations are being used. Example 1, for instance, combines II^1-V^1-I^1. Then analyze the way I've revoiced each chord to get the best sonority and smoothest voice-leading. Then play the music, *and listen to the sounds you make.*

When you've worked your way through the whole set, begin working on your own. Try out new combinations and new voicings. Then (graduate exam!) set up your own "cube" of altered II-V-I chords *in another key!*

Ninth Chords

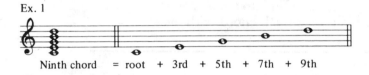

pop piano

by Raphael Crystal

The higher numbered chords — the ninths, elevenths, and thirteenths — have an important place in popular music. They contribute color, richness, and a pungent touch of dissonance. Most importantly, they introduce a new range of expressive possibilities. As a popular pianist you should be familiar with the names and principles of construction of these chords, as well as their characteristic sounds and their positions on the keyboard.

Higher numbered chords, like their simpler counterparts, are built in thirds. A ninth chord consists of a root, third, fifth, seventh, and ninth:

Ex. 1

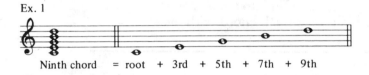

Ninth chord = root + 3rd + 5th + 7th + 9th

At the keyboard ninth chords are often played with the root in the left hand and the other four notes in the right. All four possible voicings of the upper four notes are used, but the most common is the voicing with the ninth on top (a). In stride piano style the left hand plays a root in the lower register and then leaps up to play a voicing of the remaining four notes in the middle register (b). Of course it is also possible to divide up the notes of the ninth chord between the two hands (c). Almost always the root of the ninth chord remains in the bass, and it is usually *not* present in the upper voices.

Ex. 2

The major ninth chord can be constructed on the first note of the major scale. It consists of a major third, perfect fifth, major seventh, and major ninth, and is symbolized as maj9 or △9 (a). A related chord is the 96, which includes a major sixth but does not include a seventh (b). The chord that is known as the "add 9" includes only the third, fifth and ninth. Here the ninth does not ordinarily appear in the top voice; it is usually placed just below the third of the chord (c).

Ex. 3

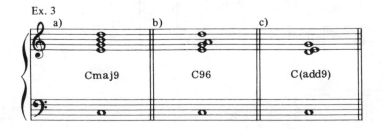

Cmaj9   C96   C(add9)

A group of major ninth chords moving in parallel is a familiar big band brass section sound. The device is also effective on the piano:

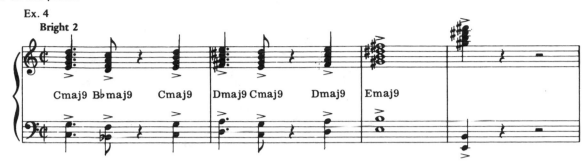

The 96 has a more settled, stable sound; it is often used at the end of a song:

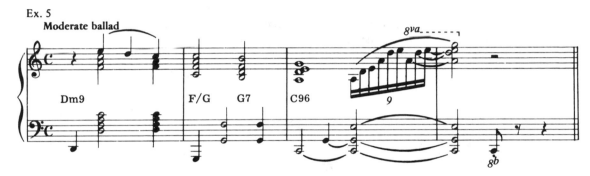

In the "add 9" the ninth has the effect of coloring and softening the sound of the major chord. The "add 9" is often associated with a country or folk-rock feeling.

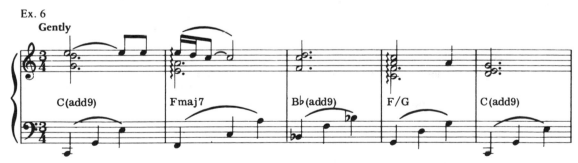

The minor ninth chord can be built on the second degree of the major scale. It includes a minor third, perfect fifth, minor seventh, and major ninth, and is symbolized as m9 or —9 (a). When a minor ninth chord is used on the first degree of a *minor* key it often has a raised seventh (e.g. B in a C minor chord). This chord may be symbolized as m9 (maj7), m9 (△7), or m9+7 (b). There is also a minor 96 chord; notice that it has a *major* sixth (c). And there is a minor ninth chord (d).

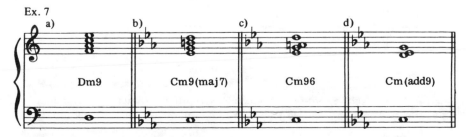

Continued on next page

The minor ninth on the second degree of the major scale typically moves to a dominant V chord and then to a major I chord. This is one of the basic progressions in popular music — it is used in all styles and genres. Here we see it in a disco setting:

Ex. 8

The minor ninth with a raised seventh has a sharper, more biting sound, because of its greater dissonance. In this example it appears on I and IV of the minor scale. Notice the effect when the Fm9(maj7) in the third bar gives way to the much softer Fm7 of bar four:

Ex. 9

The dominant ninth can be constructed on the fifth degree of the major scale. It consists of a major third, perfect fifth, minor seventh, and major ninth, and is symbolized simply as 9 (a). Dominant chords are especially subject to alteration, and dominant ninths are no exception to this rule. The dominant chord with a flatted ninth, symbolized as 7-9, is very common (b). The dominant ninth with a raised fifth, symbolized as 9+5, has a particularly strong pull toward the tonic (c). The fifth can also be lowered; often this is combined with a flatted ninth, resulting in a 7-9-5 chord (d). And the ninth can be raised, creating an augmented ninth chord, symbolized as +9 (e).

Ex. 10

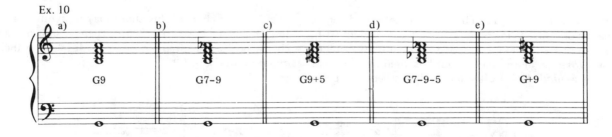

The +9 chord deserves some special attention. Although it is theoretically a ninth chord, it is often written as a seventh chord with both minor and major thirds (e.g. a chord on G containing both B♭ and B♮). It frequently appears in a blues or blues-derived context, where the minor/major third combination creates the feeling of a ''blue note'':

Ex. 11

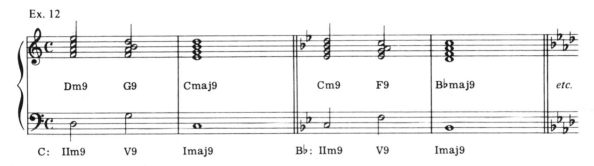

If you would like to become fluent in the use of ninth chords, you can begin by practicing the IIm9—V9—Imaj9 progression in all keys. Our next example shows a convenient way of doing this. First play the progression in C major. Then turn the final C chord into a Cm9, which becomes the first member of a II-V-I progression in B♭ major. If you continue this chain you will run through the keys of B♭, A♭, G♭, E, and D, and then return to C. Try to keep the beat going through the entire series — play it as a single progression.

Ex. 12

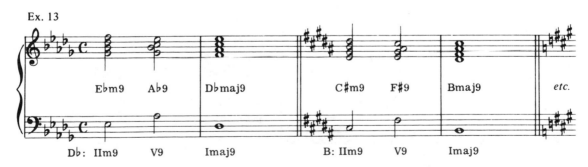

To cover the other six major keys, begin the progression a half-step higher, in D♭ major. (Notice that when we transform the D♭ maj9 into a minor chord it is changed enharmonically to a C#m9, taking us into the key of B major, rather than the less common C♭ major.) This series will move through the keys of B, A, G, F, E♭, and back again to D♭.

Ex. 13

Ninth chords are more common in popular songs than you might imagine from looking at sheet music. This is because when the ninth is in the melody, the chord symbol is often given as a seventh chord (i.e. it only covers the notes *accompanying* the melody). As you play through the sheet music for a song, be on the lookout for those ''hidden'' ninth chords. You will find that they all have characteristic and familiar sounds — sounds that you have been hearing all along without, perhaps, knowing exactly what they were. Happy hunting for hidden ninths!

POP PIANO

by Raphael Crystal

Dominant chords constitute the most vital harmonic force in popular music. The dominant seventh seems to have an irresistible urge to resolve to the tonic (a), and this creates a strong sense of movement and direction. There are many colorful alterations and elaborations of the dominant chord; among the simpler of these are the augmented seventh (b), the dominant seventh with a flatted fifth (c), and the dominant seventh with the addition of a flatted ninth (d). And there are a large number of dominant ninth, eleventh, and thirteenth chords that extend this repertoire further.

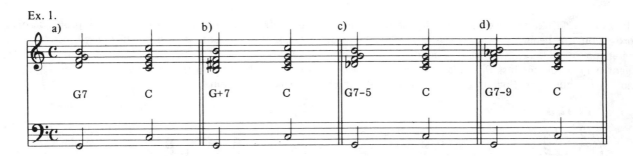

What makes dominant chords especially common is that they are not only used on the fifth degree of the scale. Our next example is in C Major, but in the second bar there is a C7 chord. This functions as a dominant for the F chord which follows. For a moment F is treated as if it were a tonic, although it would not be correct to say that the music has changed keys. In harmonic analysis the C7 chord would be called a "V of IV," i.e, the dominant of the IV chord. In popular music it is more convenient to refer to the chord simply as I7, bearing in mind its dominant function. This kind of chord — a 7 chord on a root other than V, that functions as a dominant — is called a "secondary dominant."

Since the only dominant seventh that occurs naturally in the major scale is the V7, secondary dominants always require the use of accidentals. In the case of the I7 there is always a flatted seventh in the melody or an inner part. The I7 is probably the most commonly used secondary dominant. Notice how it provides a smooth but strong preparation for the IV chord.

Next in frequency to the I7 is the II7, which serves as a dominant for the V chord. In the II7 the third of the chord must be raised (in C, this means using an F#). The II7 is often used in the sixth or seventh bar of a tune, to create a "half cadence" on V. Imagine that this example begins with the fifth bar of a tune:

Ex. 3.

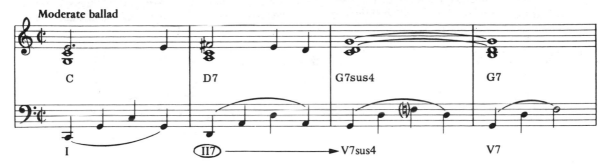

Another typical use of the II7 is to nail down the cadence at the end of a song with a strong II7-V7-I progression:

Ex. 4.

The III7, serving as a dominant for the minor VI chord, is another common sound. It is especially typical of gospel and gospel-derived music, since it has a "churchy" connota-tion. Notice that in this example the VIm is followed by another secondary dominant, II7, which then leads to a V7 chord:

Ex. 5.

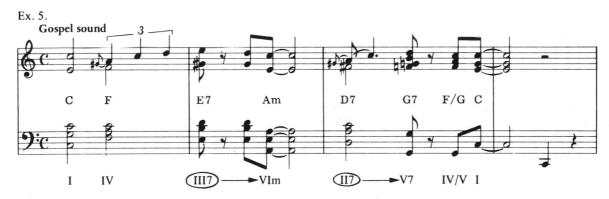

The IV7 is not ordinarily used as a dominant in a major key. In C this would be an F7, which resolves to a B♭ chord, leading us out of the key (a). Of course the IV7 is a basic chord in the blues, but in that context it does not function as a dominant at all, but rather as a "blue-note" chord (b).

Ex. 6.

Continued on next page

The VI7 serves as a dominant for the minor II. There is a class of tunes that begin on the IIm chord, and these often have a VI7 chord as a pickup, as in our next example.

Notice that here the dominant includes a flatted ninth, especially appropriate when approaching a minor chord.

Ex. 7.

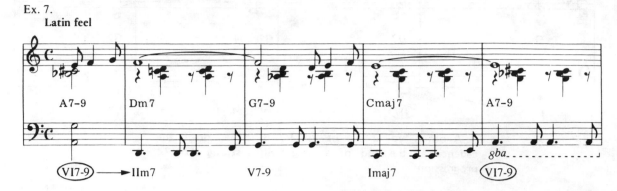

Another familiar function of the VI7 is to introduce a "one-more-time" repetition at the end of a song. Here the VI7 leads back to a II7-V7-I cadence.

Ex. 8.

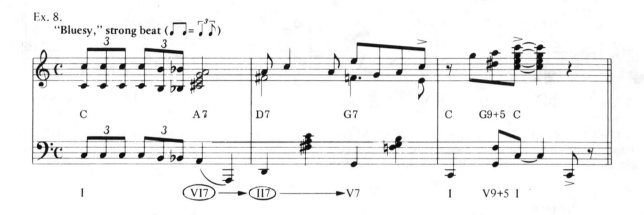

The VII7, which functions as the dominant of III, is not quite so common as the others. Perhaps this, together with the fact that it involves two accidentals (D# and F# in the key of C) accounts for its greater "shock value." Of all the secondary dominants, it is the one that seems most foreign to the key. In this example the VII7 initiates a string of secondary dominants, in which each chord serves as the dominant of the next:

Ex. 9.

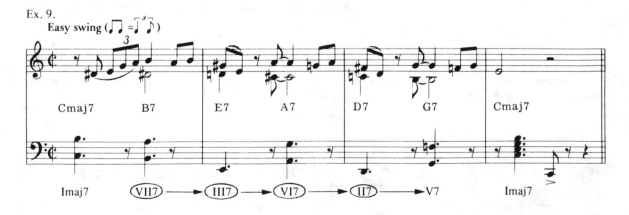

To become familiar with the sounds and positions on the keyboard of the various secondary dominants you should practice some chord progressions that illustrate their use. Our first progression proceeds up the scale, touching on all the secondary dominants used in a major key. Notice that in the sixth bar a IV7 chord appears, which resolves to what may be called a ^{b}VII chord; this has been included in order to continue the sequence in a consistent manner, but it is not something you would ordinarily encounter in a pop song.

58

The progression should be practiced in all major keys. It would also work well with 7-9 chords. In order to transform the dominants into that form, simply add flatted ninths in the right hand voicings, in place of the doubled roots (i.e. in the second chord of the first bar use a B^b in the right hand, in place of the A).

Ex. 10.

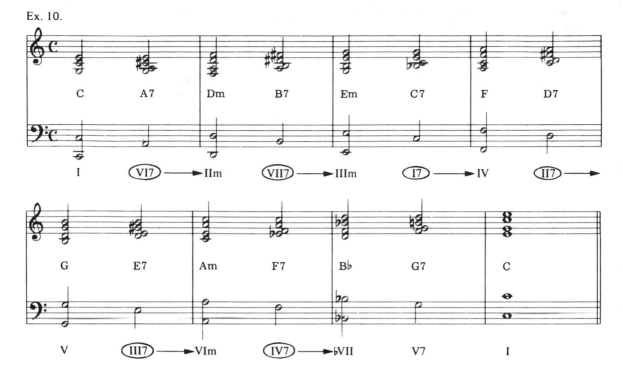

Our next progression is a descending one. Here, for the sake of variety, the secondary dominants are augmented seventh chords, which resolve to major, minor, or dominant sevenths. Like the previous example, this progression should be played in all major keys.

Ex. 11.

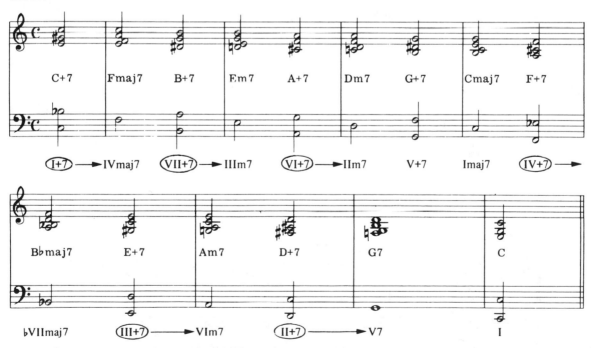

Secondary dominants can become an important part of your resources as a popular pianist. You will find them very useful when you are harmonizing a tune by ear — often the chord that is especially hard to find turns out to be a secondary dominant — or when you are elaborating the sheet music arrangement of a song. By introducing notes and chords that do not appear in the basic scale, secondary dominants broaden the harmonic scope of a tune. And by creating many new dominant-tonic relationships they give strength and harmonic direction to the music.

pop piano

by Stuart Isacoff

"Slash" Chords

Several readers have written asking for an explanation of those "slash" chords you often see in contemporary music: symbols like C/G and D/E. These are a form of musical shorthand, and they are used in two types of situations: both have to do with the composer's or arranger's wishes for a particular kind of sound.

Sometimes these symbols are used simply to eliminate long and complicated chord spellings. For example, suppose the arranger wants an F# chord with the dominant seventh, ninth and eleventh added, but with the fifth omitted. He or she might notate it as:

$$F\#^{11} \ (no \ 5)$$

Now, many keyboardists will be confused by this symbol. Experienced players will know to leave the third of the chord out, and may not find it too difficult to pick out the seventh, ninth, eleventh, etc. But think of how much simpler it is to read the following:

$$E/F\#$$

The directions are clear: Play an E chord and place an F# underneath it in the bass! Voila: you have the harmony exactly right.

There is yet another purpose for these slash spellings, though. Chords can be played in many different ways. For example, a C Major triad might be struck with the root, the third, or the fifth on the bottom. These variations are known as "inversions."

When chord progressions are played without the use of inversions, the bass line often hops around quite a bit; the sound is not always pleasing or "professional" enough.

By using inversions — with notes other than the root of each chord on the bottom — a smooth melodic line can be created in the bass.

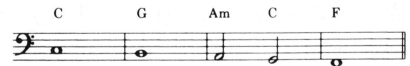

The symbols for the chord progression here — with explicit instructions built in to indicate the bass line — appear over the next example.

Other lines could just as easily have been indicated in the music. If you saw the following:

$$C/E - G/D - Am/C - C - F$$

it would mean that the composer wanted this bass line:

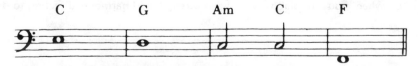

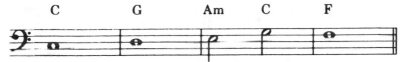

$$C - G/D - Am/E - C/G - F$$

indicates the following rising bass line:

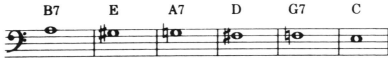

Sometimes this notation is helpful in producing a very specific sound. The progression of $C - E^7 - Am$, for instance, takes on a Gospel flavor when it is played as

$$C/G - E^7/G\# - Am$$

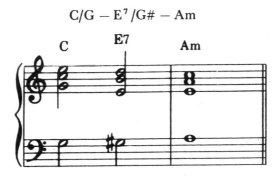

The idea of this kind of movement in music is very old. The cycle of fifths appears in a Bach Menuet in the following way:

The last example shows how the music might have appeared if Bach had written in "slash chords":

Menuet

J.S. Bach

TIPS ON HARMONY

GETTING MORE OUT OF YOUR CHORD PLAYING:

POLYCHORDS

by Ed Shanaphy

In previous articles we have talked about chord substitution; that is, replacing the chord indicated in the sheet music with one of your own choosing. Such a device is a very important step toward creating your own style or interpretation of pop music. Once you have familiarized yourself with that device, the next step would be experimenting with what are called *polychords.*

What a polychord is. A polychord is nothing more than the playing of two chords at the same time. On the keyboard it could mean that the left hand plays a C7 chord while the right hand plays a D7 chord. Or, the left hand holds down a C7 chord while the right hand arpeggiates a D7 chord.

What a polychord does. The introduction of polychords to your own playing will produce a whole new sound, a more contemporary one, and it will add a great deal more depth and interest to your personal style be it rock, jazz or pops. The same principles would be employed for all three types of music, rock, jazz or pop, but the chord voicings would be slightly altered in each instance. Of course, there are rhythmic differences between rock and pop, or rock and jazz, but the polychord technique is basically the same for all three.

The example below (Ex. #1), shows

a typical polychord, a C7 chord in the bass clef and a Bb7 chord in the treble.

The voicing in this example would be appropriate for a jazz or pop style. For rock, however, it would be preferable to have a more open sound, a simpler one where the bass clef (played by electric bass) is a simple note C rather than the full chord, and the treble clef is a pure Bb major chord rather than a Bb7.

EXAMPLE #2

Bb / C

Note the chord symbols on each of the above examples. Much of the new music you buy nowadays will have double symbols because the new composers are utilizing polychords as a regular device.

Now that we have shown how a rock-styled polychord might be voiced, with the more open sound, take a look at example #3 which is a simple rock riff employing the same chords, and then play through example #4 which uses a few more polychords.

Example #5 is more a pop or jazz styled melody with the kind of chords you might find on a standard piece of sheet music. Play it through once or twice to get familiar with the melody.

Now that you have played it, and have heard the standard chord progressions, you will be quite surprised how much more interesting this simple

melody can become by using a few chord substitutions and polychords. Play through example #6.

If you have been following our previous articles on keyboard and harmony, you will notice that we have employed chord substitutions here exactly as previously discussed, and we have used the extended ending device as well. But the polychords have added even a greater dimension to the song. Notice, for example, that the melody in measure #3 is a sequential repetition of measure #1. However, using the A/G polychord in the third measure makes you forget that it is a repeated phrase altogether. It gives you the feeling that the melody is now about to move somewhere else. And it does. To an E in measure #4. When simple 7th chords are used as in measure #7, they are now refreshing in their openness and simplicity, and very effective. Since we have used stepwise chord progressions in this measure, there is enough interest without having to use polychords.

The arpeggio in the next-to-last measure is a perfect example of using polychords to create a run. The left hand plays a G7 arpeggio while the right hand alternates with it on an A7 arpeggio.

As you experiment with polychords you will find that they work more readily when the right hand plays a chord that is: 1) a whole tone above the left hand chord; 2) a whole tone below the left hand chord; 3) a flatted 5th above the left hand chord. For example, a G7 chord will sound best with 1) an A7 chord, 2) an F7 chord, 3) a Db7 chord. There are many other possibilities, but we suggest that your initial experimenting be confined to these three types. The melody note will more or less dictate which polychord, if any, can be used.

You must be patient with polychords. They will take some time to master. But the more you play with them, the more interesting your playing will become. For the moment, at least, you should be able to understand the principle involved.

Just as a closing note, and to prove that kids say the darnedest things, my 8 year-old son just asked what I was writing about. He's an eager little piano player himself. When I told him I was writing about polychords, and then asked him if he knew what they were, he answered smugly, "Sure. You use 'em to tie up parrots!"

If you are ever asked what a polychord is, you have his permission to use that line. ♩

EXAMPLE #1

Bb7/C7

EXAMPLE #3

Continued on page 78

63

pop piano

by Stuart Isacoff

Give Your Friend A Fifth for The Holidays

Many contemporary keyboard artists have turned to fourths and fifths when voicing their chords, to obtain an open, warm sound. Here are some suggestions on how to construct this kind of harmony.

1) For a major harmony with no seventh, begin the series of fourths on the third of the chord:

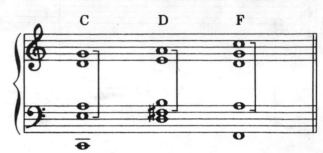

2) For a major harmony with a major seventh, begin on either the third of the chord (placing the seventh on top), or the sixth (placing the third and seventh on top), or the major seventh:

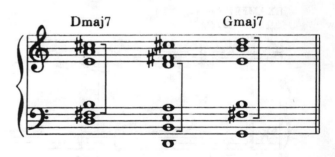

3) To avoid clashing with the melody note or covering it over, the top note of the chord can be moved down:

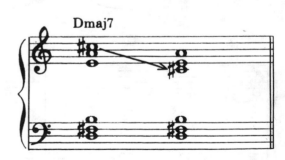

4) For a dominant seventh harmony, begin on the dominant seventh—or else be sure to place the sixth and ninth of the chord either above or right next to the seventh:

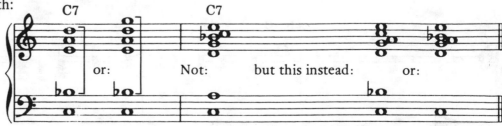

TIPS ON HARMONY

A PRIMER ON THE CYCLE OF 5THS

by Ed Shanaphy

In past articles we have used the term "cycle of 5ths", and some of you have asked us to elaborate on just what it is, and how it works.

The cycle of 5ths is the most natural progression of one tone to another. If you sound the note C, the most natural tone to follow that C is an F, a perfect fifth below. As they say in "Star Wars", there is *a force*. And the strongest force in music harmony is probably this: the tendency of one tone to progress to a tone a 5th lower. As an analogy: you are at a party and have just introduced yourself to a perfect stranger. What is the most natural question to ask to get the conversation going? "Where do you live?" "Where are you from?" It's a much more natural progression than "Are you a Democrat?" This kind of question can set up a much more interesting conversation, but should it have happened so soon?

We call it the "cycle" of 5ths because the progression from one tone to another, always moving a fifth below, will eventually return to the starting tone. And this progression passes through all the twelve tones of the chromatic scale. It's a *local*, making all the stops. If you progressed a minor third away each time, for example, you would reach the starting tone after just four tones.

One thing to remember is that the progression to a root tone a perfect 5th below is identical to a perfect 4th above. The C goes to F, which is a perfect 4th higher, or a perfect 5th lower. It depends entirely up to you which direction to take. But the result is exactly the same as far as the "cycle" is concerned. You are still progressing to an F, no matter which octave you select, therefore you are still utilizing the *cycle*.

So much for the theory behind the cycle of 5ths. Now, how will you use it? Once you have become familar with it, and we have included some exercises to get you started on playing through it, you will find it extremely vaulable for playing by ear, composing your own songs, improvising, and understanding the theory of music much better.

For example, let's play a song by ear. In order to do this you have to know what a dominant 7th chord is. (At the very least, you must know your major chords. Check your chord dictionary in the Nov. '77 issue.) The song is in the key of C, and the melody starts on E. The name of the song is *Five Foot Two, Eyes Of Blue*. What you will do is simply sing the melody while accompanying yourself with chords. We'll give you the first two chords only, and then you will use the cycle of 5ths to get you through the rest of the song. The first chord is C: Play it with the first words *Five foot two . . .* With the words *eyes of blue*, your chord is an E7. It's a dominant 7th chord. (You may also use the plain major chord.) Now you are on your own. Your next chord is a 5th below the E7, and it's a dominant 7th. The following chord is another dominant 7th another 5th below, same for the next chord. The last chord is a major chord, a 5th below, because you are back to home base. Tonic. That's the first eight bars. The second eight bars is an exact repeat with different lyrics.

The middle section of the song, or the bridge, which starts with the words *"If you run into a five foot two . . ."*, your first chord is an E7 again. And again you simply progress a 5th below each time (or a 4th up), to find your next chord. The second chord of the bridge comes on the words "covered with fur . . ." Of course you know what chord it is!

The final eight bars are exactly the same as the first eight. Shazam! You've played a song by ear! Now if you have had a little difficulty following this exercise, our final example on the opposite page is the progression for this song. Use it as an aid if you have to.

Memorize the cycle by using the circle illustration. Play through the cycle by utilizing the circle illustration as well as the examples we have provided. Make it part of your practice schedule. Experiment with it. It will sink in without you even realizing it. You'll be amazed how many songs use the cycle of 5ths progression in one form or another. You'll be playing them by ear before you know it!

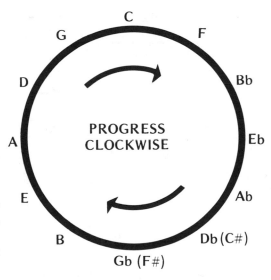

Continued on next page

CYCLE OF 5THS MUSIC EXAMPLES

1. Major chords

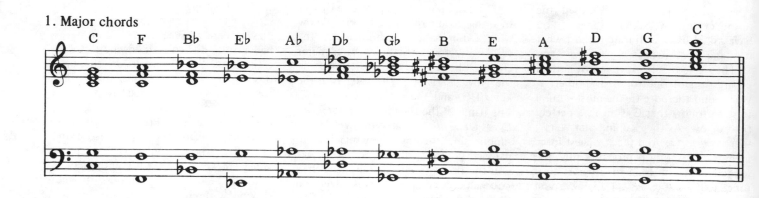

2. Dominant 7ths

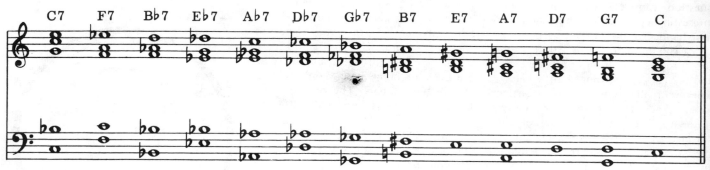

3. Minor 7 and Dom. 7 combination

4. Song Progression

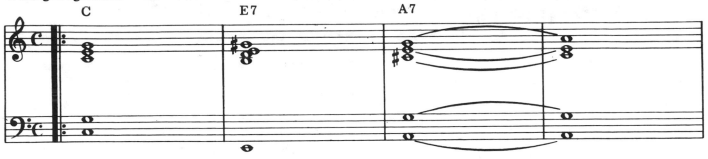

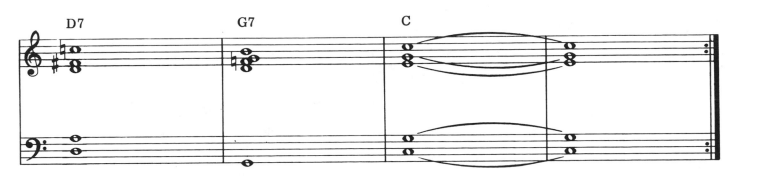

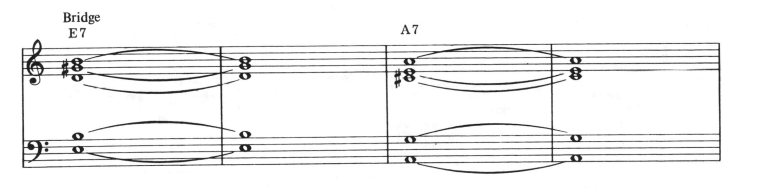

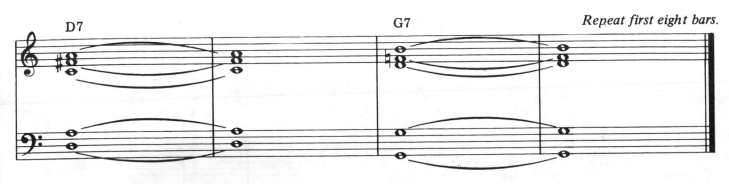

Repeat first eight bars.

67

MUSIC THEORY WORKSHOP

HOW TO USE THE CIRCLE OF FIFTHS

By Ed Shanaphy

After years of constant harassment, my mother finally let me quit the piano at age 12. It was a six year battle but I finally won. At last I could walk home from school on Tuesdays with the rest of the kids instead of sideslipping over to the piano teacher's house for another go at "Spinning Song" and "Edelweiss Glide." That was freedom.

Not long after, a couple of "horn men" wanted to start a band and remembered I had taken lessons. "Do you guys know 'Spinning Song'? 'Edelweiss Glide'?" It was obvious I had a little to learn about pop stuff, and as I remember it, I picked up a book by 'Bugs' Baer on the Circle of Fifths. Suddenly I was discovering things about music I had never dreamed existed. One of the great discoveries I made was how to use it for chord substitution and for passing chords.

Below is the 'circle' arranged in clockwise progression i.e., each chord name always leads clockwise to another chord name which is a perfect fifth below. (Some people prefer a counterclockwise order.)

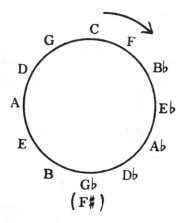

An exercise to help familiarize you with the 'circle' is to play it on the keyboard as single notes, selecting any random locations on the keyboard. For example: starting at the top of the circle you play a C, any C. Say Middle C. The next note in the circle is F. Play any F. It doesn't necessarily have to be the F below Middle C. Next play any Bb, to any Eb, etc. *Memorize* it as you play. Once you've done that you know the fifth below every note in the scale and you are on your way to changing your entire concept of pop harmony, which is really traditional harmony as epitomized by Bach.

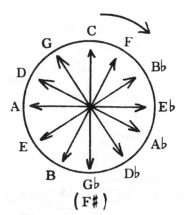

The illustration above is the one you will use to find chord substitutions and passing chords. Here are the three rules to remember:

Rule 1: You can often use the chord directly across the circle as a substitute for the chord you are playing.
(Example: if you are playing an F7 chord, follow the arrow across to find the likely substitute: B7.)

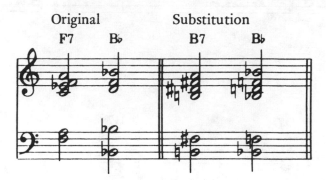

Rule 2: You can often use that same chord, the one directly across the circle, as a passing chord in addition to the original chord. (Example: if you are playing an F7 to a Bb progression, as written in a piece of sheet music, you can slip that same B7 in between as a passing chord.)

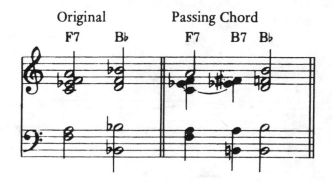

Rule 3: You can often precede the chord you are playing with the chord which precedes it in the circle. (Example: you are playing a G7 chord for two beats and would like to "fill" a chord before you hit the G7. Delay the G7 until the second beat and play the chord which precedes it in the circle on the first beat. The chord which precedes it in the circle is a D. In the example below we use a Dm7.)

Let us now apply these rules to a portion of Jerome Kern's "All The Things You Are."

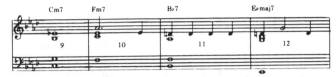

Before we substitute chords, take a quick look at how Kern composed this song around the circle of fifths, and also uses the 'jump-across-the-circle' technique we've discussed. His first chord is Fm. Next chord a Bbm (next in circle); his next chord Eb7 (next chord in circle); next chord (can you guess?) is also the next chord in the circle, an Ab: the next chord is (how can you miss?) a Db, the next chord in the circle. (You could practically play this song 'by ear' if you knew the circle of fifths.)

On the next chord, Kern throws a little curve. He gives us a G7. The G7 is *not* the next chord in the circle after Db7 . . . but it *is* the chord which is located directly across (follow the arrows) from the Db7. He has used the 'jump-across' technique to continue his song. And now he starts using the circle all over again beginning on the G7. The next chord is C. It changes to Cm before going on to Fm, the next circle chord. Analyze the rest of the example yourself to see Kern follow the circle and jump across.

Now let's put in some of our own chords using the rules we discussed here.

In the third measure we will use another chord instead of the Eb7. To find a possible substitute, look directly across the circle. An A7.

Now that we have that A7, let's apply Rule 3 to put a 'filler' or 'passing' chord in front of it. Find the chord which precedes A7 in the circle, and use it just before you use the A7.

By using the circle, we have substituted two chords for the Eb7, and now you are leaving the sheet music arrangement for your own styled interpretation.

In measure 11, there is a Bb7 chord and we can apply the same technique. First find the substitute by looking across the circle. The substitute is E7.

Now use a filler chord by finding the chord which precedes the E7 in the circle. A B chord. Since there's a D in the melody, Bm chord is the logical choice.

And finally   , in the 14th measure, we can apply all three rules.

There is a D7 for four beats. An Am7 played before the D7 (Rule 3) and an Ab7 played after the D7 (Rule 2):

Or you can simply ignore the original D7 altogether by substituting the Ab7 for it (Rule 1) but still keeping the Am7 as a filler chord.

This demonstrates how the filler chord (Am7) for the D7 can also become the filler chord for the D7's substitute. Another DISCOVERY! Ah, the circle is full of 'em! ♩

pop piano

Modulation

by Stuart Isacoff

Modulation is the process of moving to a new key, either temporarily or for the duration of a piece. Singers often like to raise the key of a song one-half step for the final verse — to add dramatic flair to the performance. Sometimes, when a whole series of songs are to be performed without stopping — in a medley — the musicians will *modulate* from the key of the first song to the key of the second, etc. This means that instead of simply ending one song and beginning the next.

a way is found to lead smoothly into each new key from the one before.

There are endless possibilities for leading into new keys, but musicians most often use a few "standard" harmonic patterns that occur in the tunes themselves. One of these patterns is the cycle of fifths:
V goes to I. The I becomes the V of the next chord, and so on.

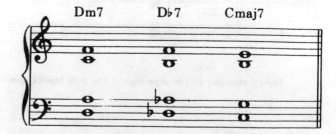

Another common pattern is II-V-I. This is really just a little segment of the cycle of fifths, confined to a particular key. For example, in the key of C, the pattern D to G to C represents a cycle of fifths progression, but the D chord in the key of C is minor and the G chord is a dominant 7th:

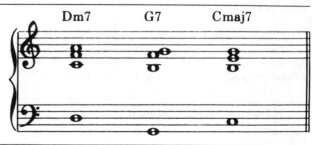

Let's look at other common progressions. I-VI-II-V-I should sound familiar enough:

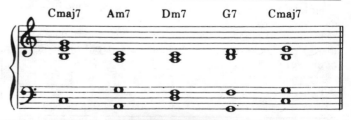

And half-step movement also works well. For example, instead of using the V or G⁷ chord to lead into C in the following example, we have used a Db⁷ :

70

How can all this be used in modulating from one key to another? I'm glad you asked. Let's try a few modulations.

Suppose we wanted to play SUNNY SIDE OF THE STREET, followed by CHEROKEE.

We would end on a C major chord, and begin again on a B♭ chord! Here's a simple way to make the transition: the V of B♭ is F⁷; the V of F is C⁷. So, we can use the cycle of fifths to lead us from the key of C to the key of B♭:

Another way of accomplishing the same thing would have been to use the half-step or *chromatic* movement of C to B⁷ to B♭:

How about moving from IN THE MOOD (key of G) to CHEROKEE? Here's an example of half-step motion leading to the V chord:

The various patterns we've listed could be broken into fragments and strung together for longer or more roundabout routes. Below is a transition from CHEROKEE to IN THE MOOD:

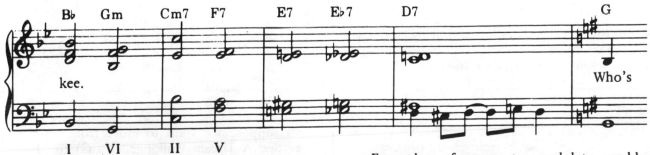

Examples of ways to modulate could fill several volumes. In the next issue we'll look at *voice-leading* in modulation.

Musical examples used by permission of Shapiro, Bernstein & Co., Inc.

Modulation
Part 2: Voice Leading

Moving from one musical place to another involves much more than simply following a harmonic progression. A series of chords "works" only because there is an underlying melodic strain that "leads" from one voice to another. For example, let's take the common progression V - I. In the key of C, we will play G^7 to C:

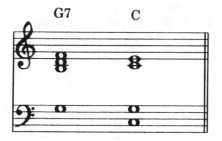

This movement sounds as solid as it does because the F in the G chord moves to the E in the C chord (a whole step); the note G acts as a "common tone" between the two harmonies (a common tone is the *strongest* possible connection between two musical moments); and the note B moves easily to the note C (a half step).

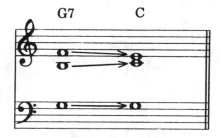

Such *voice leading* occurs often in popular music, and it can be spotted by looking for *stepwise* motion. The progression C to A to Dm, for instance, might appear this way:

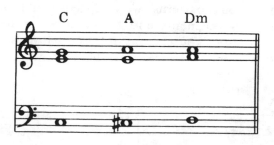

You'll notice that the bass line is moving chromatically stepwise, and that the right hand maintains a common tone: first the E, then the A.

This approach can be used in modulation, too. Last time we looked at certain chord progressions used to modulate from one key to another. This time, we'll explore the *voice-leading* approach.

Let's suppose we want to move from "Did You Ever See A Dream Walking?" (in G) to "Life Is Just A Bowl Of Cherries" (in B♭).

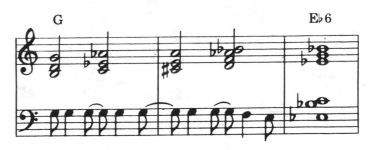

One way is to keep a common tone. The next example keeps the G in the bass, while the chords above move chromatically until reaching a B^{b7} chord.

Here's another possibility, along the same lines: the common tone is in the uppermost voice, and the bottom voice descends. The last chord before the new E^b harmony is a form of B^{b7} — the V chord of E^b. The inner voices I chose just as a matter of personal taste. They could have appeared in endless combinations. Usually, however, *dominant* sounds are most successful.

The next examples omit the common tone altogether. Here, the method is to set up what is known as "contrary motion." The upper voice moves up toward the B^b note of the new song,

while the bass voice moves downward towards the E^b.

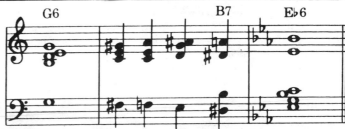

Again, the inner harmonies are strictly a matter of choice. A B^7 harmony moves strongly to an E^b harmony; like the V to I progression, the flat VI to I has both a common tone, and good voice leading.

Musical examples used by permission of Chappell Music Co., Inc.

The following article is designed as an introduction to transposing at sight. When you are finished with it, you will not be able to transpose at sight, but you will know how it's done. The prerequisites for getting the most out of this article are: you should have a working knowledge of major and minor scales, and you should know how to construct a chord and/or be able to identify chord names from written music.

The article has been divided into three phases. If you have never had any experience in transposition, take this introduction in small doses. Work on the first phase, and keep working on it until you thoroughly understand it before going on to Phase 2. Memorize as much as you can. Go very slowly. Remember this is a whole new thinking experience, and at times can be as frustrating as a Chinese puzzle. Have patience. Don't be afraid to get up, walk away, and come back later.

Although the article focuses on keyboard transposition, the overall system and logic is applicable to any instrument. So whether you are a guitarist or a piccolo player, if you want to understand basic transposition, this is a good place to start.

If you ever go to a recording studio and watch a group of professional studio musicians at work, you can begin to understand how much musical savvy it takes to be one of them. It is an enlightening experience, especially if you do it in Music City, U.S.A., Nashville. More often than not, Nashville musicians don't even use music. They record what are termed "head" arrangements. The composer of a song might play it a few times for them, let them know what kind of feeling he wants, when they should change key, and some other details. After a couple of run-throughs, the featured artist, Dolly Parton say, walks up to a mike and glides into the next month's #1 Country Hit. And it sounds like they rehearsed it for weeks.

How *do* they do it? Well aside from eating, sleeping and breathing music, and having musical ears as large as an elephant's, the boys in Nashville also have a system. A numbering system. And in order to get you into transposing, we are going to use a modified version of that system.

Firstly, you have to understand exactly what a *key* is. The *key of C*, the *key of G*, etc. Simply put, it is a frame of reference for a particular song, a module, if you will, where the song exists. Usually, a female singer cannot sing a song in the same range as a male singer. The entire song would have to be "lifted" to a new range in order to accommodate the female voice. By doing this, you can automatically change the entire complexion of a song. For example, a song played in the key of C can sound much more colorful and vibrant in the key of D-flat. Each key has a personality of its own, and most musicians agree that the key of C has a rather dull personality, and D-flat an interesting and alive one. If you have a good piano, try an experiment. Play some whole notes, slowly, using only white keys. Now play a similar phrase on black keys only. The black keys have a roundness of tone that is decidedly different than the whites. Bell-like. Therefore, when a key is used which has more sharps or flats, it usually is more exciting and interesting to listen to.

For our purposes, however, we will stick with the relatively simple keys, and leave it up to you to apply the theory to all twelve keys at your own speed. Let's get on to the numbering system.

PHASE I:

Example 1:

Key of C

In the above example of the C scale, each tone is assigned

the ROOTS of

a number. C is the tonic of the scale. The tonic always = I.

Let's look at the F scale:

Example 2:

Key of F

F is now the tonic, it gets the numeral I. (C is no longer the tonic, and loses its I status. Being the fifth note of the F scale, we assign it a V.

Exercise: Write out the scale in the key of G, placing the proper numbers under each scale tone. (Don't forget that there is an F# in the key of G.)

In our initial experiments with modulation and transposition, we will use a song with only two chords. We will use the Tonic chord which is built on the tonic of the scale (I), and the Dominant chord which is built on the fifth tone (V).

Exercise: Write out the D scale but only put the numbers I and V under their correct notes. (D has two sharps, F + C.)

Now that you've read this far, and have done the written exercises, you have, whether you know it or not, accomplished basic transposition. You have taken a basic scale pattern and shifted it (on paper) from G to D.

Let us now transpose our first song.

Example 3:

Key of C

Recognize the above melody? It is, of course, the old war horse, "Chop Sticks". It only uses three tones of the scale. It starts on V, Moves to VII, ends on I. (Memorize this number sequence.)

Exercise: Write the Roman numerals for each melody note *under* the above example.

Now take the G scale which you wrote out earlier and find the same numbered scale tones (V, VII, I).

Play the same melody in the key of G without peeking at the example below.

PHASE II:

Example 4:
Key of G

Now let's add a single note bass line on the first beat of every measure. (Stay in the key of G.)

The bass line starts on II. Can you play it (left hand alone) with just the numerals. (Thumb on II, down to V with the pinky.)

Bass line: II, V, I, V, II, V, I.

Example 5:
Key of G

The following example uses no notes whatsoever. It's the same piece of music with just Roman numerals. Can you play it in the same key (G) by only looking at the numerals? Keep at it until you can.

Example 6:
(Any Key)

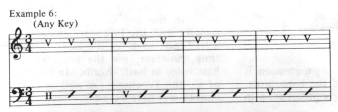

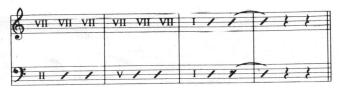

Once you get it in G, take a good long look at it and, before you try to play it, think it through in the *key of C!* Unless you have had some experience in this kind of thing, you might find this somewhat difficult. If you have trouble, play the hands separately. *But whatever you do, forget the notes and think of the numbers!*

Once you have it in C, refer to our example above of the F scale and find the correct notes for V, VII, I, and then for the bass (II, V, I). Now play it through in the key of F, both hands.

PHASE III:

There are only two chords in "Chopsticks", the V and I. What we will do now is forget the melody, and create a chordal accompaniment which we will transpose into several keys.

Here is our accompaniment in the key of F. Note that we are using the same bass line.

TRAN♫POSITION

by Ed Shanaphy

Example 7:
Key of F

The numerals between the staves indicate the chords being used (I and V). In the key of F, the V chord is a C chord, and the I chord is, of course, an F chord.

In order to transpose this accompaniment to another key, three things have to happen in your head in the following order:

1) You have to recognize which chords are being used (I, V, IV, II, whatever.)

2) You must analyze how the chords are being voiced. The easiest way to do this is to identify which scale tone is in the top voice of the chord, II, V, I, VI, etc.

3) You must know the numbers of the bass tones.

Continued on page 79

EAR TRAINING

by Ed Shanaphy

Training your ear is much the same as training your dog: you keep shouting orders at it until it recognizes what a certain sound means. For example, if someone sat at your piano and kept playing major chords without interruption for two straight days, you would no doubt recognize a major chord any time one sounded during the remainder of your life. Or you might have the same dedicated friend strike nothing but major thirds: C and E, D and F#, F and A, etc. And the next time you heard your car horn you would probably exclaim, "Eureka! It's a major third." (Most car horns are "factory-tuned" to a major third.)

Once your ear is trained to decipher certain sounds, you can pretty much drive all of those around you to a padded cell with your recognitions. "Hear that train whistle? It's a perfect fourth!" Or when a car horn passes you on the highway producing the sliding Doppler effect: "That car just produced a tritone portamento descending!"

In spite of that, many of you have written requesting some tips on ear-training, so here goes.

A DEDICATED FRIEND

The first order of business is to find that friend who will sit and pound out the sounds for you. The best one that we can recommend is your tape recorder. Or a cassette recorder. It should have a numerical counter on it so you can rewind to a specific spot

accurately. (Thanks to the electronic age we live in, we can all become better musicians than would have been possible some years ago.) The tape recorder should be set up on a table close enough to your instrument so that you can operate it with the least amount of hassle.

You now must record a series of sounds which you wish to learn. The question is whether to start learning melodic intervals, chords, rhythms, progressions, whatever. Most teachers would recommend starting with melodic intervals such as skips of a major third, a perfect fifth, major sixth, etc. However, it is not necessary to start here, and I, for one, think that starting with chord progressions is a lot more fun, and gets you right into the thick of things immediately. You can train your ear in melody easily enough by continually picking out melodies of songs on your instrument. The operative word is *continually*. And later on in your tape recorder exercises you can record easy melodies which you will later take as musical dictation. But let us now skip right on to the progressions.

THE GREAT AMEN

Before recording any progression, it is advisable to record the tonic note. I.e., if you are doing a progression in

the key of C, record the single note of C followed immediately by the progression. This will orient you to a 'home base' and make things a bit easier.

Our first progression will be what is commonly called the "Amen" progression: IV to I. The fourth tone of any scale is called the subdominant, so technically speaking this is the subdominant to tonic progression.

Keeping the common tone in the melody (if you are in the key of C, C is the common tone and should remain as the top note in both chords), record the IV, I progression in the following keys: C, Eb, Db, G, E, Ab, F, A, Gb, Bb, D, B. Record the same series twice, and don't forget to record the tonic note before each IV, I progression. (Note: the bass voice should use roots of each chord.)

Before your listening exercises begin, there's some more we must record. Record the exact same progression again in each key as outlined above, but with a melody change. Use the sixth tone of the scale in the IV chord ascending to the tonic in the I chord. (In the key of C this means your melody goes from A to C.) Record the series of keys only once this time. Again, use the roots in the bass.

Your last recording will be to change the melody whereby the fourth tone of the scale descends to the third tone. In the key of C, it will be F melody with the IV chord, descending a half-tone to E for the I chord. This time, however, use the tonic as the bass voice in both chords. In the key of C, the IV chord (as well as the I chord), will have a C bass.

Now we are ready to play it back. Listening to the entire series of this progression (you should have 48 of them on tape), just close your eyes and let the sound of the IV, I progression sink in. This might read like an instruction in a book on meditation, *because that is exactly what you are doing.* You are meditating on musical sound.

The second time through, listen for the bass, and be certain that you can hear it as you progress through each key. Sing along with the bass part. This is good.

On your third and final listening, concentrate on the melody line, singing along with it for each progression. (What should eventually happen as you listen to the single note tonic being sounded, is that you will be singing the correct melody notes even before the tape recorder sounds them out.)

PROGRESSIONS FOR PROGRESS

The IV, V, I progression.

It's back to the *record* button. This time we will introduce the V chord (dominant), and place it between the IV and I. Again record it in all keys as in the previous series, and with bass and melody notes for each series as follows:

1st series of twelve keys:
Melody: I — VII — I
Bass: IV — V — I

2nd series of twelve keys:
Melody: VI — VII — I
Bass: IV — V — I

3rd series of twelve keys:
Melody: I — II — I
Bass: VI — VII — I

At this point, you should be getting some idea of the regimen, i.e., there should be a minimum of three series for each progression, with melody and bass changes for each series. Listed below are more progressions which should be recorded in the identical manner. They become progressively more complex as you go along. Incidentally, this is a program which can easily take you some weeks, even months to complete. So don't be in a big hurry. But do it *continually* lest your ear become lazy! It's up to you now to decide what the melodic variations should be as well as the bass movement. Keep it consistent within each series so that you can pick out the top and bottom voices without too much trouble. You will be wise to keep the bass in the roots for now.

You can go into inversions at some later time.

Progressions For Recording

1. II, V, I
2. I, V, I
3. I, II, V, I
4. V, IV, I
5. I, VI, IV, V, I
6. I, III, VI, II, V, I
7. IV, IVm, I, V, I (m = minor)
8. I, VII(Maj), III, VI, II, V, I
9. I, VI(Maj), II(Maj), V, I

(The above progression is called the "We want Cantor" progression. Also the chord changes are sometimes called "Rhythm changes" since it is the progression used in "I Got Rhythm".)

MANDATORY EXERCISES

I. Record the following chord progression a few times, each time varying the voice leading, but keeping the roots in the bass line. This is what is called the cycle of 5ths, utilizing the dominant seventh type chord. Recognizing this progression by ear, going through all the keys, will be the greatest boon to your ability to play by ear in the future.

C7 — F7 — Bb7 — Eb7 — Ab7 — Db7—
Gb7 — B7 — E7 — A7 — D7 — G7 — C

II. A variation of this would be to utilize the minor 7th chord in conjunction with the dominant 7th:

Cm7 — F7 — Bbm7 — Eb7 — Abm7 —
Db7 — etc. through the cycle.

There's plenty here to keep you busy for a spell. However, there might be times when you would rather sidestep the routine and have some fun, still deriving ear-training benefits. Here's a suggestion: record a song from the sheet music, one you haven't played very much, and listen to it play back while following the progressions and voice movements on the sheet. Later on, listen to the playback without the sheet. How much of it can you decipher? If there are progressions within the song that you can't get, look them up on the sheet, and keep playing them back on the recording until you have it. Do this with other songs. It's an enjoyable exercise, and will help you immensely.

His Mentor's Voice

Polychords — *continued from p. 63*

Roots of Transposition — *continued from p.75*

Let us take each of those three steps and explain them in detail as we again look at the example in the key of F.

Example 7:
Key of F

Obviously you can play this as written. But what we are going to ask you to do is to look at it as you play it in a new key. Play it in C as you read it in F.

Step 1: *You have to recognize which chords are being used.*

The first chord is a C chord in the above example. Which number is that in the key of F?

Answer: V chord (or Dominant).

What is the Dominant (V) chord in the key of C?

Answer: G chord.

Play a G chord with your right hand. (G-B-D) (With the G as the lowest note, this is called ROOT POSITION.)

Step 2: *You must analyze how the chord is being voiced. The easiest way to do this is to identify which scale tone is used in the top voice.*

In our example above, the top voice or note of the chord is a C. That is the fifth tone of the F scale (V). What is the fifth tone of the C scale?

Answer: The fifth tone of the C scale is G.

Play the G chord with the G on top. (B-D-G). (This is no longer ROOT POSITION since the root of the chord, G, is not on the bottom. This is an inversion.)

Now play the G chord in this inversion in the exact rhythm of the first measure above (right hand only).

Note: the second measure is exactly the same for the right hand.

Step 3: *You must know the numbers of the bass tones.*

In the first measure the bass note is a G, the II scale tone, and the bass note in the second measure is a C (V).

What are the II and V tones in our new key of C?

Answer: II = D; V = G.

Play the bass line of the first two measures using the II and V tones of the new key (C).

Now play the first two measures, both hands, in the new key of C. Keep looking at the example, even though it is in F, as you play these measures.

A good exercise at this point is to play the two measure units in its original key (F) several times, and then play it in C several times. Keep switching back and forth. It's like working a switch, a "transposing switch" in your brain, to get it working more easily.

Proceed to measure 2 and 3 and apply the same 3 steps. Once you have the first four measures down, you have the whole routine since the last four are an exact repeat. Again, once you have accomplished the transposition, play it in its original key, and start working the "switch" again. Why not try playing "Chopsticks" in the key of G?

What does it take to become facile at this transposing business? First of all, you should do a little every day. Even if it's one or two measures of a song. Secondly, you must commit to memory all scales and chords, and all the corresponding numbers. This must be second nature to you. I.e., you should be able to answer questions like the following without even thinking:

What is the III tone in the key of A-flat?
E-flat is the IV tone in which key?
What is the II chord in Fm?
A# is the VII tone of which key?
" " " III " " " " "

KEYBOARD STYLES & IMPROVISATION

PIANO TIPS FROM THE PROS

DEVELOPING YOUR OWN STYLE

by Ed Shanaphy

Before the advent of Rock, that is before music became a groupie thing, musicians strived more for individuality by developing their own style of playing, as *soloists*. With Rock, the *groups* have their individual sound, but not the musicians within the group. Any good rock drummer, for example, wouldn't necessarily be missed in a prominent rock group if another good rock drummer sat in his place. But if Gene Krupa wasn't playing with the Benny Goodman sextet, lookout!

Keyboard styles, especially piano styles, are more easily discernible from one another. Anybody who knows even a smattering of piano stylists could tell the difference between George Shearing and Count Basie. And for some of you who have good memories, how about the contrasting styles of Frankie Carle and Carmen Cavallero?

Carmen developed a sizzling style of playing in double octaves which became his unmistakable trademark. (I still think he played octaves faster than anyone I've ever seen.) I was also told that he had his piano tuned sharper than standard A-440. And that it became progressively sharper up the keyboard. That, supposedly, enhanced the glassy effect of crackling ice that his octave sound produced. Perhaps. Shearing also was noted for a moving octave sound, but of a completely different color. He would fill in chord tones between the octave span and the melody moved in what is called "block chord" style. He diffused the effect even more when the guitar and vibes doubled his melody and "shadowed" every move he made. Absolutely beautiful.

Well, you ask, what about developing my own style? How do I go about it? (Most professional pianists answer the question "Where did you get your style?" just about the same way: "Well, I was fooling around on the piano one day . . ." *Don't you love that?* They try to tell you it happens in one day. ". . . and I just hit upon it." What they don't talk about is all the other days, YEARS, they just fooled around. But there is something there. Playing the piano has to have some "fooling around" time. If one wants to stylize, he or she must fool with a song, play around it, ignore the melody, substitute a chord, add a run. Once you become a slave to the written notes, you have dismissed any chance of being a stylist, be it jazz, pops, or even honky-tonk.

The purpose of this article is not to start you on a course in piano styling. That would be very dull. We'd have to start with playing by the chord system and all that. That's something that can be very easily achieved by going out to your local music dealer and picking up some chord books. (Playing by chord symbols is the easiest thing once you put your mind to it.) However, you don't have to play by chords to "fool around." And THAT's the purpose of this article . . . learning how to fool around on the piano.

We'll teach you two runs. From there, using the same principle, you invent a few of your own. Once you have invented even one, your styling days have begun!

The two runs we'll learn have several things in common. First of all they are built on a major chord like C-E-G, or Bb-D-F. (For you people who know what a dominant 7th chord is, you may make them into a dominant 7th by adding a Bb to the C chord, an Ab to the Bb chord.)

Another thing they have in common is that they consist of coupling two elements together. Once you have memorized the two elements, then you simply make them into a full keyboard cadenza descending by mere repetition. Let's call this system the "couplet run system" therefore, since the run is really made up of two tiny runs.

Note: To get you away from the written notes, we are not using examples on the staff. You will find that you'll memorize the run faster and will think it through better using this method.

RUN # 1: (Built on a Bb chord, dom. 7th):
Element # 1:   Pinky on a high Ab, descending to F (3rd finger), descend again to D (2nd finger), and

finally descend to a Bb with your thumb.

It's a simple Bb7 arpeggio descending for all you people who know your chords. Before you move on to element #2, just practice this simple arpeggio until you get it going in rapid succession at a very fast clip.

Element # 2: O.K., your thumb is on a Bb, the last note from element #1. Your pinky (5th finger) comes down to the D above that Bb; that D descends to B (natural) (3rd finger), then to G# (2nd finger), then to E with the thumb. Again a simple E7 arpeggio descending.

The Full Run: You now have the two elements: a Bb7 arpeggio moving right into the E7 arpeggio without a speck of a delay. Practice the two in rapid succession a few dozen times. Now all you have to do: your thumb is on E, bring your pinky down to the Ab above that E and start the couplet all over again an octave lower. And keep repeating it over, an octave lower each time, until you've reached a good bass note E. And then resolve the E to an Eb. End of piece!

The Left Hand: The best thing for the left hand to do is just hold a low Bb octave and let the right hand do its thing.

Where To Use: Obviously, we are in the key of Eb. And a Bb chord almost always is the next to the last chord in an Eb song. The last chord, naturally is an Eb. It's called TONIC. The chord built on the fifth note up from TONIC is called DOMINANT. DOMINANT ALMOST ALWAYS LEADS TO TONIC no matter what key you are in. So the best place to put this run is at the very end of the piece just as you hit the next to last chord (Bb DOMINANT 7th).

RUN # 2:

KEY: F

CHORD: C DOMINANT 7th

(To be more specific: C-E-G-Bb.)

Element # 1: A high Bb with your 4th finger (ring finger), descending to A (3rd finger), descending to Ab (2nd finger), descending to G (thumb). A simple chromatic 4-note run. Repeat it in rapid succession until you've got it fast and smooth. Set your metronome at 130 and play the entire element in each click. That's fast enough. (If you can't play it that fast, don't despair, work on it later.)

Element # 2: Your thumb is on G from element #1. Cross your 4th finger over the thumb to the very next note F. This is the first note of element #2, descending to E (3rd), then to Db (2nd), and C (thumb). Practice the two together slowly to get that cross-over smooth.

The Full Run: After you play the two elements in rapid succession, cross that 4th finger over again to the Bb and start the couplet all over again going right down the keyboard.

The Left Hand: Again, a simple C octave in the bass is probably best. A C7 chord will work fine too.

Where To Use: Just about anyplace a C7 chord exists in a piece, and your good judgment says it's right.

Now you can invent one yourself. The rules are: 1: You must build your run on a DOMINANT 7th chord. 2: The run must consist of two elements as above. I.e., you must use the *couplet run system*. Hint: try one ascending.

This is your start of "fooling around" and inventing your own style ideas. We've laid down the rules here just to give you some framework in which to create.

COUNTRY-STYLE AT THE KEYBOARD

by Stuart Isacoff

The popularity of country music has grown so swiftly over the past few years that almost every musical style has been influenced by it in some way. Pop and rock artists often record in Nashville, and the little slides and fills which grew in the green hills of "Opry" country have now worked their way into urban music centers with pleasant insistence and rewarding results. While the elements of this style spring from the way certain instruments, notably the guitar, are played by country musicians, these techniques are easily transferred to the piano.

Let's look at some of the phrases and "frills" you can add to pieces to give them a country flavor, beginning with basic accompaniment patterns. Country back-up rhythms are usually very simple and straight-forward (like down-home country people!):

Ex. 1

Depending on the particular song, the accompaniment may have less movement in the left hand, and more in the right:

Ex. 2 & 3

Notice the bit of *walking bass* used in switching from the C chord to the F. Other forms of this movement occuring in country-style piano include the use of a *drone* note above:

Ex. 4

or parallel 3rds or 10ths:

Ex. 5

or triplets which arpeggiate or break up the individual harmonies:

Ex: 6

The walking line can move down, as well as up.

Ex. 7

Ornaments play a big role in this music and many of them duplicate sounds characteristic of the guitar. For example, guitarists sometimes "hammer on" notes, by striking a vibrating string down against the fingerboard; or they "pull off" notes by plucking a string with their fingering hand. The equivalent sounds on piano are these:

Ex.'s 8, 9, & 10

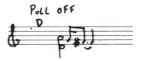

82

Ex. 13

Floyd Cramer is famous for using these devices. The moving note always ends up on the third of the chord, starting from the second or the fourth.

Those *drone* notes can be used in many situations, and they often are:

Ex. 11

Other country sounds are the *tremelo* (used in slow songs very effectively):

Ex. 12

the quick chord *arpeggio* (like a guitar strum):

and guitar-like "picking patterns":

Ex. 14

Applying these country "flavorings" to a song is simply a matter of looking for places to plug into the chord progression one or several of the "riffs" we've explored. It's important not to over-do it, but filling in with these sounds can be great fun:

Ex. 15

Playing With Blocks

by Stuart Isacoff

Playing with blocks isn't always kid stuff — especially when the "blocks" we're talking about are a type of chord "voicing" made popular by jazz great George Shearing (and duplicated by hundreds of nightclub pianists around the world).

Every professional keyboardist knows that the very same notes can produce dramatically different sounds, depending on where they are placed. In order to play a C maj. 7 chord, for example, we might choose a voicing that stretches the harmony across the length of both hands:

Ex.1

Cmaj7

This is a fairly "open" voicing. A "close" voicing of the same chord would look more like this:

Ex.2

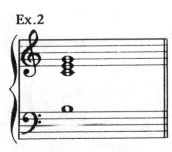

Continued on next page

83

The notes here are close to each other; in fact, they're fairly cramped.

The block chord is a form of "close-voicing" that usually accompanies each note of the melody, and produces an unmistakable "cocktail" sound. Here's how it works.

When playing a melody in block-chord fashion, we take the melody note and duplicate it one octave below.

Ex.3

We now have the top and bottom notes of our chords. All that's left is to fill in the other chord tones. We started with five voices, so we'll maintain the same number throughout.

Ex.4

If we were to eliminate the 6th or 7th from the harmony the sound would fall apart. The block chord effect depends on the bunched-together quality that occurs when those chord tones are added. (Notice that we end up playing an F maj. 7 instead if F6 in measure 2, and an Fm (maj.7) instead of an Fm6 in measure 3. That's because we are doubling the melody note, which happens to be the 7th of the chord, and we are limiting our harmonies to five tones. The result is perfectly fine.)

It's possible to use even thicker chords (adding 9ths, 11ths, etc.) when playing block style. (Example 5 alternates the F6 with an occasional 7th or 9th.) But this is a good start, and it can provide many hours of fun and exploration. Get your friends to tinkle some glasses in the background, dim the lights and you'll be all set.

Ex.5

PEDAL POINT
by Stuart Isacoff

Many of the devices used by contemporary pop keyboard players have their origins in the classical tradition. These include ostinatos (repeating bass lines), syncopated rhythms, and a colorful harmonic twist called *pedal point*, which goes all the way back to the 12th century.

Pedal point doesn't refer to the pedals on your piano. It is an effect which occurs when one tone is held in the bass while various harmonies move over it — some of which are dissonant. These dissonant sounds appear only briefly because the harmonic motion never rests for too long, and the result is interesting and attractive:

Two kinds of pedal point are found frequently in contemporary music. One, called *tonic* pedal point, occurs in the example below. Carole King and other rock artists make it a part of their style:

Familiar sounding? (It's called a "tonic" pedal because the bass note stays on the root of the tonic, or I chord.)

This effect can be used wherever a musical phrase begins and ends on the same chord. For example, look at this melody:

If we were going to play it with a simple root-movement (playing the root of each chord) in the bass, it might come out this way:

But a large part of the phrase begins and ends on the same chord: C.

$$C - G - F - C$$

Since we know from the start that we are going to end up once again on the C, we can simply hold it on the bottom, creating a pedal point:

It sounds so much more impressive, yet it takes less effort!

Pedal points work just as well with arpeggio patterns:

The second type of pedal point is called *dominant*. In practically all Western music there is a strong movement of V to I (dominant to tonic):

The dominant pedal keeps the 5th of the chord in the bass, so it is especially useful as a musical introduction leading into the first chord of a song:

Experiment with both kinds of pedal point on several different tunes. It is a simple device that will make your playing sound surprisingly sophisticated.

TAKING IT ALL IN STRIDE
by Stuart Isacoff

Thomas "Fats" Waller, composer of AIN'T MISBEHAVIN', along with countless other jazz greats, was an expert in *stride piano,* a style of swing-bass playing developed in Harlem in the 1920's. The name *stride* probably resulted from the use of single notes or octaves in the bass, followed by a stride upward to hit a chord before bouncing back down again. Some of the great stride players included Willie "The Lion" Smith and James P. Johnson, but even lesser-known musicians of that time helped to make it a popular and longstanding technique. One of the last surviving pianists of the stride school, Joe Turner, offers this explanation for both the name and the popularity: "I guess it was because it's just like striding down the avenue when you play it."

Stride takes the concept of bass-chord-bass-chord (the standard accompaniment pattern for thousands of show-tune arrangements), but adds fire to it by placing all of the accompaniment in the left hand:

A further twist on the old pattern is used: the chord doesn't always follow a bass note. And frequently short melodic lines, played in octaves, move from one chord to another:

That's not too difficult! Let's go even further. Try playing tenths instead of a single note. (If you can't stretch to reach the tenth, hit the bottom note slightly ahead of the beat):

Did you notice the fullness of the chord at the end of the last example? Combining the tenths with full, close-positioned chords gives us a real stride sound:

As you can see, inversions also play a part in this style. They can ascend, as in the previous example, or move downward, as in this one:

One last trick and we'll be ready to move on to the tune itself. In order to connect the left hand movements, stride pianists sometimes use chromatic motion (1/2 step motion), by taking a chord progression such as this one:

and inserting chords in-between (they often use the VII chord of the chord they are moving to, or an inversion of the V, in order to lead in gently:

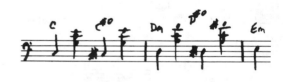

Keep it bouncy, and try your hand at continuing the song in this style. With a little effort, I'm sure you'll come up with plenty of fun variations.

RAGTIME RIFFS

By Stuart Isacoff

In the introduction to his *Etudes,* Scott Joplin lashed out at those who threw bricks at "hateful ragtime," and announced with some pride that it is a music of often painful difficulty. He created his set of ragtime lessons, as he wrote, "to assist amateur players in giving the 'Joplin Rags' that weird and intoxicating effect intended by the composer."

Keyboardists who attempt ragtime rhythms are more likely to face confusion than intoxication, but with a little practice the weirdness of the music will seem no more jarring than falling down a flight of stairs. A good way to begin is to examine the music to see what the shortest note value is. If a sixteenth note is the shortest, count the entire measure in sixteenth notes.

Ex. 1

Using the sixteenth notes as a basis, the tricky rhythms that contradict the natural accents in each measure become less of a problem. Usually the left hand keeps up a steady, even pulse (although it will at times play a raggy countermelody).

The right hand riffs of ragtime will most often fall into a few rhythmic combinations, all based on the syncopated feeling of example 1. These combinations place the "syncope" either before or after an even group of eighth or sixteenth notes; one of the key features of ragtime is the contrast set up between the syncopated figures and the "straight" figures surrounding them.

Ex. 2a

Ex. 2b

These combinations become a little more complicated through the use of ties.

Ex. 3a

Ex. 3b

Ex. 3c

Ex 3d

- or -

Ex. 3e

Again, the way to practice these is by counting them in sixteenth note divisions. Go through all the combinations above and then make up some additional ones yourself. After practicing each of the rhythmic possibilities, you'll be set to tackle any ragtime piece. ♩

Perhaps you are one of those people who play an instrument by chords, and you find that you just play the chords which are indicated in the standard sheet music. But when you happen to hear the same pieces that you play, played by a professional instrumentalist, for some reason the chords sound much different. It's sounds as if there are a lot more chords in there than you learned. How so?

The answer to that is usually that a substitute chord has been used to either replace the original chord, or the substitution has been used *in addition* to the original chord. There are other methods regarding chord substitution and alteration, but in this article we will touch only on replacing the original chord, or finding a second chord to use with it. Look at example #1.

In the first measure we have a Cm7 chord progressing to an F7 chord. In the second measure we have a Bb chord. This progression is indicative of a cardinal rule in music: ALL MAJOR AND MINOR CHORDS TEND TO LEAD TO A CHORD WHOSE ROOT IS A PERFECT FIFTH LOWER. THIS RULE IS ESPECIALLY TRUE OF DOMINANT SEVENTH CHORDS.

Therefore, before we begin substituting and adding chords to this little phrase of music, look at the following table, and without trying to memorize it, just try to understand it fully. The left-hand column shows all the roots of chords that can exist in music. If they are anything but diminished chords, the odds are that they will lead to a chord whose root is a perfect fifth lower (right hand column.) Now you will find a million instances where a chord leads elsewhere, that's true. And a chord can go anywhere a composer darn well wants it too. However, there is a kind of gravitational pull for a chord to resolve itself a perfect fifth below.

Chord letter	Tends to lead to this chord
C	F
F	Bb
Bb	Eb
Eb	Ab
Ab	Db
Db	Gb
Gb (F#)	B (Cb)
B (Cb)	E
E	A
A	D
D	G
G	C

(The above table has been arranged in

TIPS ON HARMONY

Chord Substitution and Fills
by Ed Shanaphy

such a way, that if you read either column straight down, you will find the same answer. I.e., rather than having arranged them alphabetically, we have arranged them in the "cycle of fifths." There's a term, cycle of fifths, that you should keep in the back of your brain for future reference.)

To look back at our musical example, therefore, we find a classic example of our cardinal rule, and our table, at work. Cm chord leads to F7, a perfect fifth below. And the F7 leads to a perfect fifth below as well, Bb.

Okay, so what substitution may we use? To arrive at a substitution, it is important that we see what the next chord is. We must really look at two chords at a time. If the second chord is a fifth below the first, a chord we may use in place of the first chord is located one half-tone above the second chord.

Example: 1st chord F7
            2nd chord . . . . . Bb

(One half-tone above the second chord is B. Use a B7 instead of the F7.)

Try it on the musical example. (#2).

Let's review the rule:

In a two-chord "cycle of fifths" progression, we may replace the first chord with a chord located one half-tone above the second chord.

Here's a trick: You may use the substitution we have just arrived at *in addition* to the first chord. In other words, you don't have to throw the original away altogether. In this case, the new chord is a filler chord, not an actual substitute. Your progression on the musical example can be, therefore: Cm F7 B7 Bb. (Example #3).

Try it a few times. Experiment with the voicing of the chords until you are satisfied with the smoothness of sound leading from one chord to another. (We will deal with chord voicings many times in future articles, but experimentation is

the best teacher in the beginning.)

Review this principle we have just discussed, and experiment with it in other keys and progressions until you feel you are fairly familiar with it.

Now let's go on to another simple, yet effective chord filler. Whenever you have a Dominant 7th chord, say a G7, chances are you may precede it with a chord whose root is a fifth higher. (If you think about this, you will realize that it's nothing more than a reversal of our cycle of fifth table. Just read the table from right to left.)

The only addition to this rule we might add here is that the chord you use to precede the dominant 7th chord will usually be a minor 7th chord. In other words that G7 chord would be preceded, or led into, with a Dm7 chord. An F7 chord would be preceded by a Cm7 chord. In fact, if you look at the first measure of our musical example you will see an F7 being preceded by a Cm7 chord.

Let's review this rule:

A dominant 7th chord may often be preceded by a minor 7th chord whose root is a perfect fifth higher. We will call this minor 7th chord a filler chord.

Let's use it in the example: In the second measure, on the third beat we have a G7 chord. What we will do is use a Dm7 chord on that third beat instead, and use the G7 on the fourth beat. Try it slowly. (Example #4).

What about that last chord, the G7? Where does it go? To a Cm7 in the third measure. (See #1.) It goes to a chord a fifth lower. Therefore, let's apply our rule that says: in a two-chord "cycle of fifths" progression (G7 to Cm7) we may replace the first chord with a chord located one half-tone above the second chord.

Instead of the G7 we will use a Db7.

Now our first two measures look like this:

Cm7 F7 B7 Bb Dm7 Db7

Note: Try a Dbm7 too. Both sound fine. I prefer the Dbm7. (Example #5).

You may recognize our musical example by this time, it is the bridge for *Angel Eyes*, located in this issue. *Angel Eyes*, in addition to being a beautiful song, is perfect for our purposes of chord fills and substitutions.

No. 6 is an example of the complete bridge of the song, using chord fills and substitutions which utilize the rules you have learned as well as some other tricks which we will discuss in future issues. (Example #6).

TIPS ON HARMONY EXAMPLES

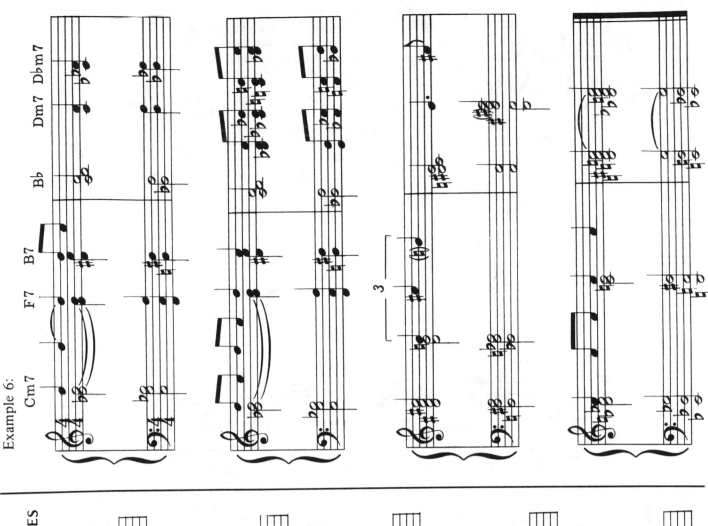

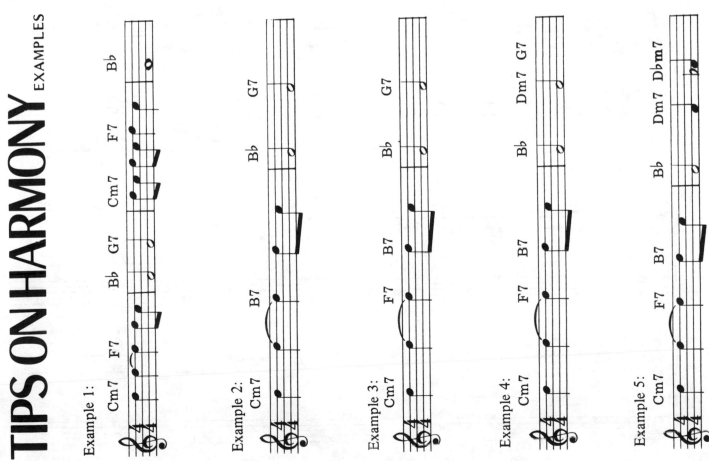

TIPS ON HARMONY

Extended Endings

More often than not, a standard piece of sheet music ends with a very simple straight ending. However, many instrumentalists prefer to improvise their own ending as they do with an introduction or "intro." There are many types of endings, but the one we will deal with here is the extended ending. The purpose of an extended ending is to delay the TONIC chord beyond the point where the listener expects it. In so doing, the instrumentalist creates a special improvised conclusion in keeping with the mood of the song, which also serves as a surprise bonus for the listener. Any listener, no matter how naive, feels that last TONIC chord coming. And when it doesn't happen exactly where he feels it, you've got his attention until the very end.

One tip: whatever chords you use in your ending should harmonize with the last melody note of the song. This is especially true when accompanying a vocalist or melody instrument.

The last melody note is a C. A singer could hold that C right through the entire ending in either case, because all the chords in the endings harmonize with C.

Study these endings closely as far as chords are concerned. We are in the key of C, the first example substituting an F# diminished chord (fourth measure) for the C tonic. It is a diminished chord built on the augmented fourth scale tone of the key. And it keeps moving down chromatically until it finally winds up on a C chord. Try it in another key, with another song of similar mood. Do the same with the second example.

Also note the voice leading in example #1. The more you can use stepwise voice leading under the melody, the smoother the entire piece will be.

Learn these endings in several keys, and use your own creativity to improvise some others using the same basic principle: delaying the TONIC chord.

by Ed Shanaphy

Alberti Boogie

by Stuart Isacoff

Alberti Bass is a classical compositional technique, but it has much to do with contemporary left hand styles in rock and boogie-woogie, so it seems worthwhile to devote a column to it.

In classical music, Alberti bass refers to left hand accompaniment figures like the following, made up of broken chords:

They were named after Domenico Alberti, an 18th century composer who used them extensively, although similar patterns can be found in earlier music. One of the most famous examples of Alberti bass is in the opening of this piano sonata by Mozart:

Readers who have played early rock and roll or boogie-woogie will see some similarity here to left hand patterns which typify those pop sounds; the difference is often just a matter of dotting a note here and there. For example, this Alberti pattern:

can become this pop pattern:

The whole catalogue of left hand figures used for this sound is simply a set of variations on this basic idea. Here are some that should be familiar:

etc.

Continued on page 101

Disco At The Keyboard

POP PIANO

by Raphael Crystal

The disco sound is currently the hottest thing in popular music, and promises to be so for some time to come. We usually associate this style with big band arrangements, sophisticated recording techniques, and lots of percussion and electronic effects. Nevertheless it is possible to play disco songs at the piano. We are not talking about duplicating the total disco sound, of course, but of finding a workable solo keyboard equivalent.

Above all, it is necessary to capture the quality of disco rhythm. Let's begin by listing some components of this rhythm. Disco is always in 4/4 time, with a tempo somewhere around ♩ = 120. (There are slower and faster disco songs, but they all remain within the same general range.) There is a very strong quarter note beat, played by the bass drum, usually with accents on the second and fourth beats (a). Often the snare drum plays a pattern consisting mainly of eighth notes. This may have a very pronounced "marching band" flavor (b). And there is usually a sixteenth note pattern as well, often played on a synthesizer, or by Latin percussion instruments (c).

At the keyboard it is not necessary, or possible, to maintain all these levels of rhythmic activity at once. But they should all be suggested, or implied, in your playing. A strong foot beat is almost indispensable, to maintain the quarter note pulse. And you must tap your foot on *every* quarter-note — never on just the first and third beats.

Often the left hand part expresses the beat very clearly. Here, in a basic kind of disco arrangement, the left hand plays repeated notes on every beat. The bass should have a springy quality — accented but not staccato. Notice that the right hand adds eighth note offbeats at places where the melody is not active.

Our next example shows a somewhat more complicated bass part. Now, because of the syncopated rhythm, the left hand is not playing directly on every quarter note. So the strong foot beat becomes all the more necessary. Here the rhythm begins to have a Latin feel — another important ingredient of disco.

A popular disco device is the climbing octave bass line. Here the left hand provides eighth note motion as well as a strong quarter note beat. (Incidentally, this pattern is very similar to a boogie-woogie bass line, but with the important difference that in disco the eighth notes are always even.)

In a variant of the previous pattern, the left hand subdivides the second half of the beat into two sixteenth notes. Now another level of rhythmic activity is present in the bass:

By now it should be clear that one thing you would not use in disco style is a stride piano accompaniment (a), since this creates a cut time feeling. Also to be avoided is the kind of rock bass line that consists of dotted quarters and eighth notes (b). This rhythm does sometimes appear in disco sheet music, but it can cause problems because, in the absence of a bass drum playing every beat, it also tends to suggest cut time.

At the ends of phrases, or during long notes and rests in the melody, you can add disco-style "fills" in a higher register. These often feature repeated chords in syncopated sixteenth note patterns. They are meant to suggest the sound of backup singers or figures played by a brass section.

As we have pointed out, the eighth notes in disco are always even; they are never played as "swing eighths." But a jazz swing feeling is often present at the sixteenth note level. Try playing our next example using "swing sixteenths":

Continued on next page

Ex. 8

This last example brings up a problem which many musicians have with rock and disco: the prevalence of sixteenth notes and sixteenth note syncopations sometimes makes the music hard to read. This is mainly a notational problem. A passage which might look difficult, such as (a) in our next example, would appear much simpler if re-written with the note values doubled, as in (b). This is a useful way of dealing with problem spots, but we don't recommend it as a usual practice. The real solution is to become accustomed to sixteenth note patterns, and not be daunted by all the black marks on the page.

Ex. 9

a)

b)

Disco songs are usually recorded in both short and "extended play" versions. In the extended versions, statements of the tune are separated by long interludes made up of vamps, repeated figures, and sometimes jazz-like solos. These are all based on two- or four-bar patterns, often drawing on motives or progressions from the tune. Typically, a four-bar pattern will be repeated four times, to make a 16-bar section, and then another figure will be superimposed on it, or the music may move on to a different pattern.

Part of the fun of playing disco lies in making up these repeated figures to use as introductions, interludes and closing sections. They can be quite simple. Somewhat mechanical patterns can create a synthesizer-like sound, as in this example:

Ex. 10

Another kind of figure involves the use of rapidly repeated chords. Notice the effect of *not* playing on some of the beats. Remember that these phrases must be played four or eight times to get the true disco feeling.

Ex. 11

The harmony in disco changes rather slowly; usually there will be only one chord to a bar (and often a chord is held for much longer than that.) As in much contemporary popular music, there is a tendency to avoid dominant sevenths. On the other hand, the diminished seventh chord — usually on the raised seventh degree of a minor key (a) — seems to be making a comeback. Minor ninth chords are common, especially moving in parallel (b). And a very popular chord is what is sometimes called an F chord over a G bass. This chord is often used on the fifth degree of the scale, in place of a dominant seventh (c). It may also appear on the flatted seventh degree of a major key (e.g. B♭ in the key of C major) as a way of approaching the tonic without using a dominant (d).

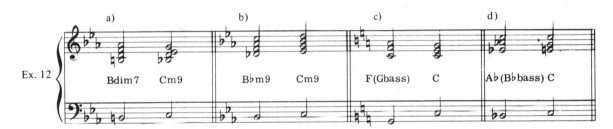

Ex. 12

Bdim7   Cm9   B♭m9   Cm9   F(Gbass)   C   A♭(B♭bass) C

One of the challenges in playing disco is to create endings for songs in place of the "repeat-to-fade" endings found on records. You can do this by prolonging the last note of the tune, after repeating the final phrase several times. Or you can go back to material from the introduction, and end with a sharply accented chord. The trick is to make your final section come out to eight or sixteen bars, so that it seems natural. In this example, a two-bar phrase that might come from the introduction to a song is played four times, and brought to a close at a convenient spot. Notice that it is not always necessary to end on the tonic.

Ex. 13

play 4 times

Disco should always be played very precisely, in order to convey its "machine-made" quality. The beat must be unwavering, the rhythms exactly in place, and all the notes of a chord must be struck at just the same moment.

If you want to sharpen up your disco technique, most of the examples in this article can be used as exercises. It has been said that disco dancing is really part of a national physical fitness craze — perhaps disco music can have a similar function for us keyboard players. So get into your musical jogging shorts, set your metronome at 120, and join the disco generation!

pop piano

STARTING OVER

by Stuart Isacoff

Turnarounds are a way of turning a tune or a section back to its beginning again. You'll most often find a turnaround at the end of a song, or at the conclusion of a "first ending" within the song. Here's an example from the original sheet music to *The Lady Is A Tramp*

We might substitute any number of progressions here, as long as we bring the music back to that C chord once again. One commonly used progression is I-VI-II-V-I:

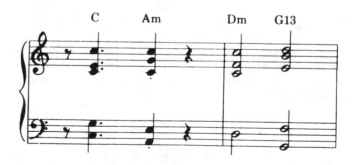

By using chord substitution we can freshen this up a bit:

Melodically, bits of the original song can be used (*sequence* is an especially enjoyable effect):

or, we can build ascending or descending patterns based on other tunes, or on exotic scales:

Remember, our aim is to construct a bridge between the final chord of a section, and the chord which begins the section over again (they are often the same chord). Try your hand at creating new turnarounds. You might make friends with a sound you never met before!

pop piano

CREATING COUNTER-MELODIES

By Stuart Isacott

Counter-melodies (you don't have to be in a coffee shop to play one) can add new depth and color to your arrangements, and there is a simple way to go about making them up. Let's use IF I LOVED YOU /for practice:

Ex. 1

The first two measures present a very primitive type of counter-melody. Here the chord is simply being arpeggiated, or broken-up. But most melodies make use of smaller steps, and more varied motion: moving up and down and weaving in and out. To begin creating a more interesting line, think of the scales from which the chords are derived:

Ex. 2

Ex. 3

The arpeggiated chords serve as a good foundation, which we can keep and build on. Let's take the first interval of the counter-melody:

Ex. 4

and insert another scale tone:

Ex. 5

That's a little more interesting already. But if we continue in the same way we'll simply end up with a scale. So we'll place a note *above* instead of in-between the next interval:

Ex. 6

Now that we've placed one note in-between an interval of the broken chord, and one above, we can try adding a note *below* the next interval:

Ex. 7

Applying these possibilities to each measure makes it easier to come up with an unlimited supply of counter-melodies. Remember to vary the rhythm and the range. If you begin on the downbeat of one measure and play up the keyboard, try starting on an upbeat and playing downward on the next phrase.

Ex. 8

In a future column we will explore the use of accidentals (notes outside the scale), which can lend added color to your counter-melodies.

PART II — ACCIDENTALS

Last month we looked at a technique which can help you create counter-melodies in any song. This time, we'll take this approach one step further by adding notes which do not belong to the particular key or scale implied by the chord being played. Notes which lie outside the key are often referred to as "accidentals." They can add color and charm to a piece—provided they don't sound accidental!

Let's work with the song SUMMERTIME

Any measure in which the melody comes to rest on a held note is ripe for added melodic movement in the bass or mid-range:

Ex. 1

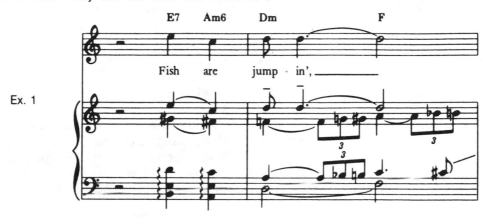

As you'll remember from the last column, a good way to begin adding melody is to think of inserting a note below, above or in-between a chord interval:

Ex. 2

We can use the same technique with notes that don't fall within the expected or "correct" harmonies:

Ex. 3

The out-of-key notes should generally fall near a chord note so that the melodic movement is smooth; it is also important to land on a chord tone often enough to remind the ear once again where the foundation of the song lies.

These "chromatic" movements (half-step motion is known as chromatic movement) can be strung together, repeated on different pitches, or played backwards or upside down to form counter-melodies—just as we would use material which comes directly from a major or minor scale.

Here are some more examples applied to SUMMERTIME. Try your hand at arranging some of the other songs in this issue in the same way.

Ex. 4

Musical examples used by permission of Chappell Music Co., Inc.

Style at the Keyboard

Playing Ellington Tunes

by Raphael Crystal

This music belongs to the jazz tradition, so a "swing eighths" rhythmic approach is called for. What is written as a string of even eighth notes should be played as a series of alternately long and short notes, creating the effect of 12/8 time. Our first example shows the opening phrase of *Do Nothin' Till You Hear From Me* as it appears in the sheet music (a) and rewritten in 12/8 (b).

Sometimes a dotted eighth and sixteenth note pattern appears, but it should also be given that 12/8 feel. Our next example is from the middle section of *Just Squeeze Me*.

The keyboard arrangements in Ellington sheet music are excellent, but you still may want to make up your own. At slow to moderate tempos, the "stride piano" technique is a basic resource. The left hand plays roots and fifths on the first and third beats, and middle-register chords on the second and fourth. Here are the opening bars of *Do Nothin' Till You Hear From Me* with a stride accompaniment:

Another important resource is the "walking bass." The left hand plays a bass note on every beat, while the right hand supplies melody and chords. The bass line is made up of chord tones, together with some passing tones between them. (This style is especially adaptable to the organ, where the bass line is played on the pedals, and the left hand is free to play fuller chords.)

Walking bass provides a nice change of pace for the middle section of *Do Nothin' Till You Hear From Me*.

During long notes in the melody you may want to add "fills." One particular fill is standard for *Don't Get Around Much Anymore,* and it is useful in many situations. Here the melody has been moved up an octave, while the fills appear in the middle register. (The organist can play the melody with the right hand and the fills with the left hand and pedals.)

One final tip: keep the lyrics in mind. They can give you ideas for phrasing and for melodic and rhythmic variations. As you play the song, think of how you would sing it.

Musical examples used by permission of Big Three Music, Inc.

Alberti Boogie — *continued from p.91*

c)

Our other Alberti bass can easily be transformed from:

Ex. 6

into any of these:

Ex. 7

pop piano

All That Jazz

by Stuart Isacoff

Improvising jazz at the keyboard is not as mysterious as some people believe. You don't have to be born with the ability: it *can* be learned, and it is less complicated than, say, Sanskrit. Of course, it is next to impossible to give a whole course in improvising in these short columns, but we'll offer some approaches you can take in beginning to create your own melodies while playing your favorite songs.

Here's an improvised line to be played over the chords in the first two or three measures of *Don't Blame Me:*

Ex. 1

Let's look at how that melodic line came to be.

If we start with the original melody:

Ex. 2
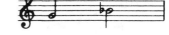

We can begin to embellish it in a number of different ways. We may want to add a note between the G and the B♭:

Ex. 3

Or a note that is higher than the interval between G and B♭:

Ex. 4

Or one that is lower:

Ex. 5

Usually, we'll want to add more than one note between the original melody notes. So, let's turn to the scales that work with the harmonies of the song. The chord progression for these measures is C - Gm^6 or E$^{\emptyset 7}$ - A - A^7 - D$^{\emptyset 7}$. (I know the progression in the written music is somewhat different, but this is the one used by most professionals.)

If we use a C scale as our material for the part of the melody that goes with the C chord, we'll want to experiment a little with building melodic patterns out of the scale tones:

Ex. 6

By breaking up scale patterns into zigzag-like lines we can create more melodic interest:

Ex. 7

And, by inserting a few chromatic tones in between, we can add a little more zip:

Ex. 8
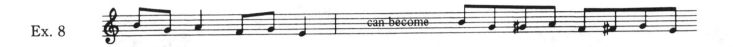

The melodic line in example 1 was built by using scales and a few chromatic tones to embellish the original melody of *Don't Blame Me*.

Next, we'll take these ideas step-by-step in order to explore all the different ways improvisers work at the keyboard.

Musical examples used by permission of Big Three Music, Inc.

improvisation

Chord Scales

by David Berger

In the early 1940's a young saxophone player named Charlie Parker (nicknamed "Bird") rose to prominence in the jazz scene. One of his accomplishments was to introduce a new concept of improvisation that radically altered contemporary approaches, and which has influenced musicians ever since. This new concept (embraced by the term "Bebop") emphasized chord *scales* rather than chord *tones* in improvising over a given chord progression, with the result that the improviser had a greater vocabulary of notes to choose from.

For example, in this passage from "Pennies From Heaven", two scales are used:

Ex. 1

The first is the Major scale:

Ex. 2

And the second is the (Dominant) Seventh scale (major scale with the seventh degree flatted):

Ex.3

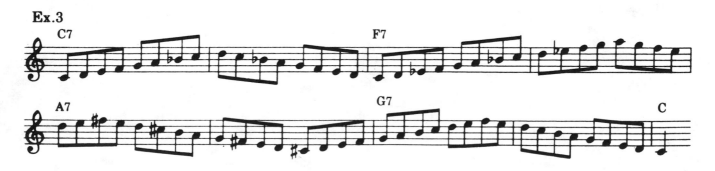

Scale passages may begin on any note in a scale; they can ascend or descend, or change direction at any time. It is essential to know all twelve major and all twelve seventh scales thoroughly, since these scales apply to 90% of American music. It was Bird's personal observation that the best improvisers were those with the greatest facility with seventh scales.

Determining Chord Scales

*Mr. Berger is a free-lance arranger/composer and trumpet player in New York City. His credits include various Broadway shows, movies, records, jingles and concerts. He is the author of *Contemporary Jazz Studies*, vol.1 and 2, *Contemporary Jazz Duets* and *Contemporary Jazz Chord Progressions*, published by Chas. Colin Pubs.

In order to improvise melodies, we have been using chord scales, which are in most cases more simplified than the chords given on the sheet music. For instance, the chord scales for the first four measures of "Love Walked In" would be:

Ex. 1

These same four bars in the sheet music version show an Eb6 in measure 1 and an Ab in measure 4. Since the only difference between Eb and Eb6 is C (which is in the Eb scale), an Eb chord scale will do fine. However, the Ab symbol in the sheet music is actually misleading. If the chord is read from the bass up, it is seen to be a Bb7 with a suspended fourth. So, we use a Bb7 chord scale here. Many times, especially when playing from a lead sheet, the bass notes will give you vital information missing from the chord symbols. Let's look now at the last eight measures of "Love Walked In." The chord progression used by most jazz players is:

Ex. 2

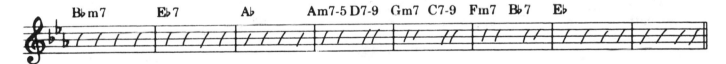

Let's figure out some chord scales to use for improvising a melody over the chord progression in Example 2. Bbm7 is the chord on the fifth step of Eb7, Eb7 is O.K., Ab is O.K., Am7-5 is the chord on the third of F7; for D7-9 we can use D7; Gm7 is the chord on the third of Eb; for C7-9 we can use C7; Fm7 is the chord on the fifth of Bb7; Bb7 is O.K. and Eb is O.K. Generally a minor seventh chord, whose root moves down a fifth to a seventh chord, takes the same scale as the seventh chord (Bbm7 Eb7 = Eb7; Fm7 Bb7 = Bb7). Gm7 C7-9 is an exception in the above example because at this particular place in the tune an Eb scale sounds better, and since Gm7 is the chord on the third of Eb, we use Eb for the first two beats of the bar. The resulting chord scales for Examples 2 are:

Ex. 3

Remember, chord scales apply to creating melodies and are not for playing left hand bass notes or voicings.

Musical examples used by permission of Chappell Music Co., Inc.

improvisation

Chords Derived From Chord Scales

by David Berger

We discussed the construction of scalar passages based on major and seventh chord scales. It is also possible to play arpeggiated figures utilizing the notes from these chord scales. These arpeggios are formed by using *every other* scale tone.

Ex. 1

Major scales use arpeggios on I, III and VI. Seventh scales use I, III, V and VII.

Ex. 2

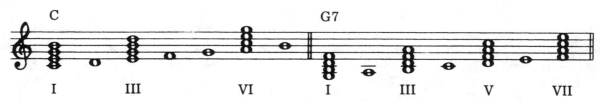

Arpeggios may be played ascending and decending in all inversions. They may also alternate with scale-wise passages. The following example utilizes all these techniques

Ex. 3

Upper and Lower Neighbors

In addition to scale passages and chordal passages built from chord scales composers and improvisers employ neighbor tones to build melodies. Neighbor tones are notes that are a step above (upper neighbors) or a step below (lower neighbors) a chord tone.

Ex. 1

In example 1, "D" is an upper neighbor (UN) to "C", and "B" is a lower neighbor (LN) to "C". In the second measure both neighbors are used before resolving to the "C". Both "D" and "B" are in the "C Major" scale (the chord scale for "C"), so they are labeled diatonic neighbors. Ex. 2 shows the same situation with chromatic neighbors (a half step above and below regardless of chord scale).

Ex. 2

Ex. 3 demonstrates the usage of neighbor tones for an improvisation based on the first 8 bars of "In the Shade of the Old Apple Tree". You might analyze the melody of the song for neighbors—there are both upper and lower as well as diatonic and chromatic!

Ex. 3

improvisation

Chord Style

by David Berger

What do you do when you get to the end of the tune? Most tunes last between one and two minutes. The average record is three to four minutes in duration. One could simply repeat the melody. Another possibility is to play the verse and then go through the chorus again.

During the 1930's it became popular for instrumentalists to improvise over the chord progression of a tune to provide a link between the opening chorus and the final recapitulation. Most players used a basically arpeggiated style (running up and down the chord tones). Here's an example of what might be done with *CHEROKEE*:

Ex. 1

It is possible to play scale passages by adding passing tones:

Ex. 2

x = passing tones

A good improviser tries to achieve a balance between rhythmic phrases (Ex. 1) and eighth note phrases (Ex. 2) as well as a balance between chordal passages (Ex. 1) and scale passages (Ex. 2).

Musical examples used by permission of Shapiro, Bernstein & Co., Inc.

Eight Note Scales

When improvising, it is essential to play notes in the chord *on the beat*. This can be a problem with our conventional Major and Seventh Scales.

Ex. 1

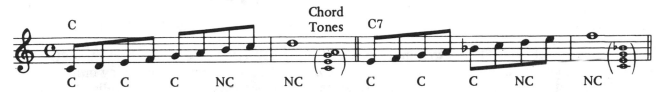

I have marked each downbeat as to whether it is a chord tone (C) or a non-chord tone (NC). In order to make more chord tones fall on downbeats, we can add an extra note to each scale. The extra note is added so that the scale will alternate between chord tones and non-chord tones. To the Major Scale, we add the half step between 5 and 6 (raised fifth or flatted sixth) and to the Seventh Scale the half step between 7 and 8 (major 7).

Ex. 2

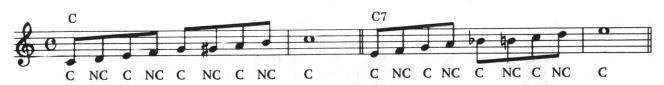

Learn these scales in all twelve keys (they have a pretty sound). Ex. 3 is an improvised line on the chord progression to *Auld Lang Syne* using these added notes.

Ex. 3

improvisation

Minor Keys

by David Berger

To date, we have looked at how to improvise in major keys, using major scales. In the workshop, *Determining Chord Scales,* we reduced chord progressions including minor chords to simpler major chord progressions for the sake of improvising. A common progression, ii(minor) - V - I, is visualized as V - I, using a *seventh* scale for the V, and the *major* scale for the I.

Now, let's look at a ii - V - i progression in G minor (in which the tonic chord is minor):

Ex. 1

To begin with, it is helpful to remember that G minor is the relative minor scale of Bb major. So, the Am7-5 chord can be played as an F7 scale, beginning on A. F7 is the V7 Chord of Bb, and you can think of the F7 scale as simply a Bb scale beginning on F.

For D7-9, we can use the G Harmonic Minor scale (D7 being the V chord of the G minor scale), and for G minor we can play either the G Melodic Minor scale, or a C7 scale. Play them both, and let your ear decide which you prefer. The first four measures of the bridge of "They Can't Take That Away From Me" can be played like this:

Ex. 2

In the workshop *Chords Derived From Chord Scales,* we discussed major scales. So is the case here. Referring to the chord progression in Example 1, we can arpeggiate the chords built 1, 3, 5, and 7 of the F7 scale (Remember that we are using an F7 scale for the Am7-5 chord). On D7-9 we can likewise build chords on 1,3,5,7, and -9. On Gm we can build chords on 1,3,5 and 6; or, if we prefer using the C7 scale, we can build the chords on 1,3,5 and 7 of the C7 scale.

Ex. 3

Example 4 is an improvisation on the entire bridge of "They Can't Take That Away From Me". I have employed everything we've covered thus far: scales, chords, and neighbor tones.

Ex. 4

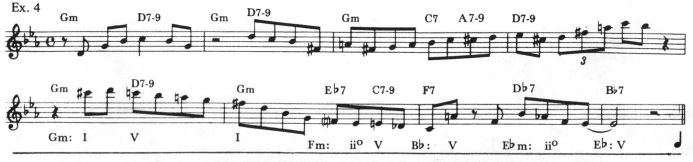

TECHNIQUE

IMPROVE YOUR FINGER DEXTERITY
...IN HALF THE TIME

by Ed Shanaphy

There's no doubt about it, if you want to achieve good finger technique at the keyboard, you must devote a certain amount of time to doing five-finger exercises.

Certainly one of the most popular, and most successful series of studies in this area is Hanon's *The Virtuoso Pianist.* In creating these exercises, Hanon was working to give each finger total independence. And the Hanon exercises can very well accomplish that, as well as increasing finger speed. In fact it is still one of the best methods in becoming a true virtuoso pianist, as its name implies. However, we have recently discovered a new approach to Hanon, teaching the old dog some new tricks, which improves finger dexterity in half the amount of time usually spent, and creates greater finger technique and independence in the process.

We call this method the Hanon-Szabo Method since it was brought to our attention by pianist Eugene Szabo. The method applies different rhythm patterns to each Hanon exercise, thereby shifting accents within each to benefit each finger individually.

If you can work your way through the first twenty exercises, or Part I of Hanon's *Virtuoso Pianist,* doing two each week, say, at tempos that are comfortable for you (blazing speed is not a necessity), you will be another pianist in 10 weeks. If you are a slow learner, and cannot learn two new ones, or even one new one each week, keep reviewing the old ones every day, in all the patterns described here, and your technique and speed will still improve drastically.

PATTERN A: (Dotted 8th and 16th)

Applying this to Hanon study #1:

And Hanon #2 would be played thusly:

PATTERN B: (16th note pickup to dotted 8th)

(This pattern completely reverses the accents of pattern A, to strengthen the alternate fingers, the 2nd and 4th.)

Hanon # 1:

Hanon #2:

PATTERN C: (Triplet and quarter note)

Hanon #1:

Hanon # 2:

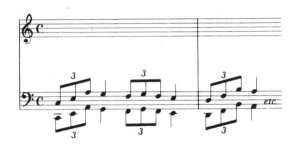

PATTERN D: (8ths and 16ths combination)

Hanon #1:

Hanon # 2:

PATTERN E: (Straight staccato)

(*Note well:* this should be a *finger* staccato, no wrist or arm.)

The final pattern, PATTERN F, is to play it as Hanon wrote it, but using a very light touch (think of a feather.) Only use the fingers, and play it up to your maximum speed, whatever it is. Stay within your limits. However, we promise that if you utilize this method of technical practice regularly, your limits will expand greatly.

REACH, Don't Stretch

By Robert Dumm

How often do students ask a teacher: "What can I do to increase my stretch?" Mine do every now and then, before they know me. Or worse, they proceed to demonstrate the latest medieval torture, gleaned from somebody else's teacher. The nineteenth century produced a full, mostly anonymous crop of crippled hands from their misunderstanding of how the hand works as a whole, notably Robert Schumann, who permanently maimed his right index finger in the attempt, forced by a mechanical device, to work it apart from the rest of his hand. (Yes, his *index* finger, not the fourth. Records show his military exemption later came because of his not being able to pull a trigger!)

To speak, or even think of *stretching* your hand is negative, self-defeating, and *dangerous*, especially for the fine network of ligaments that "steer" the direction of finger action from their roots in the knuckles of the hand. Most pianistic ailments derive not from overwork, but from an overexertion of small muscles where larger muscles are needed. Instead of *stretching*—a negative suggestion that implies *willing* your hand beyond a natural limit— think of yourself as *reaching,* for that is what the hand is made to do. For example, if hunger causes you to reach for a bunch of grapes high on a vine, you just might get them. On the other hand, if you make a grab for the grapes your hand (and all your body with it) contracts, shrinks, and probably misses. You may impose your will (grrr!) and force your success, but not without strain and little chance of succeeding every time on demand.

To sense the natural way of the hand, try this experiment. Sit tall in a straight-backed chair, legs uncrossed, feet flat on the floor. Get comfortable. Close your eyes and place both palms flat down on your knees. Allow them to rest there, motionless. Now, breathe in and out, slowly and deeply. As you enter the broadening rhythm of each breath phase, mentally tell your hands to *grasp* on the inhale. As you exhale, think *give*. Continue breathing easily in and out, and very deeply, gradually changing your mental command to grasp-*ing* (on the inhale), and giv-*ing* (on the exhale), imagining that extra syllable being a softly sung *crescendo* to the very end of the breath phase. As you alternate these mental commands, notice the changing sensations in the very pit of your palms.

Instead of holding a position, you are beginning to create a *process*. This is what playing hands must be every-ready to do: flexibly adapt to the changing keyboard shapes of the notes. Hand positioning should be thought of as a moving picture, and any "still shot" taken for a better view of its action is simply a springboard *to its next* position.

To "open" our hand we must always picture it as moving *as a whole*—when it rests at a trill, lifts at a rest, or rolls between two chords. Do not impose strain on any finger (or pair of fingers) by isolating its action.

For example, say you have trouble trilling with fingers 4 and 5. The first thing to do is plant your hand weight onto the heavier thumb, shifting it away from four and five. That simple gesture may prove enough. If not, remember that your muscular networks are wired and woven for cooperative action. For every action (tension) there must be an opposite, natural *re*-action (release) somewhere *else* in the hand. Therefore, you might further free the action of fingers 4 and 5 by working fingers 1 and 2 in some easy, unforced rhythm.

In my studio lies a life-molding of Chopin's left hand, one of three made after Clésinger's original in Paris. When I offer it for students to place their hand upon it, they will exclaim: "My hand's bigger than *his!*" I then point to the telltale valleys between the sinews that lift each finger, to show how Chopin's hand had been rendered flexible "as an empty glove," down *into* the wrist. Here are five exercises that will help pianists of all ages to "open" their hands (I call them "warm mittens"). Each is to be worked up, and then down, in all keys. I have given my explanations as I might say them at a Lesson.

KEYBOARD POSITION

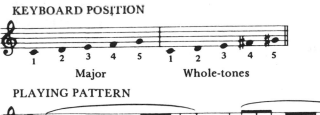

Major   Whole-tones

PLAYING PATTERN

You will note that in this unusual meter signature of 5/8 an extra beat lets your hand rock *three* times onto the fifth finger, after it has rocked twice on the thumb. This easy, back-and-forth rocking from thumb to 5 keeps your wrist free enough to build the "frame" of your hand, fingers 1 and 5. As you roll, let the weight of your hand shape each two-note slur. As your *outer* fingers become able to roll your hand-weight *into* the keys, your inner fingers (2, 3, and 4) will feel loose and begin to play freer from their roots in the hand. This helps every note you play to sound full and vital.

KEYBOARD POSITIONS

PLAYING PATTERN (up)

etc.

(down)

etc.

Since by keeping the wrist free to bob as the keys dip and rise *allows* the hand to open, raise the wrist a little for this one and let the hand dangle freely down from it. Let your hand roll limply as it plays, leaving this shape on every two-note slur:

1 2 2

mf > *mp*

After you are comfortable with that fingering, use this one, which even more applies your hand to *shaping* to the sounds:

2 3 2   or   1 2 1

KEYBOARD POSITION

Easy   Intermediate   Advancing

5th   aug. 5th   maj. 6th   min. 7th   maj. 7th   octave

PLAYING PATTERN (up)

(down)

Continued on next page   115

Nothing like a jingling tune to *swing* your hand *around* from those "frame" fingers, 1 and 5, onto the *inner* voices of a chord. Stress those inner voices (marked here with bigger notes), by a vigorous roll of your hand from the wrist: left to right. This will get your whole hand "into the act," so you can sense that its shifting balances "bring out" this or that note of a chord. By the way, on changing from one position to the next inversion of the same chord, stay *in touch* with the keys. Think: 1. "*Replace*" the last finger by the first finger of next inversion; 2. "*Place*" your hand quietly over the next inversion; and 3. "*Play*" that pattern freely, since you already "feel" its notes. As you work through every inversion this way, your hand will "remember" what you are "programming" to it and will leave your eyes free to watch the page.

KEYBOARD POSITION

PLAYING PATTERN (up)

This one is fast, so begin with those starter up-beats to a free *drop* onto the first downbeat, to spring right off it again. The increasing dynamics will urge you to sink more freely into the keys at each round. Once you feel free, "tell" your hand to "splay" just as a kitten, falling from a tree, will automatically outthrust its four legs before it hits the ground. Fling your fingers, from their roots, in the same way. Once that splatter registers on the ear as four bright tones, in a *splurge* of colorful *crescendo*, you may then try the wider "reach" of a tenth. Who *said* you had a small hand?

KEYBOARD POSITION

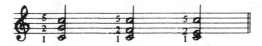

PLAYING PATTERN

KEYBOARD POSITION

More advanced

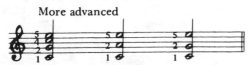

PLAYING PATTERN

Robert Dumm was named Dean of the Boston Conservatory when he was only twenty-five, and became a critic for The Christian Science Monitor a year later. He served fifteen years as head of graduate Piano Pedagogy at The Catholic University before retiring in 1979. Mr. Dumm is active as a teacher, contest judge and writer on musical subjects.

KEYBOARD CLINIC

DEVELOPING FINGER TECHNIQUE

by Ed Shanaphy

"I think you should write about finger exercises and how the average player can improve his dexterity by using them properly. You seem to be pooh-poohing the idea of good old fasioned five finger exercises and scales." So writes a woman from New Jersey.

Well, actually, we are not putting these exercises down, we just think that new students, especially the young impatient ones, would stick to that piano or organ for a longer time if they were not subjected to the boredom of scales and such. At least not in the beginning. But the point is well taken. There are some great finger exercises that can yield tremendous results, and they don't really have to be boring or tedious. They can be fun. The trick is to get yourself a plan and stick to it for a few minutes every day. It's the daily practice that counts, whether it be 15 minutes or eight hours. Scales can be fun, believe it or not. They can be played in different rhythm patterns, different directions, different intervals, etc. The more variations one can apply to scale practice, the better the results, the less ledious they become.

To look at the examples of scales we have included: you may practice one scale in 10 different variations as we have shown here. (We only show two octaves, you should use four octaves.) Set your metronome to a tempo you can handle, no matter how slow, and practice these variations. Hands separately, hands apart. First variation: strict quarter notes. Lift fingers high. Second variation: eighth notes with accent on first note of each couplet, (don't accent with your arms, let your fingers effect the accents.) Third variation: Eighth notes again, switch the accent to the second note of each couplet. Fourth variation: triplets. Good clear accent on first note of each triplet. Fifth variation: sixteenth notes, accent on first note of each four. Make that accent unmistakenly punched home. (No arms.) Sixth variation: accent on second note. Seventh variation: accent on third. Eighth variation: accent on fourth. Ninth variation: eighth notes again, but dotted with sixteenth. Tenth variation: sixteenth notes, no accents, play as smoothly as possible. Do not lift fingers high. Keep close to keyboard. If you practice just two scales a day this way, playing each variation twice, it will take about eight minutes. You're more than half through your 15 minute schedule for technique exercises.

There is a book of five-finger exercises for keyboard called *Schmitt Five Finger Exercises*. We highly recommend it for those of you who wish to acquire good finger technique. It is easier to get into quickly than Czerny studies, or Hanon. You will be able to read the exercises more readily, not having to get bogged down with learning the exercise before it starts doing you any good. It will also start you with simple transposition since all the exercises are written in the key of C, and are to be transposed by you to all other keys. It is easier than it sounds actually. Each exercise is a repetitive finger pattern, and transposing that pattern to another key is not very difficult at all. In your practice time, you should start with these Schmitt exercises before practicing your scales. About ten minutes of Schmitt and your hands will be loosened up nicely. Your local music store should be able to order the Schmitt book if they do not already have it in stock. If you have no success please write to us and we will try to help locate the book for you.

One other aspect of practice for finger technique which we will only mention briefly, since it would require an entire article of its own, is the practice of arpeggios. Primarily, the practice of four-note arpeggios: major sevenths, dominant sevenths, minor sevenths, major sixths, and augmented and diminished sevenths. Regular practice of these is indispensable if good finger technique is desired. They are for the more advanced students. For now, stick to the scales and the five-finger patterns, and you will be making enormous progress.

Continued on next page

KEYBOARD CLINIC MUSIC EXAMPLES

Var. # 1

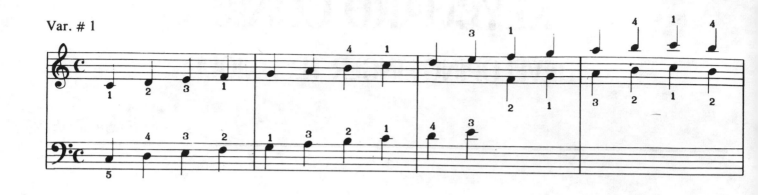

Var. #2

etc. (ascending and descending)

Var. #3

etc.

Var. #4

etc. (3 octaves. . .asc. & desc.)

Var. # 5

etc.

Var. # 6

(l.h. octavo)

etc.

Var. #7

etc.

Var. #8

etc.

Var. #9

etc.

Var. #10

etc.

119

ETUDES

Etudes is a department which features technical exercises composed by masters throughout history.

Liszt told his students to avoid playing from the arms and shoulders. He asked them to play from the wrist, using a "dead hand"—which was to fall onto the keys with total elasticity. In scale playing he demanded an impeccable evenness. The pressure was not to come from the fingertips near the nail, but from the "palm" of the finger, where the flesh could act as a cushion.

Liszt did not hold his fingers in a curved position because he claimed this could create a dryness. He recommended a pliability—neither stiff and curved, nor flat. As you play these exercises, try to maintain a relaxed hand posture, and check to make sure you are not raising and tightening your shoulders!

FROM LISZT'S TECHNICAL STUDIES

For gaining strength and independence of each individual finger with a quiet hand.

FRANZ LISZT

Technique

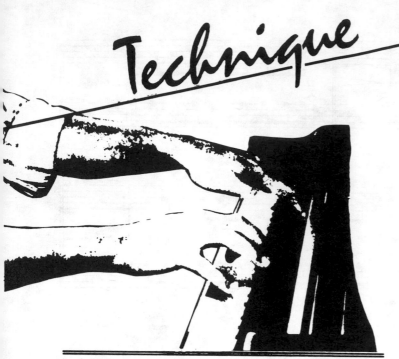

by Robert Dumm

I should like to put forth an idea or two about how to *approach* the piano: how to sit and feel, develop readiness to play, find the right position at the instrument. First, let's consider the piano keyboard. Modern keys are covered with white plastic, while older ones are genuine ivory. If the latter, you are lucky, because ivory "breathes" with your fingers, and absorbs their moisture, so that you experience the adhesiveness of human skin when you play on them.

Either way, treat the keys as the "skin" of the piano. If you poke them (try it on your hand), they answer with a start: the sound is bright and sudden, it even "barks" a little. If you stroke them, the sound seems softer, but it is rounder and fuller. It sounds mellow, like "purring strings" and it will carry farther. Of course, the full range of music will at some time call for every tone color there is. But for your basic, everyday, "good" piano tone—one that attracts the listeners' ear and keeps it pleased—we might say: "Stroke, don't poke, the keys." But it's not only the visible movements of the fingers that make the sound. More than fingers, the hand, moving at the wrist, is involved. You have only to play a two-note slur with a rich, full tone, to feel your hand drop-pulling, then rolling from one key onto the next; like the stroke a painter might use to brush this expressive line:

Getting back to stroking tones from the keys (as a string player "draws" tones from a string with his bow), place either hand *flat* on a table top. Open out your thumb wide, then stroke the table top with all four fingers at once, leaving a streak on its surface.

Try it again. Open the hand full-flat-out. Think *reach* rather than *str-e-e-etch*. That will do it. Now you can feel the under-surface of your full palm "belly-floppers" flat-as-a-mat on the table. From this flat position, draw the fingers slowly toward the thumb. Continue to draw them together, then up vertically, till the top of your hand is raised like an arch and the fingers point almost straight down. It's like raising a tent by pushing up on the centerpole. Now you will feel your stroking action coming from deep inside your palm, back towards the wrist.

This is simply a way to give you the feel of a good piano touch. You can practice this movement with every key you play, till it becomes second nature. Then you can stroke the keys being sure to use *very little movement* (it might seem motionless to someone watching). The *sense* of your motion, however slight it is, should be a drawing-to of the key: as Count Dracula might raise his hand in a slow gesture ("Come to me — Come to *me*"). This gesture will, for one thing, even all voices of a chord.

While you were drawing-in your hand, did you notice how long and flexible your thumb had gotten, while being dragged flat on the table surface? In this pliant condition, resting flat along its key, the thumb can rest your hand, since it is the bone-heaviest finger. It carries the hand weight and frees the other fingers for lighter work. Above all, loosen that thumb! Let it hang from the hand, like a tail. Many pianists, under tension, lock it solidly *into* the hand, its first bone fused with the wrist. They play, then, only with the first two bones of the thumb, not at its "hinge" in the wrist; or they poke the thumb at an angle *down* into the keys. Either way, the thumb remains frozen, the wrist is locked, and the hand must be moved clumsily (with a bumpy, uneven sound) from the forearm, acting from the elbow.

Paderewski (and he was not the only one) considered the freely-skilled movement of the thumb the key to piano playing. We'll focus again on "touch" in the next issue. For the moment, here is a little "thumb oil" to make you aware of how often (but how little) it does move when you play.

Robert Dumm is the former head of Piano Pedagogy at Catholic University and publisher of **The Robert Dumm Piano Review.**

Technique

Touch and Tension

by Robert Dumm

In the last issue, we looked at ways to improve your piano "touch." This time, we'll cover similar ground by focusing on ways to *stay in touch,* both with the keys of the piano and with your own musculature.

Since the modern grand piano action is fairly deep, there is a *round-trip* to every touch. After you draw the key downward, you should sit on it, and then *ride* back up as if on a seesaw. Your "partner" on the other end is the weight (and friction) of the key-action.

There is a crucial point, about a third of the way down the key descent, where you will sense a slight resistance. Technically, this is called the escapement point, but I like to call it the "tone spot." This spot is the point at which you punt, bump, or pop the hammer on the last lap of its motion toward the string. Thus it is the last point at which you can still aim for the tone you want. What you do *right there* determines how mellow (with slow strokes) or bright (with a quicker pop of the key) your tone will sound. So staying in touch with the keys is very important for musical expression.

There is another more subtle kind of "staying in touch" that is just as crucial to good playing. Many pianists hold back shyly from the keyboard. Their fear of hitting a wrong note causes their shoulders to rise and their necks to jam; thus they play while locked into a sort of harness which cramps their movements, causes pain, and numbs the finer muscular sensations. Most of us carry this overload of tension without knowing it, but it affects us nonetheless.

To find and release inner tensions, both physical and psychological, try sitting quietly at the piano, straight up, your lower back supported by a chair. Slowly inhale as much air as your lungs will hold, feeling your chest widen, your upper body grow tall, and your back broaden. Feel your shoulders settle down into their natural place—the socket joint that lets them move in circles.

Then begin to exhale slowly. As you think "let it go," feel each muscle relax in ripples, as if water were running down your body in a shower. After your shoulders settle into place, continue to exhale. Soon you will feel your neck growing "longer," like a sunflower growing toward the sun overhead.

You are now in the right position—and condition—to play the piano. But wait. So pleasing is the sensation of an ongoing release of tensions that you will want to breathe in again, more deeply. Let the air out more slowly this time, like a big tire with a slow leak. As you do, try to feel the little tensions ripple down your trunk, into your arms and thighs, and on and on, all the way to the tips of your toes and fingers. Even when your body seems absolutely still, imagine this process going on, like a wave spilling slowly over a broad, deserted beach.

Now you have not only made yourself ready to play, but in your mind you are already playing. An artist who is "in touch" uses this sense of weight flow all the time. Through the breath, he or she feels it move first down the arm, then into and *through* the keys as they are drawn down. More of this later. Meanwhile, send me your problems and share your good ideas!

Robert Dumm is the former head of Piano Pedagogy at Catholic University and publisher of **The Robert Dumm Piano Review.**

Technique
by Robert Dumm

We ended the last column with some ways to adjust your position and affect your condition to play the piano. We inhaled deeply, then exhaled, long and luxuriously. As your lungs slowly emptied of stale air, you felt your neck, back, and shoulder muscles let go. Your arms hung whole and slack from the shoulders, and your shoulders themselves settled into a natural position of rest.

Other effective techniques for conscious breathing are given by Dr. Win Wenger, in his valuable paperback *Beyond OK* (order from Psychegenics Press, P.O. Box 332, Gaithersburg, MD 20760). Wenger gives the same "stuff" to those tensions, strains, and pains the body does not need. See that "stuff" being blown away — out your fingertips — by a powerful fan; imagine it turn to sparks on contact with the air.

Once you've got yourself both sparking and emptied in this way, "sling" your arms outwards and upwards from the shoulders, in a simple curve, until both forearms hang cradled over the keys (still balanced from the shoulders). Hover there over the keys, your hands dangling freely from both wrists.

In this "lighter-than-air" position (and condition), try easily rocking your arms in and out at the elbows, away from, then towards the body. Gradually convert your sideways rocking to a back-and-forth rocking: *back* towards the elbows, then *forth* into your dangling fingers, like the rhythmic pump-arm of an oil derrick, or the two-man long saw of big timber country.

As you continue to "rock in the cradle" in this way, bear in mind the insight of Ludwig Deppe (1828-1890), a pioneer teacher of arm weight: "Elbow like lead, wrist like a feather."

To put this into practice, look at the opening chords of Chopin's 20th *Prelude* in C minor:

Now, return your arms to the "sling" position in which we left them hovering. Let them flow gently down into the keys, as a hot air balloon lets its basketful of people down onto a mossy field. Or, think of yourself descending to the bottom of the ocean. The lower you sink, the more the water buoys you up. It helps to laugh a little.

It is this balanced, weightless contact with the keys that Debussy must have been referring to when he spoke of "feeling the keys rise to meet your fingers" with the merest brush of a "kiss." Now try *that* over on your piano!

As you play the Chopin *Prelude,* you will sense the keys' buoyancy as you rise and then depress them with each succeeding chord.

Think of the *fortissimo* marking not as force, but as a big sound, like summer thunder, magnificently rolling down the hills and into the valleys. If you prefer a brighter sound, "send" your sound-boom as a fisherman casts his fishline, far out over the trout stream; its lead sinker landing just where he aims it (at the time-spot for each note).

Now try this exercise:

By energizing (in your mind) those 16th-note subdivisions of every beat, you inject a "magnetic" force into the piece, as if a powerful magnet up ahead were pulling you forward, *into* the music. That mental magnet will help you to convert your drop/lift movements (for each chord) into a sustained, horizontal carrying of the arms. This will help stabilize your time sense in any piece, especially in a slow one.

*Robert Dumm is the former head of Piano Pedagogy at Catholic University and publisher of **The Robert Dumm Piano Review.***

a son ami J.C. Kessler

PRELUDE IN C MINOR
Op 28, No. 20

Largo

Frederic Chopin

PIANO TIPS FROM THE PROS

"HOW TO BECOME A BETTER SIGHT-READER!"

by Ed Shanaphy

If you are like most people, your performance of a piece of music "at first sight" could probably stand some improvement. Oh, to be able to breeze through a brand new piece without all the stops and starts! What you may not realize is that sight-reading is an art in itself, separate and apart from pianistic ability. Many conservatory musicians, even many soloists, are not the great sight-readers you might expect. Sight-reading is a special craft within the art of music that won't come automatically. You must work at it just as you work at technique, or interpretation. You could have the technique of a Horowitz on the keyboard, or a Segovia on the guitar, but still be a laughable sight-reader.

There are many tricks to the sight-reading game, no matter which instrument you play. If these tricks can be used properly, and with regularity, two things will happen: 1) your sight-reading improves, of course, and 2) your over-all technique automatically improves. And if you regiment yourself to a daily sight-reading program, even just fifteen minutes' worth, your entire outlook on your instrument will change drastically in a matter of days! If you practice scales, for example, you only improve your ability in playing scales. Nothing more. However, with sight-reading practice, you improve your scale playing technique, your octave technique, your arpeggio technique, because you are using actual pieces which can encompass all of these techniques and more.

Let's talk more of those "tricks" that will get you on the road to better sight-reading. First of all, you need a metronome. That's trick number one. You can get a pretty cheap metronome that will serve our purposes, or you can start calling a few neighbors who probably have one stashed in the attic that they never use. Check out garage sales. There has usually been a metronome at every garage sale I've ever been to.

WHAT A METRONOME DOES FOR SIGHT-READING:

Have you ever played chess, or watched people play chess by time-clock? The object of time-clock chess is that each player has a stipulated amount of time in which to make his move. He CANNOT exceed the amount of time allotted, or else the bell will sound and he will be penalized. This is exactly how we use a metronome in sight-reading. We must make our "move" to the next note, or next chord, within a set time period. And that's the trick that gets our reflexes going. Sight-reading is nothing more than training our reflexes. In order to do this we have to fight the time-clock. In the case of music, our time-clock is the metronome. It's an absolute necessity if you are serious about becoming a good, or better sight-reader. Besides that, you will find it invaluable for other practice purposes, which we will deal with in future articles. (It's a great boon for insomniacs who don't have a grandfather's clock handy.) There are all kinds of reasons for having a metronome. So you might as well invest.

We'll get back to the actual usage of the metronome, but first we should discuss the kind of music your sight-reading program should start with. No one knows your present ability better than yourself, and your selection of the music based upon degree of difficulty must be your own decision. However, for the purposes of this article we will presume your sight-reading ability is virtually non-existent.

Now's the time to dig out those old beginner books. The John W. Thompson graded books, or any of those beginning graded books will do very well. Look through these books and decide which grade is best suited to your sight-reading ability for a starting point. Don't be afraid to start with something you will play easily. We are after faster reflexes in our exercises, not great performances. Go to the first piece of the book you choose and look through for the most difficult section. DON'T PRACTICE IT . . . JUST LOOK AT IT! Now decide, with the help of your metronome, how slow the tempo must be to get you through this section with relative comfort. Do not, no matter how great the temptation, put your hands anywhere near the keyboard. You very well might have to set the metronome right up near the top for an extremely slow tempo. That's quite alright. In the beginning, the slower, the better. And the fewer mistakes you make, the better. SO START SLOW!

Here's trick No. 2. Once you have decided the tempo at which you can handle that first piece, say it is 40 on the metronome, stick with that tempo for the rest of the book. There will be sections of the piece you are playing which are so simple you might say to yourself, "This is ridiculous . . . I'll just whip through this part quickly, and slow it up back to 40 when I reach the hard part." WRONG! You are training your reflexes against a constant of TIME, and when you reach the hard part, your chances of getting through it more smoothly will be greater if you have been working with the metronome steadily from the beginning. The tempo is being drummed into your head, your fingers, your pulse, your everything.

MOST IMPORTANT . . . if you make a mistake, KEEP GOING. Don't, whatever you do, stop the tempo and the progress of the piece. If you forgot the F#, forget it until the next time through. If you do stop to go back and fix, the entire purpose of the sight-reading drill is lost. That purpose is: SPEEDING UP THE REFLEXES! And that cannot be accomplished unless the strict tempo is adhered to for the entire piece, beginning to end. Something you might think about while you are playing the easy parts . . . the parts you would rather speed through: Are my fingers curved properly? Am I contacting the keys with the ball (the fleshy tip) of my fingers? Are my upper arms relaxed? Is my wrist flat? Do my hands look good in their playing position? In other words, work on your technique too. It can't hurt.

Now that you have played that first piece through, go right on to the next piece in the book. So you made three mistakes . . . who cares? You must not go back, only go ahead. The metronome stays ticking away at 40. Look at the next piece. Time signature, key signature. Try to hum the first two measures in your head. Look ahead for the most difficult phrase or section. Play.

Continue this procedure for the entire book. Never going back to a previous piece, only ahead to new ones. If you are allotting yourself only fifteen minutes of sight-reading practice, you probably will not finish all the pieces in the book. Mark the page, and pick up where you left off next time. DON'T REVIEW OLD PIECES.

Continued on next page

Now you've completed the first book. Go on to the next grade at the 40 tempo. Do two pieces. At this point, go back and review the previous grade, but at a tempo 10 points faster on the metronome. 50. Do two pieces from the previous book at 50. Two pieces from the new grade at 40, two from the old at 50. Keep alternating until you reach the next succeeding grade book. Now what do you do? You guessed it: two pieces from each grade . . . the new grade at the original tempo (40), the previous grade at 50, the very first grade at 60, or more if you think you can handle it comfortably. Don't push yourself into an uncomfortable tempo. It will work against you.

Now your reflexes are getting with it. Tempo, the all-important constant of music performance, is being drummed into your playing. Your fingers, as a result are gaining more independence, and a smoother technique. You are ready to tackle some more difficult sight-reading. There are some great books on the market of easy Bach, easy Mozart, easy Beethoven. These would be ideal. After these, or a couple of them, at least, it might be time to buy a book of Sonatinas by Kuhlau, or whomever you wish. They're great fun. But don't forget . . . start slowly . . . don't go back and fix . . . forge on! Apply the same techniques as you did at the very beginning. When you finish the book, then you may go back at a faster tempo.

At this point, your sight-reading is probably giving you tremendous enjoyment and self-satisfaction. You have now gotten to the point where you can expose yourself to a great deal of new music very quickly. There's one other book you might enjoy. Bartok's *Pieces For Children*. They are tricky, and that's why I recommend them. There are sudden key changes and time changes . . . AND tempo changes. You've got to be on your toes and looking ahead.

Finding new music for sight-reading now is easy. Go to your church organist. Ask her, or him, if you might borrow some of the pieces so you can work on your sight-reading. Musicians understand one another, and I'm sure you will receive a very friendly response. This kind of music, accompaniment, is very good to get familiar with. Go to the library and pick up some Broadway show scores. If your library doesn't have them, tell them to write to us, we'll send them someone's catalog. Don't try the tougher scores at first. Avoid Sondheim and Bernstein in the beginning. Get some of the older shows of Rodgers and Gershwin and Cole Porter. Also, try to get your hands on some opera scores. Especially Mozart. *The Marriage of Figaro, The Magic Flute.* They can be quite rewarding . . . and not necessarily very difficult, especially since you are holding the metronome! You can dictate any tempo you want. If you have a light opera company in your home town, use the same line you used with your church organist! Also, try it on the music director of your local school.

And every time a new issue of Sheet Music Magazine arrives, apply the metronome technique, and read through it as slowly as you need from beginning to end. Do not miss such a great opportunity for your sight-reading program as Sheet Music Magazine provides. After all, it's new music you've never seen before, being delivered right to your home. Work it in to your sight-reading routine right from the start.

And don't be surprised, as you strike up the acquaintances of these music people in your area, if they offer you a job as rehearsal pianist. After all, there are so few people who can sight-read these days!

—E.J.S.

KEYBOARD CLINIC
MORE ABOUT SIGHT-READING

by Ed Shanaphy

In our very first issue, which is our introductory issue, we discussed the art of sight-reading. The importance of a metronome was pointed out, and how you can, by gradual increases of tempo on given pieces of music, improve your ability in a matter of a few short weeks.

There are some other tips on becoming a better sight-reader which we would like to discuss. Sight-reading at the keyboard can be very frustrating because the left hand is doing something entirely different from the right hand most of the time. It might be doing arpeggiated accompaniment, or oom-pa-pa style accompaniment, or playing a counter-melody. People often ask, how can I sight-read something like that, I'd need two heads! The answer to this is, yes, you need two heads to look at the two separate entities, treble clef and bass clef, and then translate them separately to right hand and left hand. But what if you decided to look at a specific beat of music, say the second beat of the third measure of a piece, as one single entity? Look at that beat as a single happening, top to bottom, left hand and right hand as one hand with ten fingers on it. What this requires is a total vertical analysis of what happens on that beat. Not just a look at the treble clef first, and then a look at the bass clef. Once you have this concept clear in your mind, that the two staves, treble and bass, are actually one, then you can make great strides toward rapid sight-reading.

Assuming that you understand the concept, let's go on and discuss how you can develop it, and put it to actual use. Get yourself a book of pieces and sit down in your favorite chair. We're not going near the piano for this exercise. Now for the next ten or fifteen minutes, select random beats from that book. It might be the third beat in the eighth measure, or whatever. Glance at it for a split second and close your eyes. What do you remember top to bottom? Just the top two notes? Go on to another beat. Don't repeat glancing at the same beat, you will be defeating the purpose of this exercise. If, at a glance, you are only capable of getting two notes, by all means make certain that one of them is the melody, and one is the bass. Quick glance. Close your eyes. You've got the melody note, top note that is, and the bass note. Do you remember any in between? You will. And it will be surprising to realize that your eyes actually do create a photograph. What you are trying to do is to get your brain to reproduce that photograph after you close your eyes. Now why is that? Why should you want your brain to give you that image again? Because when you are sight-reading at a good clip, your eyes will be two or three beats ahead of your playing. Your eyes take the photo, and your brain reproduces it a split second later. Try *that* as an exercise! Go to the keyboard. Look at the first beat, or even the first melody note, but do not play it until you are looking at the second. Keep moving ahead that way, not playing the beat until you are actually looking at the next. It will drive you crazy the first couple of sittings, but you are going to be a sight-reader. These two exercises, one in the easy chair, one at the keyboard, should be done a couple of times a week in addition to your regular sight-reading at the piano.

One other tip, and this has to do with hand preparation: get your hand into the shape of the notes before it even reaches the notes. For example, you are ten feet away from your piano or organ. The notes I want you to hit are middle C and the D right next to it with your right hand only. What should happen as you walk over to the keyboard is that your right hand takes up a striking position. The thumb and forefinger, second finger, of your right hand are in a position as if you were going to lift a pebble. Put the thumb over the C, play. C and D play together. If I ask you to play an E instead of a D, your fingers would prepare differently on the trip over to the keyboard. To play C and the E above it, your thumb and third finger would get into a position of picking a strawberry. Put the thumb over the C, and E plays with it. The ten-foot distance was to point out that your hand should be prepared before it reaches its destination. For example, your right hand is playing a G above middle C, and the next beat it has a C triad an octave and a half up. On its way up, the thumb, 3rd finger and 5th finger should be assuming the triad position. Don't wait until it gets there to position the fingers. Work with your hands separately on this preparation concept. Select some piece and very slowly prepare your hand for the next beat before you move it into striking position.

Continue your work with your metronome, work on the exercises discussed here, and we guarantee results!

KEYBOARD CLINIC

PLAYING AT SIGHT

by Ruth Price Farrar

SIGHT READING — What is it? Willi Apel in the Harvard Dictionary of Music says: "The ability to read and perform music at sight, i.e., without preparatory study of the piece." Mary Elizabeth Clarke in her NEW POCKET MUSIC DICTIONARY says: "Reading and performing music at sight without previous preparation." Both of the definitions imply that the performance should be reasonably musical — not just note finding.

Frances Clarke in her Question-Answer column in *Clavier* Magazine talks about good readers: "Only if we start by developing students who listen, who see and understand, and who have the technique to bring this understanding into sound, can we hope to develop students who are good readers in the total sense."

You have guessed by now that sight reading isn't just letter reading or note finding — it is making music at sight. Before we go further maybe we should ask ourselves, is sight reading an asset to keyboard players or is it just a skill we can acquire but will rarely use? No one has time to develop useless skills. If you play with a group of instrumentalists or singers or play just for fun, you will find SIGHT READING a useful skill.

Years ago I had a piano teacher in one of my advanced classes. She was very proud that she could "read anything at sight" — but she added "I have a lot of trouble with time". Was she sight reading if she read only pitch? What do notes tell us? That symbol called a note says two things, loud and clear: What key do I play AND how long do I hold it? If either of these basic elements are absent you are reading only HALF of what the symbol is trying to tell you. How long would you last on the job if you did only half of your assignment?

But playing the right pitch and prolonging the tone the right time is not all there is to SIGHT READING. If your fingering is not reasonably correct you will make mistakes in time, maybe in pitch and certainly in phrasing and tone quality. PHRASING, an important part of making music, is also a part of sight reading. If you do not phrase properly you are not punctuating properly, and you can't make sense without proper punctuation.

Then there is the matter of dynamics. You ask "Do you expect a person to think about accents, forte, piano, diminish, crescendo, etc., when they have all they can do just playing the notes? If these musical nuances cannot be applied at first playing the music is too difficult for sight playing and should be laid aside until you gain more knowledge and technique. Try it again later.

Another question that comes up as we consider SIGHT PLAYING is: How do we develop the skill? Is there a plan that can lead us surely and gradually to sight playing? There are courses of study on sight playing, there are plans we can make ourselves, but first you must have a real desire to learn — then stick to your plan.

One of the first skills to develop after acquiring a real physical feel of pulse is directional reading, called "intervallic reading." We do need to know the names of the lines and spaces and location on the keyboard, but to read by letter is very slow. Of course, it is much easier to learn directional reading and letter reading from the very first lessons, but if you are a mature person with some music background you may be encountering intervallic reading for the first time.

Intervals are distances. There are two names for each interval, a number name and a quality name. We will learn how to determine the number name first, then apply our knowledge to simple sight reading. The number name is determined by the number of staff degrees (lines and spaces) embraced by two notes.

Here are intervals all measured from middle "C". Count all the lines and spaces embraced (included). This concept of measurement is all you need to start your intervallic reading. Answer the questions "Which way am I going (up, down, or stay the same) and how far?" Every line and space is a white key. Sample:

Sample 1

Now we will apply the concept to a melody — the first few intervals are numbered. Try to finish the exercise yourself.

Sample 2

Now try saying the intervals out loud as you play this melody. Say "C — same — up a 3rd — up a 3rd — up a 4th — down a 3rd — same, etc." Think "Which way am I going and how far." Distance and direction — don't think letters.

Don't become impatient with yourself. Don't hurry — speed is the least of your worries. Anything new takes time to become a part of you. Work with melodies that are short and easy — don't burden yourself with difficult music until you can read intervals faster than you can say them. Do spend 5 or 10 minutes a day on intervals — write them, say them, play them.

Remember, try NOT to think letters. It is best to stick to reading a single line melody until you are reading subconsciously, not laboriously mentally speaking the letters. Be sure to say "direction," then "distance", like this: (Excerpt from Dona Nobis Pacem)

Sample 4

F dn a   up a   dn a   dn a   up a   dn a   dn a
   4th   6th   2nd   5th   7th   2nd   2nd

If you are just beginning to learn intervallic reading you should write the interval names like the above example — but don't forget that all these symbols must be translated into pitch and time before it becomes music — so play and sing intervals at least 5 minutes a day.

Intervals have the same number names whether all on white, black or a combination of key colors — they are measured by staff degrees. In the following example note the number name remains the same as we sharp or flat the notes:

Sample 5

3rd   3rd   3rd   3rd   3rd   3rd

All these intervals embrace 3 staff degrees, therefore they are 3rds.

There are five *quality* names for intervals besides their number name. These five qualities are:

P., perfect
M., major
m., minor
d., diminished
A., augmented

If you are reasonably accurate in observing key signature and accidentals as you read you will soon associate sound with the note and keyboard pictures. You will learn to hear what you see and see what you hear.

Now to apply your interval reading to chords. So far we have studied only MELODIC INTERVALS, those not played together — like singing. Now we will take a look at HARMONIC INTERVALS — these stacked one on top of the other and played simultaneously. Here are triads built on Middle C:

Sample 6

These triads are all built on Middle C and are stacks of thirds. True, they all sound different because they are altered with flats and/or sharps which make the *quality* different but the number names of the intervals are the same — all are thirds.

When chords are line, line, line or space, space, space, they are in their root position and the lowest note is the name of the chord. At this level of development we will still concern ourselves with simplicity and think number names of intervals.

Let's re-arrange the notes of some chords to show how other intervals become involved and how you can find the root of the chord regardless of its position.

SAMPLE 7

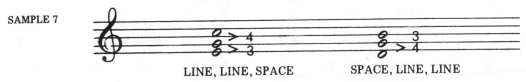

LINE, LINE, SPACE   SPACE, LINE, LINE

The letter name of the chord is the *top* letter of the *different* interval — the interval that is *not* a 3rd. The lowest interval is a third with a fourth stacked on top, so the chord a C triad — the *top* letter of the *4th.* The second chord is G — the letter at the *top* of the interval of a *4th.*

Go slowly, and become comfortable with what we've studied so far. There is more to come!

ANYBODY CAN READ
by Ruth Price Farrar

If you want to build your sight reading skills, you will want to make a master plan for step-by-step progress. I have read in books and articles "The best way to develop your sight reading is to sight read." Something like telling a person "The best way to build a house is to build a house." Don't we learn any and all skills better if you have a model or a teacher? Shouldn't we work from a master plan? Isn't it better to have some guidance, rather than learning through the trial and error method? I think so, that is why I thought you might like some suggestions on how to make a workable plan.

New music is a must. Music that has been played even once is no longer sight reading material. If you subscribe to the standard organ edition of SHEET MUSIC MAGAZINE, it might be well to receive the easy edition, because materials for sight reading must be about two levels below your study materials. There are many albums of all styles of music published in at least three levels. Buy or borrow the level below your study level. The music must be easy enough so you can read pitch and time, find the keys, think dynamics and play up to proper tempo—all without preparation. Well! almost without preparation.

This means you must build up a "vocabulary" of patterns—melodic patterns, harmony patterns, rhythm patterns AND have enough technical ability so your fingers will fall into the right places without thinking too much about fingering. Sounds like a big order. Maybe it is. But isn't all music a big order and don't the benefits received justify the effort? All of you think so or you wouldn't be reading this article.

One more word about the music you select for sight reading. Don't just play any old thing. Interesting music holds your attention longer—you concentrate better—therefore you learn MORE—FASTER. You will want to thoroughly study many of the things you first use in your sight reading plan.

You cannot work with gusto on anything that seems worthless to you, so decide. Is sight reading worth the effort? I think so. All musicians, whether professional or amateur, will profit by developing their sight reading skills. Almost all musical opportunities for the non-professional involve playing at sight. Friends drop in for an evening, bringing other instruments for the Saturday night impromptu music festival. Groups like to sing popular, folk songs and carols. Piano and organ duets are great fun. And have you ever tried playing duets at one organ?

The practice procedure for sight reading varies only slightly from your regular practice routine—if you have a routine. About the only difference is tempo. When you play at sight you MUST play IN time and up to SPEED, as well as being reasonably accurate in note reading and interpretation.

Here are a few more thoughts which might contribute to the development of your sight reading skills.

1. *BEFORE* YOU TOUCH THE KEYBOARD scan the music. Here is a procedure that works: STUDY—THINK—DON'T PLAY

   A. Title—does it suggest mood, style, speed. . .?
   B. Tempo indication—fast, slow, moderate—mood?
   C. Clef signatures—be sure of your hand positions.
   D. Key signature—not only what are the sharps and flats, but play the scale and cadences—orient your hands and ears.
   E. Scan music for key changes, accidentals, chord progressions.
   F. Time signature. Think mathematic values, then get the pulse feel of the part that holds the basic beat. Think big beat to big beat—let the divided beats fall in between. This phase is ultra important. Study the rhythm patterns of Pedal, L.H. and R.H., each as they relate to the others. Audibly tap all three parts as they fit together—Foot for pedal and each hand tapping its own part. Don't hesitate—don't stop. Tap each changing rhythm pattern—short pieces will probably have two patterns.
   G. Now the structure—the form—how are the phrases put together to form the whole piece? Are the phrases made up of four balancing measures or are the phrases uneven? Look for the like, similar and different phrases. Study each for the unusual so there will be no surprises when you begin to play.

2. Finally you are ready to play. Actually it takes longer to read the instructions about "how-to" than it does to do the scanning—once you get on to the idea. Put your music on the organ, set up your registration, decide on the tempo and you are ready to make music on a first playing. Do not deviate from the tempo you decided on. Use your expression pedal to make the music come alive but don't pump it or your listeners will get seasick.

As you play you will probably be aware that all you are doing when you sight-read is put to work, instantly, all your knowledge of theory, technique, harmony, rhythm and time patterns as well as form. So if you do your homework diligently on building a trusty vocabulary of music patterns, your sight reading skills will consistently develop without much effort.

DOES READING MAKE MUSIC?
by Ruth Price Farrar

In "Anybody Can Read" we talked about deciphering the printed page and transferring the information to the keyboard. We might say we are decoding what the composer or arranger put on the page. The symbols put on the paper by the composer are the only means he has to convey his musical ideas to the performer—and hence to the listener. But! Is decoding a page of printed music and transferring those symbols to sound really making music? Not necessarily. That is only one step. We might say that reading the notes with our eyes and playing them with our fingers and feet is putting the mechanics to work. If we stop studying the piece as soon as we are fairly fluent in playing the notes we have read, we may be good keyboard mechanics, but we may not be considered "musicians."

No doubt you have listened to an organist and come away saying, "That performance really carried me away." On the other hand you have also probably heard much so-called "music" that left you cold—that did nothing for you. Perhaps one reason we enjoy listening to "ear" players is the fact that they are listening to what they play and are not distracted by the printed page. They MUST listen to themselves or they would have no idea of what comes next. The music is really speaking to them. Always remember that until music speaks to the player it cannot communicate anything to the listener.

"Always remember that until music speaks to the player it cannot communicate anything to the listener"

What has all this got to do with reading music? You ask: "Is it wrong to try to learn to read? Since I can't play by ear, should I just forget about learning to play?"

The first question will take a bit of detail to take us from the printed page to good listening. Don't forget that the performer must be a good listener, if not the most critical of all listeners. If, as you perform, you become so engrossed in the printed notes—their pitch, their time, the touch, the dynamics—that you forget that all those things must fit together as a whole to make a good tone story, then you are a note reader, not a musician. But you must learn to read fluently if you can't play by ear.

There are comparatively few people who can play from memory or by ear everything that is on the page, fully and accurately. But, you don't hear them falter and fumble over the spots that are rough because they have learned how to *fake*—how to cover their mistakes so the average listener is not aware of their bloopers.

So go ahead—learn to be a good reader. Not just a good letter reader, be a phrase-wise reader. Be aware of everything printed on the page, but read between the lines. Like a good actor, put yourself in the role and project your feelings to your listeners. Don't let your development stop with just reading pitch and time. Include those little nuances: the delicate shadings of volume, the elasticity of tempo—the phrases that punctuate your musical story. Those are the things that make music from the printed page.

Now you know your answer. It is *not* wrong to learn to read fluently. Reading, as well as good technique, is a vital part of a musician's craft. And the more automatic your reading and technique become, the easier it will be to learn new music. That, of course, is the one big advantage the fluent reader has over the ear player—the player who reads can learn new music he has never heard.

Perhaps your second question is also answered. Of course, you can enjoy music even if you have to dig out every note phrase by phrase. A few hints may help you decide how to choose your music and how to go about learning it. First: choose music that is well within your present level of playing so you won't have to work forever on one piece. Don't worry about challenging yourself. Don't dub yourself lazy just because you play easy pieces. Who cares what grade level your music is? Just play the melody so beautifully that everyone wants to hum along. Keep the beat moving smoothly and with the proper accent so everyone will want to tap their toes. Put in enough subtle changes of volume to make the phrases speak. Deviate from the established beat just enough to enhance the natural flow of rhythm to make the music come alive.

Your next question might be: "How do I start to learn a new piece?" So glad you said "start". It is so important to start right. Learn no mistakes, so there is nothing to correct. Here is a procedure in very abbreviated form that may help you to formulate your own plan.

1. Look at the title—does it give you a clue of what the music will try to say?
2. Look at the tempo indication at the upper left hand corner—does it tell you the speed—moderate, fast, slow? It may even give you a hint of the mood of the music. What it tells you is the ultimate goal—you will start at about half that speed in order to put it all together from the beginning.
3. Study the key signature—not just to see how many sharps or flats but to establish the tonality. Play the scale and the primary chords to let your ear hear the tonality and your fingers get the keyfeel.
4. Study the time signature—get the feel of the beat, then be sure to cut the speed down to about half the finished speed for your preliminary study.
5. Now look over the whole piece to see how it is put together. Observe the rhythm patterns, the melody patterns, the harmony patterns and how they fit together to make up the whole composition.
6. Look over phrase one and decide your best hand and foot positions so you can play the beginning musical sentence as a statement or a question without a break. Preferably start with both hands and feet from the beginning. There will be some phrases that require separate hand practice. If most of the piece is too difficult to put it all together I would suggest you select easier music. There is certainly nothing wrong with pulling things apart and studying in detail. Do little sections—four or eight measures at a time. When each part goes fairly well put twos and twos together until all three (hands and feet) play with ease. While you polish this phrase you can start the next one hands alone. Let this detailed study of the more difficult pieces be only a part of your over-all practice.

The music you can start studying with both manuals and pedals at once will be finished in much less time and it will give you a sense of accomplishment. It also gives you a repertoire to play for friends. The more challenging music is definitely OK as a part of your study because it keeps you looking ahead, but if you do nothing that is well within your reach you will become discouraged. If you become too discouraged you may decide you will never MAKE MUSIC.

Don't let that happen to you! If you can think and if you can listen, you can MAKE MUSIC out of that printed page.

TECHNIQUE

by Robert Dumm

It's time to answer some of the provocative questions you've been sending. Keep them coming!

The Sostenuto Pedal

During the past five or six years, I've become intrigued with the potential value of the "full" sostenuto action (as opposed to the abominable blass-sustaining pedal). It seems to me to be an excellent tool for solo piano arrangements and compositions.

My ears tell me that I'm getting some good results; yet I've been unable to locate any competent work on the subject. Reactions from local schools of music, and even teachers, have been largely negative and of no help. They all seem not to understand what I'm talking about. If you know of any information that might enhance my own range of trials and tricks, please let me know.

Will Murphy
Portland, Oregon

Like you, I use the *sostenuto* (middle pedal, marked *S.P.*) often, especially where the glorious gong tones of the bass hold the memory of an important harmony or let it mingle through changing sounds in other registers.

York Bowen (*Pedaling the Modern Pianoforte*, Oxford University Press, 1936), greets the device as a "splendid luxury" (not to be found on English or Continental pianos), accurately dubs it the "selective pedal," and drools (his word was "mouth-watering") over its ability to "sustain a chord in the middle of the piano, so one can 'play staccato' on either side of it." He leaves it there.

W. L. Sumner (*The Pianoforte*, London: MacDonald, 1966) suggests more uses:

". . . it can sustain a chord, leave melody notes unblurred; it can catch the lower note of an extended skip, or a foundation note of an arpeggio chord can be maintained through rapid changes of the ordinary sustaining pedal (our 'damper' pedal). If a chord is sustained by both of the sustaining pedals and then the right-hand pedal is suddenly released, there is a distinct change in the tonal color-

ing. Half-damping, which is sometimes called half-pedaling, becomes easy when the piano has a third pedal. In half-damping the aim is to prolong a bass note against clear moving harmonies above it. When there is no *sostenuto* pedal this is only possible when the harmonies or melodies are sufficiently high in the keyboard and the sustained note is low in pitch."

You will find a good list of places to use the *sostenuto* pedal in Reimar Riefling's careful and comprehensive *Piano Pedaling* (Oxford University Press, 1962). Roy Harris's *Sonata*, opus 1, Samuel Barber's *Sonata*, and Bartok's "From the Island of Bali" (*Mikrokosmos*, Book IV) call on it to hold long basses.

Most specific help is given by Heinrich Gebhard, a Leschetizky pupil (*The Art of Pedaling*, Franco Colombo, 1963). First he gives many bass pedal points that may usefully be held by the *S.P.*, among them a dominant *D* bass in the final section, *presto con fuoco*, of Chopin's *First Ballade*, in G minor, opus 23, which he carries from bar 242 until near the end of bar 249. He then shows instances where *S.P.* can prolong single notes in higher registers.

Gebhard's uses of the *S.P. along with* damper pedaling for degrees of harmonic changes above the bass are most interesting. From measure 65 to the end of Chopin's *Prelude* no. 17, in A-Flat, for example, he has you depress the *S.P.* for the deep A-Flat "bells" in the bass. Once having locked your upraised damper after its tone has been sounded, you simply keep the *S.P.* depressed, open to your next "sounding."

Explore the color changes that both Sumner and Gebhard note, those that result from releasing the damper pedal from a held harmony while the *sostenuto* pedal continues. That "color change" registers in the mind as a slight swell, a precious illusion on any instrument, particularly on the piano.

Better Banana Peels

Please advise the proper way to do the right- and left-hand glissandos, glissandos starting from a written chord, and glissandos on the black keys. How did Earl Hines get that double-glissando sound? Buddy Cole had a similar sound in his playing back in the 40s and 50s.

In using so colorful an effect as a *glissando* slide, I must first sense the musical impulse behind the slide and then experiment with its timing and dynamics. Two *glissandos* came up in yesterday's teaching. The first was the emphatic, swooping scale that reintroduces the main theme for the recapitulation of the first movement of Beethoven's Piano Concerto, no. I, in C(opus 15). See Ex. 1.

Beethoven's pupil, Czerny, suggests that for the octave slide "small hands may take the run in single notes, but with an increased rapidity in order to extend it eight notes lower." Such a double-*glissando* (with right-hand fingers 1 and 5 set at the octave) would have been easier to perform on the lighter-actioned pianos of that day. On the deeper action of the modern grand one cannot apply enough weight fast enough to match the orchestral *crescendo* that occurs at this point in the piece. It is better to play it with two hands as a scale fingered 4,3,2,1 (right hand), with 1,2,3,4 (left hand) all the way down.

If the musical intent of either the double or single *glissando* is less an "eagle's swoop" and more of an "angel's kiss," then lightly "strike a match" on the key surfaces with a swift, light forearm swivel, on middle fingernails (going up), and on thumbnail (going down). As Earl Hines, Buddy Cole, to say nothing of Art Tatum and other jazz greats, tended to keep their trademarks secret, I can not say for sure how they produced their effects. But jazz pianist Billy Taylor tells us that he uses the thumb and little finger of one hand.

The second *glissando* that came up yesterday bears on your question about "starting from a written chord." Starting from the dominant 7th chord in the example below, Debussy clearly wants us to sound the chord, then *feel* the third beat pulse ("resonating" that sound) *before* the *glissando* up to C. See Ex. 2.

Ex. 1. Beethoven.

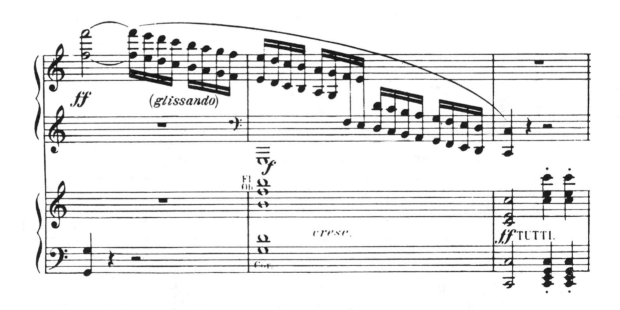

Ex. 2. Debussy.

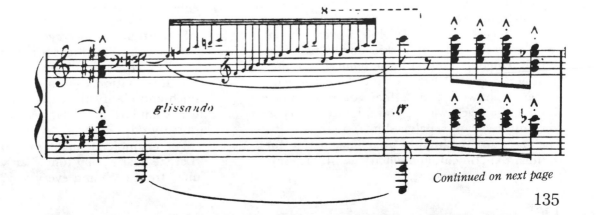

Continued on next page

Beat two takes the weight stress of the Sarabande rhythm. The slide expresses a rush of energy from *G* to *C*. I play this palm up, on the extended nails of fingers 4, 3, *and* 2, "painting" the keys with my full arm. I move from my shoulder, feeling its weight roll out toward the top of my swing.

It helps to time this slide, by playing *G* and *C* alone, right on their beats. It also helps you aim the impact of your moving arm weight *at* high *C* by thinking *past* that point, to keep your motion free. Then at the instant you "hear C" flip your right hand over onto its thumb, which "trips" your moving weight into the target note "in time."

Downward *glissandos* "skate" on the thumbnail turned under the hand, while the arm traces a single long line. The same is true for the left hand in an upward *glissando.* The first musical requirement is to hear and clearly produce the sound that *initiates the glissando,* and mentally match it with its goal sound. Then decide its timing and swell: a late swell for brilliance and an early swell for the effect of "trailing off."

Black-key *glissandos* also depend more upon musical meaning than a fear of scraped cuticle. Moving outward either way from keyboard center, I would again "skate" palms up on the extended nails of fingers 2, 3, and 4; while moving toward keyboard center, I would skid on the nail of a thumb dangling under a loose hand, like a line trailing the ground from a slowly moving helicopter. If, however, the effect you want is pale, shimmering, even wispy, you might even try a four-fingered caress, palms down, no thumb at all. The ways are as varied as your imagination for sounds. Experiment, and when you hit on a mix you like, tell us about it.

Finger Flexors

The same reader asks the following question:

How do you handle the youngster with weak fingers, knuckles that cave in, double-jointedness, etc.? Please give specifics for overcoming and strengthening.

Walter Fields
Cincinnati, Ohio

First off, the signs of weakness you note are normal in children, who have more cartilage in their hands than bone structure. A call to Dr. Rose Marie Hudson of Bethesda Health Center, confirms my experience that finger bones do not fully develop until seventeen or eighteen years of age.

One works against that fact of nature in assuming that an "on-tips" regime, however persistent, will grow bones or muscles in students before nature does. It simply elevates and exposes the wobbliness, and tightens wrists, elbows, and shoulders in an attempt to "hold a position." Dr. Hudson also warned against teachers' urging children to force their tones, since rough pressure can numb or damage sensitive nerves at the fingertips. As for numbness of the ear, one has, unfortunately, only to attend the *average* student recital.

With youngsters, it is a better idea to direct students' attention to sensations at their fingertips. Imagination can stimulate their sense of touch and clarify their nerve impulses, which in turn stimulate muscular growth (not the other way around).

For example, I might say to a six-year-old: "Let me hear a *juicy* tone. Can you 'squeeze the juice' from each and every key?" demonstrating "*this* one and *that* one" with a squeeze-press of the nail joint as I say it. Such an image connects a sound to a sensation and keeps the fingertips "in touch" with the keys, where their slightest movements translate to sounds. Their weakness is not exposed by asking too much.

In the same vein, I might ask a child to "leave your 'fingerprints' on the keys. Let's see your thumb print, pointer print, now middle finger."

In this climate of "Think-a-sound-and-feel-a-touch" I give students many short exercises with spaced stresses and clear dynamics, to "sculpture" shapes into the keys. Such shapes give evidence of musical ideas, the spur and guide to all technical progress.

A six-year-old might get *Locomotive*:

Sing: Up the hill, past the forest, to a country far away. Blow the whistle, choo-choo!

While an eight-year-old might get *The Lone Ranger*:

Sing: Galloping homeward, rider on horseback, handsome and fearless, beating the bushes. Hi-ho silver!

Robert Dumm is former head of piano pedagogy at Catholic University.

STAYING IN SHAPE

by John Browning

We asked John Browning for some advice on how to keep the hands and fingers in top shape. This is what he had to say.

If you don't practice daily, in a certain way, you will lose the ability to make it through a whole concert, so endurance is one of the chief aims of a practice regimen. Practicing has other benefits, too. It sharpens one's ears, and it helps to develop good tone. Pianists usually aim for a tone that is deep without being hard; while practicing, it is a good idea to try for this tone with both slow and fast pressure.

One of the most important points to remember is that you want to keep in shape without causing injury. It is possible to develop hand injuries by "cramming" exercises — this is the pianist's equivalent to the weekend golfer's heart attack. That's why I hesitate to recommend specific routines; everyone has to find their own. But almost everyone agrees on certain basic concepts.

One of these is that the first set of knuckles — what the Russians call the *Bridge* or *Dome* — must act as the power base so that the hand doesn't collapse. When I was studying with Rosina Lhevinne, she had me practice from the Plaidy *· exercise manual. I would suggest practicing double thirds and double sixths, using the Plaidy fingering. Use the bridge of your hand to support the tone, and try different kinds of pressure as you play.

*See page 142

"KEYBOARD CLINIC"

ARPEGGIOS: FOR FINGER TECHNIQUE AND JAZZ IMPROVISATION

by Ed Shanaphy

There are two kinds of people who should be very interested in this article: 1) the keyboard player who wants to learn how to improvise jazz, or improvise pops; 2) the student who needs to acquire a better finger technique. Arpeggios are at the foundation of both these aspirations. As a matter of fact, without in depth study and application of arpeggios, neither good finger technique and control, nor the ability to improvise jazz and pops will ever happen.

WHAT IS AN ARPEGGIO? *The Harvard Dictionary Of Music* defines an arpeggio as "a term applied to the notes of a chord when they are played one after another instead of simultaneously." From the Italian *arpeggiare*, meaning to play upon a harp, *arpeggio* has taken on a broader definition than it had say in Bach's time. Back then it was simply a

broken chord. Nowadays it can apply to any series of notes played in succession, when those notes are contained in one chord. The note pattern can be ascending, descending, or a combination of both.

Most people have the same reaction to the thought of practicing arpeggios as they do to scales. It's somewhere between *Ugh* . . . and *Yecchk!* A pair of well-deserved acclamations. If playing an instrument is to be an enjoyment, and it must be, then why get bogged down in the ritualistic boredom of repetitive exercises? The answer is, you don't really have to. Arpeggios can be fun, and they can do wonders for your playing beyond just finger technique. *They can teach you how to improvise!* That is, if you approach them the right way.

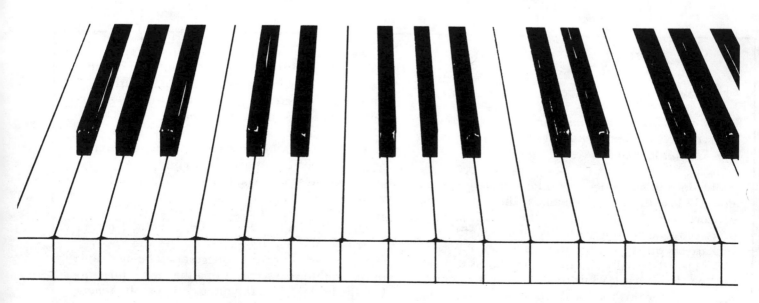

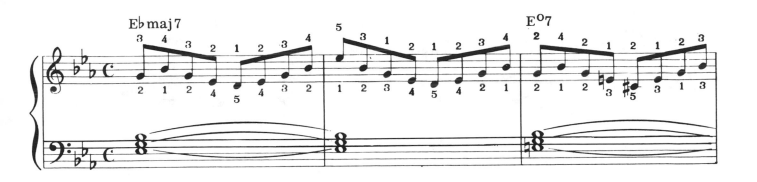

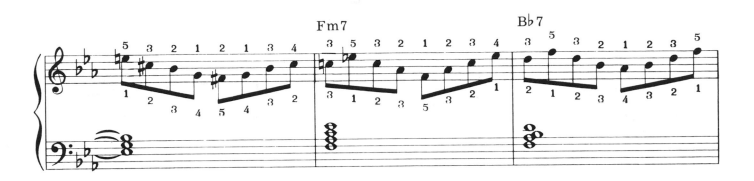

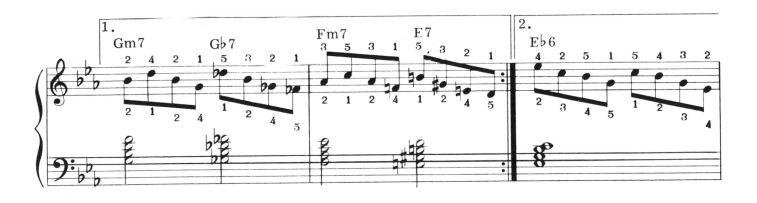

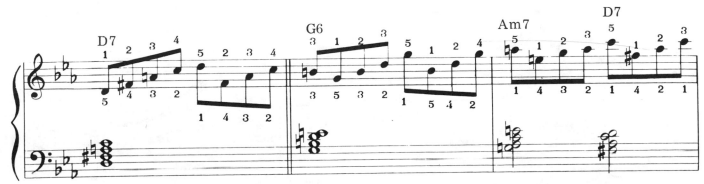

Continued on next page

140

Hence the purpose of this article: to get you to practice arpeggios without realizing it, and to show you how improvisation comes to be.

Our musical example is one long series of arpeggios in eighth notes. The notes indicated in the left hand are the basic chords upon which the arpeggios are built. At times we have inverted the chords in the left hand, or voiced them sparingly to give you a better sounding accompaniment to your right hand practice of this exercise.

Look at the first measure. The first four notes comprise an arpeggio of a pure Eb triad, combining ascending and descending directions. The second four notes are an ascending arpeggio built on an Eb Major seventh chord (Eb-G-Bb-D). For those of you who are familiar with chord progressions of various pop songs, you may recognize this entire exercise. Hint, it's by Gershwin. Take a look at the progressions, or play them through, and see if you recognize the song this exercise is built on. Then come back and read on.

If you guessed right, you'd have come up with *S'Wonderful*, a great favorite in pop as well as jazz. Except for the F# in measure 4, every note in this exercise is a chord tone. (The F# is added as a kind of jazz license. The more "outside" tones that are added to an exercise such as this, the more complex the improvisation.)

Let's look at this example first as a finger exercise, then as a jazz improvisation. As a finger exercise, it must be played at a very slow tempo. Keep your left hand in your lap, and your foot off the pedal. If you have a metronome, set it at 90 or *less*. (A metronome is a valuable asset for finger technique. We've already demonstrated its importance to sight-reading.) Play a measure at a time. Unlike sight-reading practice, try to memorize as you practice. Memorize the fingering as you memorize the notes. If this means having to play each measure 10 times before going on to the next, all the better. The hardest part of any arpeggio is where the 4th finger is involved. The last two notes of the first measure leading to the first note of measure two is just about the hardest part of this whole exercise. Have patience with it.

After you have become somewhat familiar with the exercise from beginning to end, start listening to yourself play it. And start peeking at your hands. No excessive movement of the hands and wrist. Keep it all fingers. *Piston-like.*

Think of pistons when you play. The only time your wrist elevates from a level position is when your thumb crosses under your fingers. The only time your wrist dips slightly is when a finger crosses over your thumb. So when you can take a peek look for: quiet hand, level wrist, piston movement of the fingers, and the proper wrist adjustments for cross-overs and unders.

Listen for smoothness of tone. Is every note as loud, or as soft as the next. Do some stick out like a sore you-know-what? They will. It takes regular practice at this sort of thing before you get a semblance of tone control. Play the exercise loudly with exaggerated finger movement (not hand movement). Then play it softly, feathery. NO PEDAL! From beginning to end loud . . . then soft, beginning to end.

Note: the fingering numbers above the notes are for the right hand. The numbers beneath the notes are left hand fingerings. YES . . . YOU MUST PRACTICE IT WITH THE LEFT HAND TOO. You don't have to play them together, but you must try to get a left hand technique equal to the right. At worst, 75% of the right hand's technique. Set the metronome as slowly as you want. Take your time. Your going to love the results. Your hand will start feeling the results. It will feel much stronger. But always keep striving for looseness and fluidity.

Above all, *keep a rigid tempo.* Once you have gotten to the point where you can play the entire exercise from start to finish without mistakes, and it sounds and looks good, start pushing your metronome up five points at a time. The desired tempo to strive for, even if it takes a couple of weeks, is 180 to the quarter note. If you do it every

day, it will happen. And when it does, you'll be a different pianist than you were before.

JAZZ IMPROVISATION

Now what about applying these arpeggios to the concept of jazz improvisation. If you play this exercise in a jazzy fashion, that is if you give a dotted 8th note effect, without pedal, to the whole exercise, you can understand how jazz solos are built. This is a very basic exercise; that is, it sticks rigidly to the chord tones. If it used more foreign tones such as 9ths, flatted 5ths etc., it would become a fairly typical improvisation. What a jazz musician does is to create, on the spur of the moment, a series of arpeggios and scales built on the chords of the song. A good way to get started in improvisation is to pick out a song you like, and very slowly arpeggiate every chord in the song with your right hand. Keep a constant tempo, and take your time. Change directions of the arpeggios within each measure. As you progress, you will naturally start to use tones other than chord tones in the arpeggio, and you will be changing the patterns more often. Your hands will become so familiar with arpeggiated chords, you'll be able to start sliding from one to the other with great ease. In the beginning, it takes time. And dedication.

By improvising arpeggios on a song that you like, you are, without even realizing it, improving your finger agility, improving your knowledge of harmony, taking the first steps toward improvisation, and most all, you are having a lot more fun than you would have had from an exercise book!

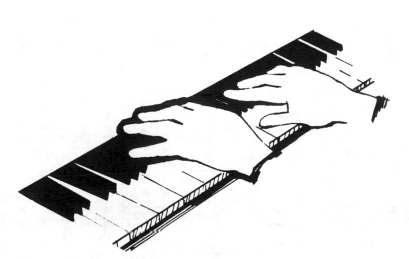

Rules for the Execution of Thirds and Sixths by Louis Plaidy

The following rules, given here only for the direction of the right hand, are equally applicable to the left in contrary motion, and are to be carefully observed in order to attain the smoothest possible connection in performing these scales. 1. In ascending, the right hand must be held a little outward, i.e. turned from the player; in descending, it must be turned slightly inward. 2. In playing ascending scales of thirds, when the $\frac{4}{2}$ has been used, the thumb must be passed under the second, and the third must be passed over the fourth. 3. The connection between the $\frac{5}{2}$ and $\frac{4}{1}$ is to be made in the same way, in scales of sixths. 4. In ascending scales of thirds, after the use of the $\frac{5}{3}$ don't raise both; the connection between the $\frac{5}{3}$ and the $\frac{3}{1}$ must be made by expertly turning the 3rd over the 5th. 5. In the same way, in descending scales of thirds, after the use of the $\frac{3}{1}$ the connection with the $\frac{4}{2}$, or the $\frac{5}{3}$, must be made by the thumb, with the fingers turning over it. 6. In scales of sixths, the perfect connection of the $\frac{3}{1}$ with the $\frac{4}{1}$ (and the contrary) is only to be made by the 3rd and 4th or the 4th and 3rd; the management of the thumb requires careful study, in order to attain an even motion.

Preliminary Exercises.

a, in Thirds.

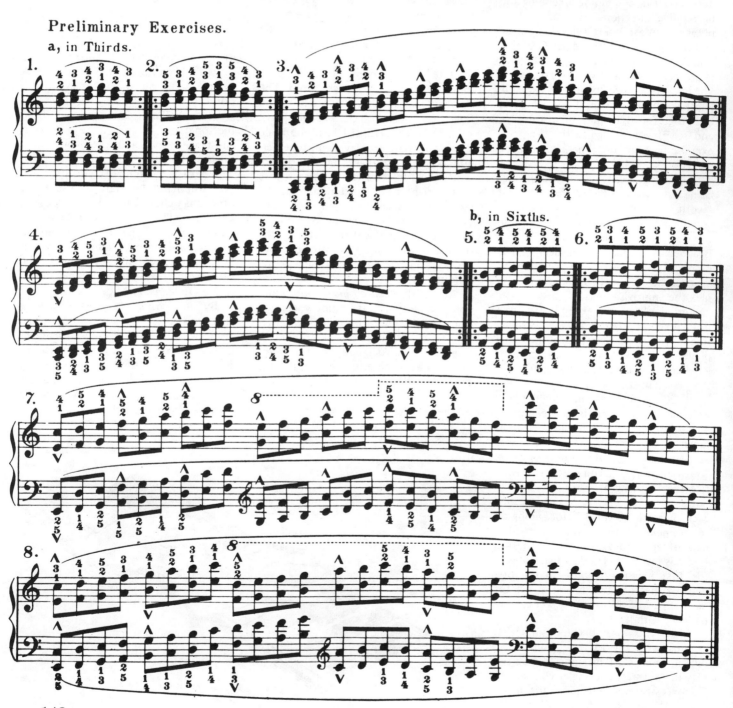

b, in Sixths.

A Fair Shake*
Some Steps to Better Trills

By Robert Dumm

Trilling is often considered to be purely finger action. When a trill sticks, lumps, or spasms to a stop, it seems logical to drill the offending fingers in a willful goose step until they *work*. At least, that seems to be the evidence of etude books past and present, which often dismisses the subject with some variant of this figure:

But so much is left unanswered. How many accents? Where? How fast? How do I speed up without tightening? It hints of gradual steps to be taken, but simply pictures an end result.

Such prescriptions ignore the rotary nature of trilling, and the *co*operation of fingers, hand, and arm. Musically, the trill should be a *thrill* in the melody. Its *vibrato* lies in the shift of energies, from one finger to another and back. We may begin trilling by oscillating each pair of fingers toward an accent. Try moving these shifts through the hand, out from the thumb and back again:

Once you have worked this figure through all the keys (at a moderate tempo), you can activate the trill-germ by a quick mordent after upbeats:

*Shake is the English word for trill.

Continued on next page

"*Musically, the trill should be a thrill in the melody.*"

And while you work, the cheerful tick of the metronome, set for the ♪, times your finger "spark." Do you recall paintings of Elizabethan girls at the virginals, their hands drooping from raised wrists, their fingers tapering whitely onto black keys? That is a picture of the arm balance and natural finger action a trill requires.

The arm hangs passively from the shoulder in an elbow "sling," while the hand dangles freely from a slightly raised wrist. The arm "slings" the hand over the note to be trilled, and the fingers, then, seem to "drop" the trilled notes, like dewdrops, from their tips. I spoke of "slinging" the arm into place to suggest its balanced weight; a passive, not a *dead* weight.

The trick is to minimize your finger "spark" so that the key is so lightly tapped that its instant rebound "springs" that finger free, ready for the next finger. To sense a near-weightless finger flick by contrast to a (hand)weighted touch, try this procedure:

While the "Trill" section of Hanon's *Virtuoso Pianist* is of the uninterrupted "drive-them-to-spasm" school, he does append two training routines by Mozart and Thalberg respectively. Both virtuosi instinctively sensed the need to deflect hand weight away from trilling fingers by changing fingers with strong beats:

Mozart's trill

Thalberg's trill

Hanon's real genius lies in an innocent skip between fingers one and two, which converts the static five-finger figure to a spiraling sequence through the changing shapes and sounds of the scales, freshening the ear while keeping the hand pliant and responsive to the continual changes of "real" music.

After Hanon, I would apply trilling figures to scales, such as:

First, work one of these jingles *through* a five-finger pattern. Then, apply it to one octave of a scale, *using the scale fingering:*

Now I hear you asking: "But, how do I get my trills *fast?*"
I might refer you to Gyorgy Sandor's stimulating new book *On Piano Playing* (Schirmer Books, 1981):

> It is best to start a trill at a moderate tempo with slightly articulated finger and forearm motions. The speed of the trill should be gradually accelerated while the player carefully guards against tension in the arm, hand, and fingers. (That's the rub!)

He even offers a reprieve:

> Trills need not be executed at a frantic pace; those that are played effortlessly at a moderate tempo are often completely satisfying.

Actually, the effect of "speed" in piano playing derives from *both* tempo *and* shape. As you work, then, gradually escalate the metronome for all the aforementioned exercises. But keep your accents! As your quick notes become lighter, your accents will become less forceful, but nonetheless piquant, like casting darts among hummingbirds. Step by step, increase the ratio of quick notes to accented "arrival" tones, but do not dispense with those "arrivals" too soon, in haste to work by "speed." You need them to discharge tension, spark the next spatter of trilled notes, and make "sense" by grouping sounds.

Robert Dumm was named Dean of the Boston Conservatory when he was only twenty-five, and became a critic for The Christian Science Monitor *a year later. He served fifteen years as head of graduate Piano Pedagogy at The Catholic University before retiring in 1979. Mr. Dumm is active as a teacher, contest judge, and writer on musical subjects.*

ETUDES

Etudes is a department which features technical exercises composed by masters throughout history.

Brahms used to take difficult passages in musical works, and practice them with accents on different notes. He gave much attention to the thumb, and to keeping a loose wrist. When he gave his students trilling exercises, he had them play in triplets and in groups of four, and demanded that they try a variety of accents in each phrase.

BRAHMS'S TRILLING EXERCISES

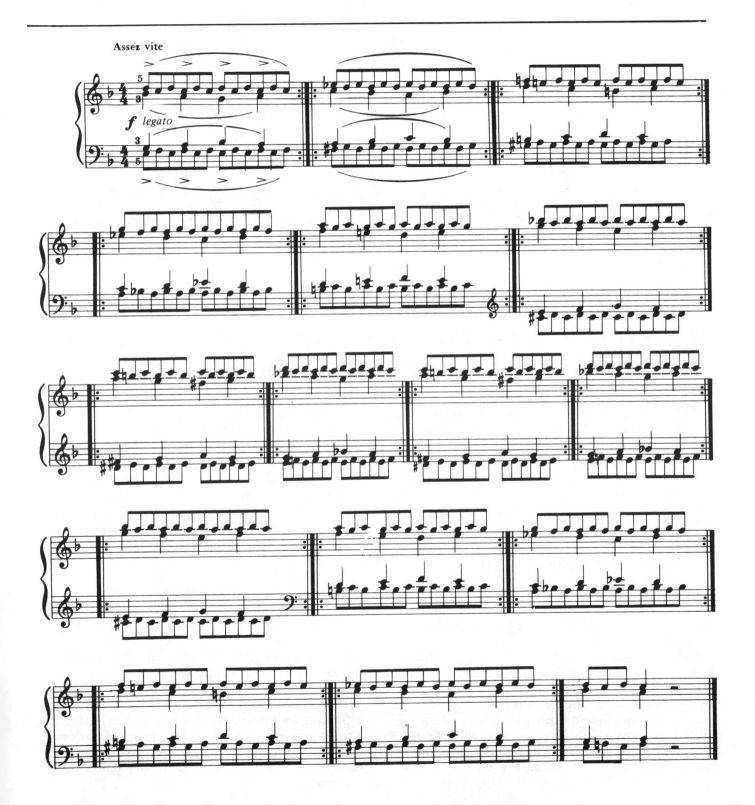

TECHNIQUE

Let Freedom Ring

By Robert Dumm

"Bell tones wing like eagles to the very back wall of a concert hall. To get them, let your arms ride gravity down, poised on a carpet of buoyant air."

The Philadelphia Liberty Bell was made for the ages. The only thing that could crack it was a fall from its tower. Otherwise, it would ring out joyously each new year till kingdom come with the free swing of clapper onto tempered metal.

It's the same way with "bell" tones on the piano. When we want a big, resonant piano sound, we have to swing something heavy very freely. "Big Ben" bell tones call for a pendular swing of the full arm (hanging free from the shoulder), while "wedding bells" drop from the forearm, and "silver" or "jingle" bells are rung by the hand or fingers alone.

One often luxuriates in the full gong tones that artists produce, which wing like eagles to the very back wall of a concert hall. Such tones cause the air of the hall to resonate like a call in a cave, and hold the ear spellbound during their natural, or pedaled, fadeaway. You may often observe how the artist lifts his arm (or arms) whole from the shoulder, and lets it descend in slow motion, pressing an invisible cushion of ever-thickening air.

For the one sitting at the keyboard, the conception of this effect might run as follows: (1) LIFT the arms, as an eagle lifts and spreads his great wings, just prior to flight. (2) Outreach your arms until your hands hang vertically down toward the keys you want to sound. (3) Then LET your arms "ride gravity down" (without slamming them), poised on a carpet of buoyant air. Aim not AT the keyboard, but well beyond and below it. See your arms riding down and INTO the floor—"down to China," as I tell my students.

To evoke from students this large and luxurious arc of movement, I also say, "A funny thing happened as my arms were sinking into the floor: I got caught by a piano!" Such an image brings your hands to the keyboard *midway* in their arc of descent, in a balanced and (seemingly) weightless condition. I never describe my arms' motion as a "fall," for that would slam them into the keys with a crashing sound, a sound we hear all too often! The operative idea is: "I am letting my arms down into a thickening sea, just as a skydiver commits his falling body not to a void, but to a billowing sea of air."

148

Historically, Russian pianists have been earliest and most consistently trained to produce this clear bell sound from the piano. I have heard six-year-olds in Moscow producing antique bronze tones from a Bach minuet, as beautiful as it is bizarre. I have often pondered the effect of those magnificently mystical Russian bell tones, rumbling in their onion domes and swathed in swirls of trapped overtones, on the young ears of Mussorgsky, Rachmaninoff, and Scriabin. Less earthshaking, perhaps, but no less affecting, must have been the piano sounds of Franz Liszt, who stirred Anton Rubinstein (founder of the St. Petersburg Conservatory) to an agonizing search to reproduce them. Liszt also imbued young Alexander Siloti (future teacher of Rachmaninoff) with his deep love for the thrilling mix of piano tone and trembling air.

Sound these first tones of Rachmaninoff's early inspiration, the famous Prelude in C# Minor (opus 3, no. 2) later called *The Bells of Moscow*. It will seem as if the whole Prelude arose as a vision after these meditative sounds:

Rachmaninoff: Prelude, opus 3, no. 2, opening bars:

The image and qualities of bell tones pervade piano literature: a "Glockenspiel" for melody tones; "chimes" for harmonies. Savor along with Schumann his programmed decay of the sixth and final clock chime that ends the ball of *Papillons*, opus 2:

Notice how swiftly Beethoven switches from fingery sounds to sudden "bells" in the last movement of his G-Major Sonata, opus 14, no. 2:

Sound each melody tone of Chopin's evanescent *Cantabile* (printed on page 36 of this issue). Imagine each note drifting to your ear over a still lake, refined by space and poeticized by distance. Above, note the mix of "percussion and singing strings" which is the magic of a well-produced piano tone.

Robert Dumm was named Dean of the Boston Conservatory when he was only twenty-five, and became a critic for The Christian Science Monitor *a year later. He served fifteen years as head of graduate Piano Pedagogy at The Catholic University before retiring in 1979. Mr. Dumm is active as a teacher, contest judge, and writer on musical subjects.*

ETUDES

Carl Czerny, the Austrian pianist, composer, and pedagogue, is famous for his technique studies. The two studies below may be used in conjunction with Robert Dumm's advice on bringing out "bell tones"

150

RHYTHM

the rhythm workshop

"Value": A

by *Ronald Herder*

WHERE HAVE ALL THE RHYTHMS GONE?

What happened to our rhythm studies along the way? Did we sleep through the wrong class? Did we lose our notebook? Weren't we paying attention?

I answer: none of the above.

The scant concern paid to the study of rhythm is one of the oddest quirks of music education, possibly its greatest mystery. Rarely has so little genuine attention been paid to a subject of such fundamental importance and inherent richness. Despite its importance, rhythm remains the least studied of the elements of music, and, as a result, is a source of trouble for far too many professionals and amateurs.

Insufficient rhythmic training hurts our ability to sight-read, to perform, and to write. We begin to depend on rote learning; and a new piece of sheet music is generally a mystery without a recording to back it up and tell us "how it goes."

A piece of sheet music, in fact, lives only through our performance of it. But to interpret it correctly we must understand its notation, and be able to respond to its signs and symbols with appropriate actions. That is what rhythmic training is all about.

"VALUE" CHARTS: MATH OR MUSIC?

At one time or another in our piano or guitar lessons, we've heard about note "values" and seen charts that look something like this:

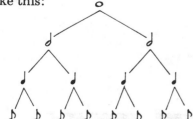

While such a chart is accurate and informative, it is plainly unmusical. For the musician-in-training, it simply fails to convey the most important rhythmic concept of all: that music is a *time* art.

There is too much of a mathematical look about the chart. What it should convey to us is not a sense of mathematics but a feeling for the *spatial relationship* of notes — *because rhythm is motion . . . the way things flow in time.*

This idea of space and time is far better communicated by this sort of diagram:

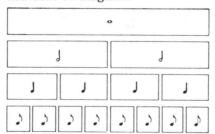

. . . or by this one:

WHAT'S A "VALUE"?

When we compare the duration of one note with the duration of other notes, we are dealing with the *values* of notes. (What are they *worth*?)

Either one of our space-time diagrams — this "family" of notes — shows that the duration of the whole note can be matched exactly by the combined durations of certain other notes in the "family":

Take a moment to experiment with this idea.

What other possible answers exist to the musical equation:

$$ o \; = \; ? $$

SLICING UP THE QUARTER NOTE

Having looked at the big family of notes — at least from the whole note down to the 8th note — let's isolate one member of that family, the quarter note, and see how it can be sliced up into smaller and smaller portions.

This space diagram uses smaller and smaller blocks to show how this is done:

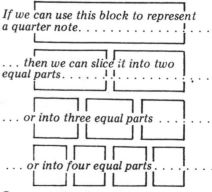

If we can use this block to represent a quarter note. . . . .

. . . then we can slice it into two equal parts. . . . .

. . . or into three equal parts . . . .

. . . or into four equal parts. . . . .

Notice that all four of these possibilities (yes, there are more) *take up the same amount of space.* For example, all four

Family of Notes

blocks at the bottom combine to match the width of that one long block at the top.

The next diagram shows how these block sizes can be translated into musical notation:

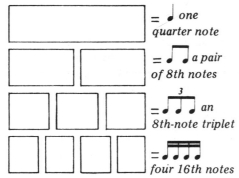

Notice that all four of these possibilities take up the same amount of time.

WORD RHYTHMS

Probably the easiest way to sense the feeling of these 2-, 3-, and 4-part subdivisions of the quarter note is to relate them to words that have 2, 3, and 4 syllables.

EXPERIMENT 1

As a starter, take the words *mu-sic* (2 syllables), *mu-si-cal* (3 syllables), and *mu-sic-mak-er* (4 syllables).

Translated into rhythmic notation — with a steady quarter-note beat as an accompanying guide — they look like this:

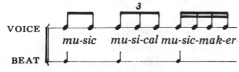

To get the feeling of this phrase, perform it on your own in this way:

1. Tap the quarter-note beat by itself:

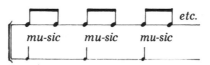

Set a slow or moderate tempo and keep the beat absolutely steady and regular. If you like, use a metronome to assure that the beat is rock-solid. Don't rush or drag.

2. Continue the steady quarter-note beat (tapping) while you say an unbroken *music music music . . .*

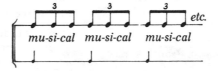

This is an exact 2-to-1 relationship: two equally spaced 8ths for each quarter. Keep the syllable flow even and continuous. Don't rush or drag.

3. Continue the quarter-note beat while you say an unbroken *musical musical musical . . .*

This is an exact 3-to-1 relationship: three equally spaced 8ths — the 8th-note triplet — for each quarter. Keep the syllable flow even and continuous. (There is a great tendency to rush triplets. Don't do it; let them *float* effortlessly.)

4. Continue the quarter-note beat while you say an unbroken *music-maker music-*

maker music-maker . . .

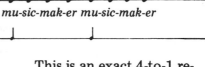

This is an exact 4-to-1 relationship: four equally-spaced 16ths for each quarter. Keep the syllable flow even and continuous. (There is a tendency to drag 16th-note groups. Don't do it; drive them forward.)

EXPERIMENT 2

Invent and perform various combinations of *music, musical,* and *music-maker* to the accompaniment of a steady quarter-note beat. Don't rush or drag; slice that quarter-note beat precisely. Practice until the rhythmic flow is effortless.

EXPERIMENT 3

Perform the "Beat Piece" printed on page **162**.

EXPERIMENT 4

Write and perform (tapping and speaking) your own experimental "Beat Piece" using an entirely different set of words.

BACK TO YOUR SHEET MUSIC

This is obviously not the end of the story of rhythmic values, but it is the end of this first glimpse into the ideas, concepts, and structural details that underlie and fill the world of rhythmic activity.

More than ever, our perception of note values — the way we

Continued on page 162

Straight Talk About...
BEAT, METER, AND TEMPO

by Ronald Herder

Our new Straight Talk series is in response to our readers' most often asked questions about aspects of rhythm. Each article in the series will be centered on a specific item; in future issues we'll focus on dotted notes, syncopation, meter and tempo, the metronome, and so on. We welcome your response to this new series, and your suggestions for additional aspects of rhythm that you'd like to see discussed.

What are they?

Beats are regular pulsations that measure musical time:

Time passes, and is measured, as the beat series goes on . . .

Meter is the way beats are grouped into measures:

a 2-beat meter:

a 5-beat meter:

Tempo is the speed of the beat. *Beats create tempo: the faster the beats occur, the faster the tempo becomes:*

a slow 4-beat meter:
(x = one beat)

a fast 4-beat meter:
(x = one beat)

What is meant by "downbeat . . . upbeat"?

All aspects of rhythm are based on one fundamental idea: *the alternation of strong and weak.*

The strong, or accented, first beat of a measure is the **downbeat.** Think of the downbeat as a release of energy. The weak final beat of a measure is the **upbeat.** It exists to prepare, or build up energy for, the downbeat that follows it.

Compare the feeling of upbeat/downbeat to the way you breathe: inhale (build energy) . . . exhale (release energy); or to your natural arm movements: lift arm (build energy) . . . drop arm (release energy); or to any number of other activities: throwing a ball, swinging a racket, walking. . . .

The rhythm of music is not an artifical concoction! It is a natural extension of how we are and how we move!

How does this work in different meters?

In 2-beat meters, the downbeat is the strong beat on "1"; the upbeat is the weaker beat on "2":

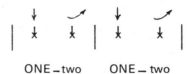

ONE — two   ONE — two

In 3-beat meters, the downbeat again (always) is on "1"; the upbeat is on "3." Beat 2 — a weak "middle beat" — simply extends the upbeat effect:

ONE two three ONE two three

In constructing meters, the 2-beat form and the 3-beat form are all we have to work with! This fact is so basic and simple that we usually overlook it: All meters either have a 2-beat form ($\frac{2}{16}$ $\frac{2}{8}$ $\frac{2}{4}$ $\frac{2}{2}$), a 3-beat form ($\frac{3}{16}$ $\frac{3}{8}$ $\frac{3}{4}$ $\frac{3}{2}$) or are created by *adding* 2's and 3's in various ways:

2+2 ($\frac{4}{16}$ $\frac{4}{8}$ $\frac{4}{4}$ $\frac{4}{2}$), 3+3 ($\frac{6}{16}$ $\frac{6}{8}$ $\frac{6}{4}$ $\frac{6}{2}$) 2+3 or 3+2 ($\frac{5}{16}$ $\frac{5}{8}$ $\frac{5}{4}$ $\frac{5}{2}$)

2+3+2 (or 3+2+2 or 2+2+3) ($\frac{7}{16}$ $\frac{7}{8}$ $\frac{7}{4}$ $\frac{7}{2}$) and so on and on.

Tempo and beat feeling

You may be astonished to hear that a time signature of, say, $\frac{2}{4}$ tells you absolutely nothing about the beat *feeling* of a piece of music. Yes, it tells you about its construction or form — that there are 2 beats per bar, and that a quarter note represents the beat. But that's all. Nothing more.

What determines the music's beat feeling *is its tempo* — the speed of those 2-beats-per-bar. This means that you will feel a certain piece "in 2," for instance, *only if the tempo lets you feel it "in 2."*

In general, the old "soft shoe" tunes have a moderate "2" feel, with melodies featuring numerous quarter notes. There are also the bright, uptempo tunes in $\frac{2}{4}$ with a driving *one-*beat feeling, with many eighth notes in the melody. And in this piece — also in $\frac{2}{4}$ and one of the gems of the classical literature — the beat feeling is neither "in 2" nor "in 1"; it is "in 4!" Chopin's tempo marking, *Larghetto,* clocks in at a speed of about ♩ = 60 — a leisurely, floating, four-*8ths*-to-the-bar feeling:

Nocturne in F♯ (Op. 15, No. 2) CHOPIN

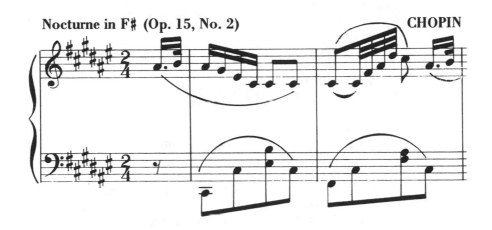

So don't trust the number game. Look at the tempo marking in that piece you're playing to know what's *really* going on.

Let's let matters sit there for now. Yes, of course there's a lot more to say about beats, meter, and tempo because we've only just cracked the nut of these fundamentals of rhythm. But we'll have to reserve the rest for a later issue or two (or three). © *Copyright 1979 by Ronald Herder*

ACCENT ON RHYTHM

by Stuart Isacoff

The difference between sounding like an amateur or a professional is often simply a matter of conviction. I know pianists who play wrong notes right and left, but they do it so convincingly that no one seems to mind. It's an old adage that a performer should never stop to correct a mistake; one can even hit all the right notes and sound just awful if a feeling of tentativeness comes across in the performance.

One of the best ways to get a self-assured quality in your playing is by developing a solid rhythmic "feel." Many of us have struggled with this for years, and some people go so far as to claim that rhythmic sense is something you must be born with. (Picture the frustration of Offenbach's valet, who lost his job despite excellent qualifications. "He always beat my clothes outside my door," explained the composer of TALES OF HOFFMAN, "and I never could get him to do it in time.") The truth of the matter, though, is that with a little practice anyone can improve their ability to play with a clear, accurate and convincing touch.

The key to good rhythm lies in the fact that some notes naturally call for more stress than others! To see how this works, try clapping your hands in a steady rhythm — then break the claps up into groups of three, making the first in every group a little louder. That accent acts as a sort of anchor, and makes it easier to keep time.

In every musical phrase there is a similar need for accentuation. In fact, musical works are built on a kind of rhythmic architecture which needs to be discovered and brought out. Let's look first at metrical accents, since meter serves as the foundation of that architecture.

If a piece is in ¢ meter, the first and third beats will normally be strongest; in $\frac{3}{4}$ meter the first beat will be emphasized.

Most songs, though, set up a rhythmic scheme on top of the normal metrical one. For example, in SCARBOROUGH FAIR we find a repeating *renaissance* dance pattern:

In other songs we might find any number of similar dance rhythms, like the tango (Example #4), or the more sophisticated Bossa Nova (see Example #5) or Hora (Example #6). (We'll deal with such complicated patterns in a moment.) Sometimes differences in pitch, rather than in note length, will bring out the particular rhythmic feeling. (Example #7.) It's not difficult to spot accent patterns in a song if you stay on the lookout for some feature which seems to repeat over and over again.

This second level of rhythmic activity (above the metrical foundation) is often translated into an accompaniment to the melody, and in future issues we'll explore how to use it in this way. For our present purpose, though, it is important to begin feeling this rhythm physically. Most pros experience it as a body sensation rather than a mental activity, and you can, too. Try beating the rhythm on a table-top; tap-dance it on the kitchen floor. Then hum the melody while you tap. If you find this difficult, use a metronome to provide a steady background pulse. Set it at a slow tempo at first, then increase the speed gradually as you get the hang of it. Remember, the idea is to recreate physically the pattern of accents found woven through the fabric of the song. (Several schools of musical education, such as the Kodaly and Dalcroze methods, are based on this "physical feeling" method.)

Now, let's look at the melody. If it consists of simple note values which clearly fit the rhythmic underpinning we've been discussing, there is no question of where the accents should be placed:

HABANERA from CARMEN   GEORGES BIZET

But some melodies (and some accompaniments) create complicated accent shifts through *syncopation*, so that notes which would normally be "weak" become purposely emphasized. This rhythmic twist shakes things up a bit, and creates a level of musical tension and excitement.

The shift sometimes comes in the form of "anticipation," in which a strong beat (such as the first beat of a measure) is anticipated, that is, played early:

Anticipated notes should *always* be accented.

Shifts also occur in melodies which begin on a weak beat, but require a real "punch" nonetheless:

Let's take BERNIE'S TUNE as a case in point for the way to approach a pop song with such sophisticated rhythms.

In this arrangement the left hand expresses a sort of dance rhythm accompaniment.

Since the meter is based in groups of four, we would expect to accent the notes falling on beats one and three:

BERNIE'S TUNE

But ties create a syncopation effect, and call for accents on the anticipatory notes:

(In order to execute these tied-note figures easily, pretend at first that no tie exists [Example # 14]. Play the melody through this way a few times, and you'll soon be ready to put the ties back again.)

EX 14

The right hand rhythm is also subject to metrical accents on beats one and three, and to accents on the notes that are tied:

But there is something else to consider here as well. Although the first melody note begins after the beat, it, too, is intended to be accented. This is because it is part of a syncopation, like the rag-time figure we looked at earlier, or the anticipations we've been accenting all along.

Once you've uncovered these accent groupings, there are several ways to bring them out, including changes in dynamics, pedaling, and touch (such as contrasting full, held tones with short staccato ones.) Experiment with each of these and you'll soon discover that music which used to sound monotonous and without backbone can take on a rhythmic solidity and excitement you hardly thought possible!

Musical examples used by permission of Atlantic Music Corp.

STRAIGHT TALK ABOUT
... TRIPLETS

by Ronald Herder

What is it?

A triplet is a group of three notes which take up the same amount of time as two notes of the same value.

What does it look like?

The three most commonly used triplets are these:

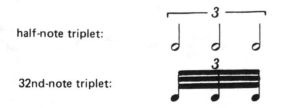

quarter-note triplet:

8th-note triplet:

16th-note triplet:

Notice that the number "3" appears with the notes. "3" always means "triplet."

Are there other kinds of triplets?

Yes, but they're comparatively rare:

half-note triplet:

32nd-note triplet:

(And it's even possible to use whole-note and 64th-note triplets.)

How can I explain the idea of a triplet to someone else?

In measuring *space,* this 3-inch block

3

... can be divided into two equal parts

1½	1½

... or into three equal parts ...

1	1	1

Notice that all three possibilities take up the same amount of *space:* in this example, they all fill up exactly 3 inches.

In measuring *time,* this 3-second sound

... can be divided into two equal parts

... or into three equal parts ...

Notice that all three possibilities take up the same amount of *time:* in this example, they all fill up exactly 3 seconds.

In music notation, this is how the divisions look: the "long" sound at the top . . . then the two-part division . . . then the three-part division:

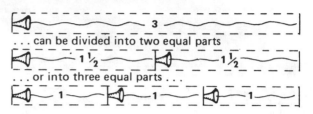

This is what is meant by the idea that "*three* notes (the triplet) take up the same amount of time as *two* notes of the same value."

How is the triplet counted?

Percussion players use the clearest counting system to get the triplet feeling and to perform it accurately. In $\frac{4}{4}$, for example, they foot-tap the 4 main beats while they recite the triplet pattern smoothly and with no breaks in the flow of sound:

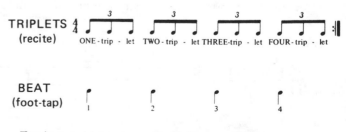

TRIPLETS $\frac{4}{4}$ (recite) — ONE-trip-let TWO-trip-let THREE-trip-let FOUR-trip-let

BEAT (foot-tap) — 1 2 3 4

Try it out. Listen to yourself. Are your foot-taps steady and even? (Don't speed up or slow down.) Are your words flowing evenly? (Don't say: "ONE trip-let . . . (pause) . . . TWO trip-let . . . (pause) . . .")

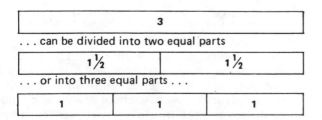

Practice Patterns

To get the triplet feeling, practice these patterns. Begin each one by "kicking off" the tempo: foot-tap the basic beat for a while; then, when you've set a firm tempo, begin reciting the pattern against the basic beat. Repeat each practice pattern until you've got it.

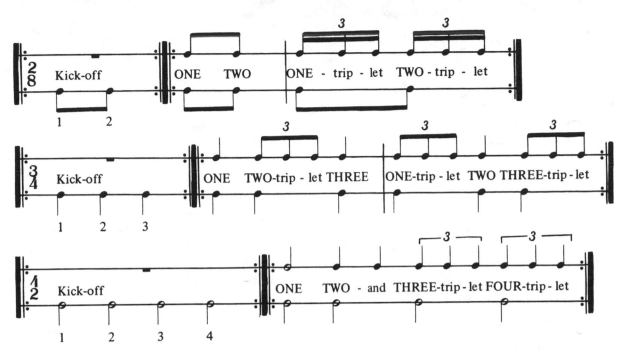

Triplet Variations

A triplet is still a triplet even if two of its three notes are tied or replaced by a longer, equivalent note value:

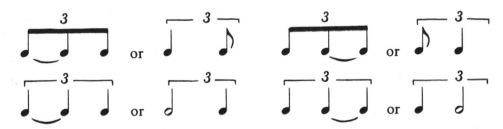

. . . or even if one or two of its notes are replaced by rests:

. . . or if one or two or all of its notes are subdivided:

. . . or if ties, rests, and subdivisions all happen together:

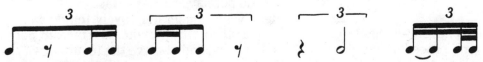

(Notice how the "3" is centered, and the use of brackets to "frame" some triplet patterns.)

Continued on page 162

159

Rhythm Workshop

by Ronald Herder

"El Vito": Working with 3/8 patterns

Outside of Beethoven's *Für Elise,* the average pianist does not often run into pieces written in a ⅜ meter. This unfamiliarity breeds a certain amount of fear because the rhythm patterns look strange, and we are not quite sure of how to go about deciphering the notation. And yet this beat pattern is one of the simplest to handle.

An effective solution is to think not "⅜" but simply "3 beats to the bar," just as we do for pieces written in ¾. This means that the basic pattern

has *exactly the same beat feeling* as

In fact a fast ¾ sounds exactly like a moderate ⅜. The listener can't tell the difference; only the player knows that the unit of beat is ♪ and not ♩. "El Vito," in short, could have been written as a fast ¾ with absolutely no change in the way the music *sounds.*

Bars 1-4: To learn the left-hand notes, practice this drill while counting "1-2-3" throughout:

Then play the original with the same counting sequence:

Bars 5-6: The practice pattern for these right-hand notes follows the same procedure: think "¾" while doubling all note values. Count aloud.

Then play the original with the same "1-2-3" count:

Apply the same procedure to the right-hand notes in bars 11, 13, and 15. Bar 19 is the same, but with the addition of two grace notes before beat 3

Bars 9-10: The right-hand rhythm pattern is just the reverse of the preceding example. This time play the practice pattern:

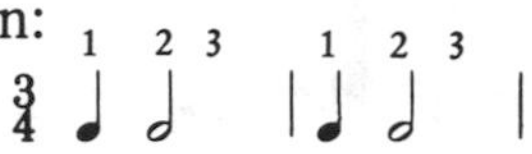

then switch to the original:

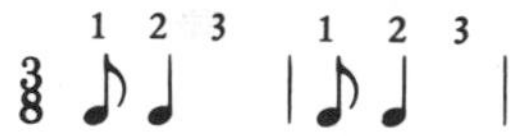

Bars 4,8,12,14,16,20a:

The pickup pattern

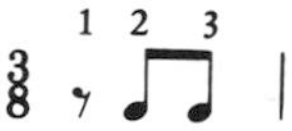

looks like this in its ¾ equivalent:

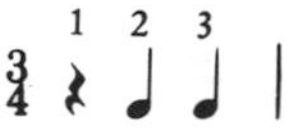

Follow the usual practice procedure, always thinking "1-2-3."

Other patterns:

For ⅜ ♪ 𝄾 𝄾 | practice: ¾ ♩ 𝄽 𝄽 |

For ⅜ ♫ 𝄾 | practice: ¾ ♩ ♩ 𝄽 |

For ⅜ ♪ 𝄾 ♪ | practice: ¾ ♩ 𝄽 ♩ |

For ⅜ ♩. | ♩. | practice: ¾ ♩. | ♩. |

The overall feeling of "El Vito" is of a lightweight, cheerful, and rather bouncy dance. You do not have to play it fast to capture that feeling. Even a moderately lively tempo works if you keep a steady beat, make the staccato notes short and punchy, and observe the tenuto marks on all of the downbeats. Keep strict time throughout, even for the sustained notes in bars 23-24. End this delightful dance with its quiet but rhythmic flourish in the last two bars.

El Vito

Arranged by Ronald Herder

Andalusian Folksong

Value: A Family of Notes — *continued from p.153*

see, hear, and feel their relationships — is supremely important to even the most casual reader of this magazine's pages. The best lyricists have always had a keen ear for language's rhythmic flow, and have paid microscopic attention to beat feeling, syllable division, and word grouping. When they slice the beat into divisions and subdivisions, they mean what they write. And the best composers have followed them right down the line, translating speech flow into a rhythmically musical line.

This scrupulous respect for rhythmic flow — evident in the best folk, pop, rock, jazz, and show tunes around — is the lyricist's and composer's half of the bargain. The other half is ours. We interpret the printed page — faithfully. We decipher the notation — faithfully. We bring it to life. □

A "BEAT PIECE" WITH MIXED NOTE VALUES

This piece shows how various note values — from the long to the quick — work against a steady beat.

Triplets — *continued from p.159*

When is a "triplet" not a triplet?

Musical notation can be confusing. But you'll always know a real triplet from something that *looks* like a triplet but isn't; just be sure to examine the meter you're in, the note value that represents the basic beat of the music (the quarter in $\frac{4}{4}$, for instance), and how the composer has written the patterns.

Here, for example, is a typical pattern found in a great number of pieces:

Is the three-note group a triplet? No! Its just three "straight" 8ths that are more clearly notated like this:

Are these triplets?
No, again. These are "straight" 8ths, six to the bar.

To avoid confusion, remember that (a) only *undotted* notes can be divided into triplets; (b) that the triplet is an *irregular* subdivision because an undotted note normally divides into two, four, eight, etc. equal parts; (c) that a triplet usually has the number "3" at its stem-end (however, the "3" may be dropped eventually if a number of triplets follow each other in a musical passage).

Where are triplets found?
Everywhere!

THE CLASSICS

The Viennese Waltz

by Robert Dumm

©T. BERNHARD 1981

So much piano music was inspired by dances that it helps to learn all we can about how people dance, and how they felt about a particular dance. In the future, film and videotape will convey the immediate sense of this or that dance, just as we can marvel today at Fred Astaire flying from garden wall to piano top in the old musicals.

For dances of the past, we must gather every clue (there are many), then try to see the dance going on in a room alive with lights and people. We must sense its movement and tempo, learn some of its steps, and imagine the feelings that animate or accompany those steps.

Goethe, in writing of his adolescence in Frankfort of the 1760s, tells of the dancing lessons his father, a wealthy jurist, gave him and his sister. First came the careful steps of stately Minuets, the positions and "plays" of *Contres* (English country dances), and "even the Waltz," with some amazement, since it had not yet been accepted by society. They "whirled around together like the spheres. It was certainly a little rough to begin with because so few knew how to dance it." Out in the country, however, "the Allemande, Waltz, and *Dreher* (a turning dance) were the beginning, middle, and end. All the people had grown up with these national dances."

Mozart, writing from Prague in 1787, tells of attending a "rustic ball, full of the town's beauties, who jumped around with sincere enjoyment to the music of my *Figaro*, which had been turned into all kinds of *Contres* and *Teutsche* ('German' dances; that is, early Waltzes)."

The Minuet was then one hundred years old and showing signs of age. Like any dance that catches on and remains popular, it began fairly fast—think of the Minuets of J. S. Bach's French suites—and wound down over the years to the slower grace of Mozart's "Don Juan" *Minuet* (1787), written as dinner music to a banquet scene:

"The turning went on in the most indecent positions.

Introduced to the court of Louis XIV of France by Jean-Baptiste Lully in the latter 1600s, Minuets acted out—by steps, gestures, poses, and bows—the chivalrous protection and guidance a knight offers his lady-in-distress. Either of two notions of the origin of the name "Minuet"—the French *menu*, meaning "small" (steps), or *mener*, meaning to lead, or guide—reflects this little drama. As THE dance of courtly society, the Minuet was stopped short by the French Revolution and swept away by the democratic impulse it set loose around the world.

The elder half of the generation gap mourned the Minuet noisily, especially the ubiquitous dancing teachers, who had lost the mainstay of their lessons. "The art of dance is dead," they wailed, and called the Waltz, which quickly replaced the Minuet, a "romp" and worse. By the end of the eighteenth century in England, one C. M. Fanshaw could wad his remorse into an "Elegy on the Abrogation of the Birth-Night [The King's, George III] Ball and the Subsequent Final Subversion of the Minuet":

No more the well-taught feet tread
The figures of the Mary Zed:
The beau of the other times shall
   mourn,
As gone and never to return,
The graceful bow, the curtsey low,
The floating forms that undulating
   glide
(Like anchored vessels on the swelling
   tide)
That rise and sink, alternate as they go,
Now bent to the knee, now lifted on
   the toe,
The sidelong step that works its even
   way,
The slow "pas grave" and slower
   "balance."

Be mine to trace the minuet's fate
And weep its fallen glory.

No matter. The new generation wanted fresh air and the freedom to dance away its energy and passion. Curt Sachs (*World History of the Dance*, 1937) sums it up:

It was no ephemeral fashion which brought the folk dance to the pulse in this most impulsive of social pleasures to shake off all borrowed attitudes, all empty forms, and to mold the new bourgeois dance on the pattern of those dances in which the old forces held sway: not studied or measured steps, but joyful, intensified movement, not stylized make-believe, but living actuality, not consciousness, but ecstatic rapture.

"Character, expression, spirit, passion—everything that the new era demands from the dance, it found in the waltz," Sachs tells us. "The dance has again become truly ecstatic: exaltation, surrender, and the extinction of the world about."

"Out of this world," for sure, and wild enough at times. Waltzing at a village ball in Erlangen, "The dancers held up the dresses of their partners very high so that they should not trail and be stepped on, wrapped them tightly in this shroud, bringing both bodies under one covering, as close together as possible, and thus the turning went on in the most indecent positions. . . . The girls, meanwhile, looked half mad and ready to swoon."

Gone were the favorite steps of the *Ländler*—girls spun around by a stamping boy, arms intertwining to "make a 'chamber' while the boy looks in" (Hansi Alt's description) in favor of the close, embracing whirl of the Waltz. And the speed! Urbanized on polished floors in shoes without hobnails the *Ländlers* and "Germans" accelerated from turning to an orbital spin. Spun from a strong downbeat in three-quarter time, the embracing couple makes one full turn every two measures, at the same time it described a larger circle around the room, "like the rotation of heavenly bodies," as Sachs puts it.

"Never," asserts Goethe (in *The Sorrows of Young Werther*, 1774), "have I moved so lightly. I was no longer a human being. To hold the most adorable creature in one's arms and fly around with her like the wind, so that everything around us fades away. . . ."

Prudishness and envy slowed acceptance of the Waltz in other countries. Lord Byron, Romantic poet par excellence but born lame, writes bitterly as late as 1812:

Continued on next page

Went to a ball at the Countess's expecting to see a Country Dance, or at most Cotillons, Reels and all the old faces to the newest tunes, but judge of my surprise on entering to see poor dear Mrs. Hornem with her arms half around the loins of a huge hussar-looking gentleman I never set eyes on before; and his, to say truth, rather more than half around her waist, turning round and round to a d------ see-saw up-and-down sort of tune till it made me quite giddy wondering why they were not so.

When he thought they would surely "sit or fall down" they walked around a little, her hand on his shoulder, and then "at it again, like two cockchafers (scarab beetles) on the same bodkin (long pin)."

Byron's "See-saw sort of tune" probably was very much like the Tyrolean yodel and bob of this "Valse" by Chopin (Brown Index 46, "though not every authority accepts it a genuine Chopin"):

The young Romantic Age took the Waltz to its heart, and composers soon adjusted the lilting stamp of individual beats (in *Ländlers,* German Dances [Allemandes], and German Waltzes), to the gliding swirl of the Waltz. The dots and slurs of these two examples by Schubert tell it all:

Landler

Waltz

Beethoven, himself no great shakes on the dance floor, remains close to the step and feeling of the German Waltz, or Allemande. The daring leaps and third-beat stresses of his *Bagatelle* in D (Opus 119, no. 3, *"A l'Allemande"*) suggest vigorous rather than sweeping motion, in spite of his 3/8 meter:

a l'Allemande

And graceful as they are, sense how close still is the "German" dance in these late "Waltzes" by Mozart. His two-note slurs clearly express the lift felt on every beat:

Schubert's *Valse Sentimentale* in A (Opus 50, D. 779) shows many more signs of urbanization than its title:

Its melody, rising and falling by small intervals, centers on the light preparation and lingering resolution of a suspension (they often called them "sighs"), sailing above the quietly gliding "dance steps" of the left hand. (I would try to play that bass on the keyboard just as feet would pace steps on a polished palace floor.)

Wagner called the Waltz 'a more powerful drug than alcohol.'

Though it is clear how Schubert's Waltzes evolved, but differed from their country predecessors, he wrote them for his friends, high in spirits but rather low in "Society," to dance. They would have gone on dancing to *Ach, Du Lieber Augustin!* (a popular late-eighteenth-century Waltz) had there never been a Johann Strauss.

It was, specifically, two Josephs—Lanner first, then Strauss—who injected the Waltz with the euphoria and high style that sent it right back to royal courts (in Vienna, that is, during the reign of the Hapsburg emperor. Waltzing was forbidden at the Prussian [North German] court until the time of Kaiser Wilhelm II, World War I).

Richard Wagner, visiting Vienna in 1832 at age nineteen, tells us in *My Life*:

> I shall never forget the extraordinary playing of Johann Strauss who put equal enthusiasm into everything that he played, and very often made the audience almost frantic with delight. At the beginning of a waltz this demon of the Viennese musical spirit shook like a Pythian priestess on the tripod, and veritable groans of ecstasy (which, without doubt, were more due to his music than to the drinks in which the audience had indulged) raised their worship for the magic violinist to almost bewildering heights of frenzy.

Wagner called the Waltz "a more powerful drug than alcohol—the very first bars set the whole audience aflame."

Madder, giddier, faster than anything yet, the Strauss Waltz dives into beat one of the bar then ricochets in a powerful spring to beat two (the two beats are cause-and-effect). Beat three hangs suspended, hardly felt at all:

In playing a Viennese Waltz, let your weight "go," or spill into that first beat of the bar, then rebound onto the second beat. The first two beats are melted in a upsurge of joy. Put "springs" behind that "surge" and you'll "go through the roof" on beat two, to heaven on a spiraling cloud, like the spiraling figure of Strauss's *"Fledermaus"* (The Bat) Waltz:

The Waltz mania swept all levels of society and whirled them happily through a century, to the first shots of World War I. Even the French *valses lentes* (slow waltzes) of that war, where the second beat lingers rather than leaps, are heavy with the haze of that happiness:

Robert Dumm was named Dean of The Boston Conservatory when he was only twenty-five, and became a critic for The Christian Science Monitor *a year later. He served fifteen years as head of graduate Piano Pedagogy at The Catholic University before retiring in 1979. Mr. Dumm is active as a teacher, contest judge and writer on musical subjects.*

VIENNA LIFE

JOHANN STRAUSS

Master Class
By Santiago Rodriquez
Granados's *Spanish Dance No. 5*

I enjoy playing this piece because of its simplicity and accessibility. It's something people can go out of the concert hall humming—which they can't always do with a Chopin or Debussy etude. The work has been transcribed for guitar and was made famous by Segovia, but its original version is this one, for piano.

Actually, I never play it the same way twice, but there are some general guidelines I keep in mind. The form is ABA, but I like to think of it as ABC—with C as a variation of A. The A section is slow and improvisatory. I play it as if I were inventing it as I go along, the way a jazz player doodles and discovers a melody. It should be heartfelt and introspective.

Contrary to popular belief, Spanish people are not very outgoing: they are introverted people. Even the bullfight is an internal sport—if the matador shows off too much he may lose his life. He must have a very personal, thoughtful approach and keep his concentration at all times.

So I play the A section in a very intimate way until the Forte, which acts like a fanfare to wake me out of my personal thoughts.

As for the grace notes in the left hand, I see them as more rhythmical than musical. They remind me of castanets or tambourines, and are used to establish a pulse and a color. They should remain strictly in the background. At the beginning of the piece, I hesitate slightly after the low E's.

The middle section suggests to me a solid touch, down into the keys, but with the soft pedal. Those chords should sound like a choir humming—but without the soprano melody sticking out. I play it slower than the beginning tempo.

At the repeat of the B-section idea, I use the second finger of the right hand to bring out the alto color (for example, the D#, C#, C#, B figure).

And I repeat the little three-note descending figure with a bit more staccato to bring out the Spanish flavor.

At the return of the A section (our final C section), I use less rubato. It is a typical Spanish dance at this point. When I play the octaves, I take more time and make it stronger. At the very end, it becomes soft and introverted once again.

Enrique Granados was an outstanding Spanish composer and pianist. He is most noted for the series of Spanish Dances he composed, and for Goyescas, inspired by paintings and etchings of Goya.

SPANISH DANCE No. 5
Op. 5 No. 5

ENRIQUE GRANADOS
(1867-1916)

172

173

Daniel Varsano Plays Bach

by Marcia Menter

At the end of Bach's *Goldberg Variations* there is a quodlibet based on two popular songs of his day: *The Cabbages and Turnips Make Me Flee* and *It's a Long Time Since I Was Close to You.* To pianist Daniel Varsano, this piece is both a musical joke and a solemn reflection of Bach's entire musical philosophy. Here the trifles of the secular world and the grandeur of God exist together — another example of the duality that is the basis for all of Bach's work.

Daniel Varsano, at 27, recently won the Grand Prix du Disque for his recording of selected Satie works. His latest project, for CBS Masterworks, pairs the *Goldberg Variations* with Beethoven's *Diabelli Variations,* both of which demand a great deal of both artist and listener. Varsano is French with Russian blood, a compelling combination of intellect and romanticism. Though his manner is easy, when he speaks about music you know he has thought deeply and meticulously about each note.

I spoke with Varsano about playing Bach on the piano,

curious as to what a student of both Rosalyn Tureck and Magda Tagliaferro might have to say. Inevitably, the first question was whether Bach belongs on the piano at all.

"There has been an argument about what keyboard instrument Bach should be played on," Varsano says. "But this question was invented by the 19th century."

Musicians of that era were preoccupied by musical color, says Varsano, while Bach was not. "If he had really been concerned about color, Bach would never have been re-orchestrating, re-writing the same works for different instruments all his life," he says.

"In fact, we now know from Bach's correspondence that he acted as an intermediary in the sale of a piano to Count Branitsky of Poland, and that the

Ricercar from the *Musical Offering* was written for piano! But the important point is that his music was based on structure. It's like architecture: if, for instance, you were to take a big cathedral like Notre Dame de Paris and suddenly decided to change the color of the stone from beige to light gray, the structure and beauty of the monument wouldn't change at all.

"This big battle over instruments is based on the 19th-century concern with color, and on the 19th-century philosophy that one has to choose the right instrument, that there is only one musical answer. For Bach, there were always multiple answers to each question.

"Bach's music is written so it can be played on any instrument — yesterday's, today's and tomorrow's. And this is not a matter just of possibility, but of duty. Bach is too great to be limited to one 80-year time period. It's not like a little Greek statue you put in a museum and admire. It's much more. We need to give it oxygen so it can breathe."

When Varsano plays Bach on the piano, he leaves out what he regards as romantic mannerisms of color, volume, and rubato. What intrigue him are the piano's possibilities of clarity and line; he seeks to give each voice a different quality. ("I don't necessarily give one voice more importance than another," he says, "I just clothe them differently.")

"To argue about the validity of playing Bach on the piano hides the real problem, which is to find the right solutions for interpreting the music," Varsano says. "And these can only be found in the structure of the music itself.

"Take the *Goldberg Variations.* I've lived forever with this work and with Landowska's very beautiful, very fascinating recording of it. At the end of the *aria* (the theme) you have a gentle flow of sixteenth notes for two lines. Then in the first variation, the upper voice is also written in sixteenths. Landowska used to say this was a graphic continuation of the aria, meant to be played gently and peacefully. But with all the deep respect I have for her playing, I don't agree at all.

"I had a lot of problems finding the right tempo for this first variation. Examining it very closely, I found that the truth is in the bass — everything is in the bass in this work. The bass is written in this rhythm:

"And this is the basic rhythmic structure of the allegros of the *Brandenburg Concerti,* and of the first movements of all his instrumental concerti. When you realize this, you have the right tempo: a firm dance tempo, not too fast, not too slow. This is an example of a musical solution in the *structure* of the music, not on the surface."

Varsano uses this same structural approach to determine in which of the *Goldberg Variations* to take repeats. He does not take them all, because he believes that would be too scholarly — and too long-winded. He does repeat the ten canonic variations. ("They offer a fantastic possibility to give different color. Since a canon is polyphonic, you can give a voice one coloring the first time, another the next.")

Dance movements are also repeated. "The principle of dance is repetition." He smiles: "Imagine Bach drinking beer at an inn with friends and starting to dance around the table. He wouldn't want to stop!"

Improvisatory, virtuosic variations are not repeated. "These have the ability to amaze and thrill the listener; a repeat might diminish the brilliance of the effect. Some things have to be stated just once."

Then there is the question of ornamentation. In this area, one might say Varsano's Russian blood merges with his French upbringing: he lets his imagination run wild — within structural limits.

"Nowadays one sees printed everywhere Bach's little table of embellishments brandished like a flag of authenticity. But this was written for Bach's son, an eight-year-old kid; it's a very simplified, primitive approach. Ornamentation is much more subtle than that. You have to interpret the ornaments differently within each piece of music.

"Eighty percent of the time I improvise in adding ornaments to the ornaments themselves. But I always work within the structure that's already there."

He illustrates with the first variation, adding an ornament (G, F#, G) that is inherent within the structure.

"There is a problem at every note," Varsano says. "And the challenge with ornaments is to emphasize things which are already inside the music. I never add from the outside."

The most important element of Varsano's Baroque style is articulation. He controls different voices with a highly developed ability to play legato and staccato in the same hand.

"There are two necessities in polyphonic playing," he says: "Being able to go from legatissimo to staccatissimo; and having total dynamic control — the ability to switch abruptly from forte to piano and back again. This is very different from the 19th-century approach. Instead of being romantic and climactic, it all has structural meaning.

"It's funny how Bach was not concerned with color when he was composing. But we have to use different colors — not for their own sake, but to clarify the structure, to serve his polyphonic ideas.

"In that final variation of the *Goldberg Variations,* Bach chose to use a song about cabbages and turnips. Well, turnips grow down into the ground, while cabbages grow up out of the ground. This music is filled with the idea of opposites, and I try to bring them out."

Thus does Daniel Varsano cultivate the seeds of polyphony in Bach's musical garden — with a Russian flare for color and a French love of detail.

Marcia Menter is a freelance writer and a graduate of the Manhattan School of Music.

Menuet

Embellishments Added By Daniel Varsano

Johann Sebastian Bach

*The ornaments in small notes are to be played the second time only,
in place of the larger (main) notes.

TECHNIQUE:
PLAYING BAROQUE ORNAMENTS

Let's use this charming *Serenade* by Jeremiah Clark (opposite page) for practicing Baroque ornaments. Before starting, notice the time signature: $\frac{3}{2}$. This indicates there are three beats per measure, with each half note getting one beat.

To begin, play the piece through without any embellishments. After you can play it with rhythmic security, try the second half of the work, this time with *shakes* (trills) inserted where the sign ⍗ calls for them. Most of the ornaments use a variation of the trill finger movement, so it's a good one to practice (right is a chart of many of the ornaments you'll see in Baroque music).

Meaures 11 and 12 may be played this way:

Since there is less time in measure 11 to play the shake, the ornament is shorter there than in measure 12.

To play the shake evenly, try practicing in "impulse groups." Slowly at first, with firm fingertips in contact with the keys, play two trill groups and then drop your hand to your lap in one impulse. Completely relax your hand as it drops.

Next, play five note groups quickly and drop your hand to your lap, relaxed.

Continue increasing the number of trill note-groups, dropping your hand to your lap at each conclusion. Soon, you'll find it easy to play this ornament. When you are completely at ease with this exercise try using other fingers (such as 4 and 3 in measure 11) in the same way.

German Ornaments

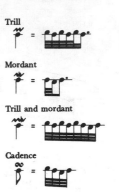

English Ornaments

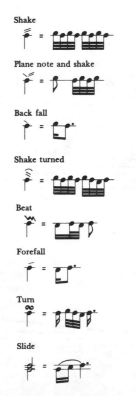

---

by May Etts

The Serenade

Jeremiah Clarke

*See table of English ornaments (beat). Second finger on C#.

CLASSICAL CORNER

CHROMATIC CHOPIN
by Ronald Herder

Chopin's haunting E-minor Prelude is the fourth in a set of twenty-four Preludes, Opus 28. In the set, there is a Prelude for each major and minor key (C major . . . A minor; G major . . . E minor, etc.), and most are but a page or two long, one as short as 13 measures. The Preludes are, in turn, serene, violent, songful, majestic, and so on, reflecting the many faces of Chopin (the troubled "poet of the piano"), the influences of his beloved Bach and Mozart, his daring breakthroughs in piano writing, and his unique talent for composing exquisite miniatures.

The world-famous E-minor Prelude — shown in full on the facing page — is one of the great examples of harmonic ingenuity. Its harmony literally "makes" the piece since the bulk of the melody is exceedingly plain. A quick scan of the unpromising pitches of the first 8 bars shows something more like a slow trill exercise than a great tune:

In fact, only 5 of the Prelude's 25 measures (mm.9, 12, 16-18) give us anything that's melodically memorable. So harmony is practically everything in this music, and Chopin's handling of its progressions is a masterpiece of subtle changes.

The key to the progressions is the strong, descending bass line, dropping chromatically from G down to B. Without its repeated 8ths, the bass reduces to this simple line:

Building on this bass line, Chopin creates a chain of chords that shift bit by bit, ever so slowly, gradually changing color. As one chord slides to the next, the smooth voice-leading always keeps touch with one or two pitches of the preceding chord, *creating an endless, interlocked chain of tightly related harmonies:*

To add still greater color to the harmony, Chopin plays with one of his favorite devices: the *suspension.* In this technique, a dissonance (that is, a *non*-chord tone) momentarily displaces one of the expected chord tones. Probably by design, most of the E-Minor Prelude's suspensions involve the pitch E: see the left hand dissonances in measures 2, 10*, 14, and 18-20.

Double suspensions — for added harmonic spice — occur in measure 9, beat 1 (G#-B are both resolved to A); and in measure 17, beat 3 (D#-F# are both resolved to E).

Looking back, it's no surprise that Chopin elected to write an extremely simple melody to join his harmonies. The harmony is so rich, so chromatic, so inventive, that nothing *but* a simple line would have been appropriate to offset the strong progressions.

Further offsetting melody and harmony is the composer's choice of rhythmic motion: the long son of the right hand against the relentless 8th-note movement of the left-hand accompaniment. To perform the E-minor Prelude, bring out the expressive long-note melody while subduing the left-hand pattern. Keep these two separate elements on two separate levels: foreground against background. Delicious as the harmonies may be, resist the temptation to bring them into the foreground. Use a light but firm touch for the repeated 8ths, with a sensitive touch of pedal for each chord change.

The tempo of the Prelude is about ♩ = 63. Anything much slower will drag the motion and weaken the subtle connections between the chords. But avoid beating out the pulse like a steady metronome; the music has drive but is far from being a mindless "motor" piece. Keep a sense of elastic give-and-take, but without exaggerated speed-ups and sugary, sentimental ritards. In short, keep the music as intimate, moving, and hauntingly beautiful as it is. ♩

Prélude

F. Chopin. Op. 28, No. 4

Prelude in C Minor
(Op. 28, No. 20)

Frederic Chopin

ROCK-SOLID CHOPIN   *by Ronald Herder*

Chopin's C minor Prelude — the 20th Prelude of his Opus 28 — has all the ingredients of an absolutely knockout popular success. It is unusually short (13 bars), enormously dramatic, melodically simple, harmonically rich — and easy to play. Don't let the size of this one fool you: It is an emotional giant, and carved out of solid rock.

Its structure is very plain. Its 12 bars of identical rhythm ♩ ♩ ♫ ♩ | are divided into three

4-bar phrases:
  Phrase 1 = bars 1-4
  Phrase 2 = bars 5-8

Phrase 3 = bars 9-12

The 13th, and last, bar is a one-chord "tag."

Harmony

Needless to say, Chopin knew how to write a great tune — but this isn't one of those times; this melody is nicely shaped, but hardly one of his most memorable. Here, the guts of the composition are its magnificent harmonies, voiced for maximum resonance on even the weakest upright piano. The chords virtually roll out of the instrument, with a sound that is as close to an organ as the piano is likely to get: big, broad, resonant, full-throated.

182

Bars 1-4 make a full, broad statement with sixteen chords voiced in root position. It is these deep roots (octaves in the left hand) that give the effect of an organ's resonant pedal tones. Bar 1 begins and ends in C minor. Bar 2 modulates to A♭ major. Bar 3 makes a passing modulation to F minor. Bar 4 modulates to the G triad (the dominant of C minor), setting up a return to the original key of C minor.

Bars 5-8 float on a lovely, descending chromatic bass line:

that makes this brief turn:

and then drops to the organ-like root progression:

Bars 9-12 are an exact repeat of 5-8. Bar 13 is the final cadence on the C minor triad.

Rhythm

If you don't bother to count, you will probably end up playing the recurring ♩. ♩ figure as either

♪ ♩ or ♩ ♪ ♩   The figure
is easy to play correctly if you practice the following pattern. As you play a measure, mentally divide each beat into 16ths, *counting out the numbers aloud and very evenly:*

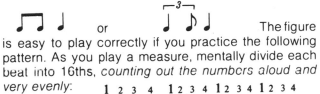

Tempo

The piece is traditionally interpreted as a slow, broad, and majestic work; ♩ = about 60. Most players hold the same pace throughout, sometimes experimenting with a *slightly* slower pulse for the last phrase (9-12) to give it a touch of relaxation and "unwinding."

Phrasing

Note that bars 1-4 have one slur per bar, and that 5-8 (and again, 9-12) are slurred from end to end. Follow the slurs, taking a barely audible "breath" (tiny phrase-break) between slurred groups without really interrupting the forward-moving drive of the piece.

Dynamics

Bars 1-4 are full and strong: a powerful opener. Play them with equal weight in both hands. Let the rich bass octaves support the harmonic weight.

Bars 5-8 create a delicate, plaintive, songful phrase. Attack it with a dramatic drop-off from the previous power to a soft level. Bring out the melody in the right hand's little finger.

Bars 9-12 — because they are a note-for-note repetition of the previous phrase — need a slightly different interpretation. (To play it the same way is simply too mechanical and unmusical.) Play this phrase even softer (*pp*), perhaps a bit slower. This time, try to bring out the inner voice of the right hand, at least for the first bar, to bring new light to the same music:

Then revert to the little-finger melody to end the piece.

The last chord works beautifully as a quiet, lingering, dying-away afterthought. (Some players prefer to make it sound big, following a brief crescendo.)

Pedalling

Good pedalling is an art in itself. Since its function is to seize and sustain color, you will have to listen very carefully to the sounds you produce. In this Prelude, many players pedal each chord separately, releasing the previous sonority a split-second before grabbing the next. If you can, work for a rapid (but *noiseless*) "release it / depress it" pedal action just before you strike the next chord. This keeps the texture clear and unmuddled.

Learning the Piece

If this two-fisted masterpiece seems like a lot of notes to grab at one time, try a couple of preliminary steps. First, you can simplify the first measure by omitting all notes played by your right thumb, and by changing the left-hand octaves to single notes. The sound will be a little thinner, but all of the notes are there.

When you've got this, add the octaves in the left hand, and then the notes played by the right thumb. (Notice that the right thumb simply doubles the melody played by the right hand's little finger.) As you need it, continue simplifying the piece, for practice, until your chord movement is fairly fluent.

The fingering is reasonably straightforward except for a couple of spots. For the third beat of bar 2, right hand, play both the D♭ and E♭ with your right thumb alone. Do the same for the second beat of bars 6 and 10: Cover the C-D with the right thumb.

Surrounding Events

Not a great deal is known with certainty about the composition of Chopin's complete Preludes, Op.28. At one time it was thought that all twenty-four of these wonderful miniatures were composed, when Chopin was twenty-eight, during a disastrous trip to Majorca. His poor health, and the depression brought on by bad food, uncomfortable lodgings, and constant rain were thought to have been the source of the drama and torment ringing through many of the Preludes. But the truth is less in the Romantic vein: The pieces seem to have been written over a longer period of time, and presented in part to his publisher, Pleyel, for an advance payment to finance the Majorca journey. The completed manuscript of the Preludes was sent to Pleyel in January, 1839.

Succumbing to tuberculosis on October 17, 1849, at the age of thirty-nine, Chopin was buried in Paris. At his service, Mozart's Requiem was sung, and the E minor and B minor Preludes of Opus 28 were played on the organ in tribute to the master.

183

Interpreting Scriabin and Rachmaninoff

by Ruth Laredo

Neither the Scriabin *Prelude*, op. 11 no. 9, nor the Rachmaninoff *Moments Musicaux* no. 3 is fraught with difficulties, but they are both very expressive—and characteristic. Each piece is songful and should be played very *legato*.

This Rachmaninoff is one of my favorites of all. The sustaining melodic lines are so Russian and so gorgeous. It's important to maintain the somber quality of the sound—the dark tonal color. It is one of the most simple of his works; the lines are plainer and there are perhaps fewer notes than in any other of his works. But those harmonies are typical Rachmaninoff, and they should be played *orchestrally*.

The Scriabin *Prelude* is one of those wonderful epigramatic little pieces. It's very similar to some of Chopin's work—especially to Chopin's *Etude*, op. 25 no. 7, which is in the same key of C# minor. Of course, the Chopin is longer and more elaborate, but it is interesting to note the similarities.

It also reminds me of the Chopin *Prelude*, op. 28, no. 6, although this piece is in a different key, B minor.

The melody in all of these is in the left hand, but when playing the Scriabin try to bring out a beautiful long singing legato *in both hands*. The harmonies must sing; they should have a wistful quality. The piece also calls for a very free speaking interpretation. Freedom of expression was important to Scriabin.

184

Prelude
op. 11 no. 9

Alexander Scriabin

Moments Musicaux
op. 16 no. 3

Sergei Rachmaninoff

Master Class
Agustin Anievas On Mendelssohn

By Lesley Valdes

Song Without Words Op. 19 No. 2

Critics often put pianists into one of two categories: the cool, intellectual school of a Brendel or Rosen, or the bravura and emotional approach of a Horowitz or Rubinstein. Agustin Anievas puts his piano playing in the latter category. "Accuracy is important but the music must speak emotionally," says the forty-eight-year-old pianist whom reviewers frequently cite for brilliant and beautiful artistry in his specialty, the Romantic literature of the nineteenth century.

As a Juilliard student, class of '59, he revered Horowitz and Rubinstein. "Perhaps Horowitz more —for his voicings and technique. But as you grow older you find out that technique isn't the only thing," laughs Anievas, who had himself traversed most of the Chopin Etudes by the age of twelve. Today it is the "freedom" of Rubinstein's style that intrigues him. "It is expressive—never gimmicky."

Although Anievas has received superlative reviews in many of the world's major cities, his career has lacked the initial visibility of Van Cliburn, who preceded him at Juilliard, and the popularity of younger Juilliard colleagues like Mischa Dicter and Emmanuel Ax. Signed by Sol Hurok immediately after winning the first Dimitri Mitropoulis award in 1961, the pianist now smiles at his ignorance of "the business of music" then. "When I got out of school I was very idealistic—and stubborn. I didn't want to push. I thought if I was good things would come after the (Mitropoulis) award. In my family, we never blew our own horn."

Moving to Europe in 1964, Anievas spent the next ten years performing, abroad more than in the States, and turning out widely praised recordings for Angel and Seraphim. Still, opportunities didn't come as rapidly as the young prizewinner had hoped. He also found himself somewhat intimidated by other Hurok clients: "All of a sudden I was matched up with Richter and Gilels!" Comparing himself to these mature giants of the keyboard made him reluctant to push his career before its time. "But careers are funny things," he adds, in a characteristically affable way. "You can be very good and never make it or not so good and play everywhere. It depends on so many things." What things? "In my case, luck—and a lot of perseverance," grins Anievas, who now averages three engagements a month. He is also a professor of music at Brooklyn College.

Last December, at Carnegie Hall, he premiered a newly discovered, one-movement sonata composed when Mendelssohn was fourteen. A conservative, monothematic work, Anievas was eager, nonetheless, to present it. He is also collaborating with Duke University musicologist R. Larry Todd, who unearthed the former work, in hopes of finding a later sonata, now lost.

"I get tremendous pleasure from Mendelssohn, but I think most people never get beyond the Songs Without Words," says Anievas who played the composer's Preludes and Fugues, the Variations Sériuses, and Liszt's transcription of Mendelssohn's Midsummer Night's Dream during the Carnegie recital. "All his works are so lyrical. They have the beautiful melodies we usually associate with Schubert." As for the Songs Without Words, Anievas says they are still among the best pieces with which to teach the lyric, legato playing demanded of Romantic literature. "Easily attainable," they don't tax the intermediate student's technique. Among his favorites are Op. 19, no. 1, "Spinning Song," "Song of the Winds," and "A Shepherd's Complaint."

Anievas finds teaching enjoyable and students cooperative about making up lessons missed due to his concert schedule. One difficulty he does encounter is in "teaching them to play with a flowing, lyric line. Some play only what they see, note to note to note," he demonstrates from the Steinway in his Victorian home in Brooklyn. "Getting them to practice is another problem. Some will go from fourteen to twenty-five hours in a week. Others won't no matter what you do."

Anievas, whom friends call Gus, practices about thirty-five hours a week. He insists, with obvious relish, that "there are still plenty of hours left for everything else": family, students, and running two miles daily!

Continued on next page

The key to this small song is legato playing, says Anievas, "always with a lilt or sense of pulse. This is music that really needs to breath. Take the tempo from the three grace notes in measure two (*the second complete measure*). They should not be hurried, fitting smoothly into whatever tempo you choose." A metronome mark between 120-126 to the eighth note is "about right." Although some may prefer the grace notes played on the first beat, in a more classical vein, Anievas always executes them *before* the beat, emphasizing the music's Romantic leanings.

To achieve the legato needed here, "the student must learn to use the wrist as a pivot for each phrase": dropping down at the beginning of each line, moving the wrist up and over to lighten the fingers' release of each phrase. "I also tell my students to hold on to each note as long as possible—some think the moment a note has expired they should get their fingers off the key. That only makes for a lumpy, unlegato sound." To underscore the melody in the left-hand accompaniment Anievas holds the main notes (C, B, A, G# at the beginning of the piece) for an eighth, instead of sixteenth, note value. Since the accompaniment forms a kind of countermelody to the main theme in the right hand, Anievas sometimes suggests "breaking it into two hands just to get an idea of which lines they want to hear." Once the left-hand accompaniment is played as written, however, he stresses a very light use of the thumb on each E (measure 1, etc.). "I only use the smallest fraction of the right side of my (left) thumb; it's an area about the size of my fingernail. And I never get off the key completely."

If the double thirds in the right hand (measure 7) present a problem, try leaning more on the top notes (B, D, C), and aim for a "full, decent sound" instead of a careful, "skimpy one." The quality of tone can help to bridge the gap between less-than-perfect and ideal double notes, Anievas maintains. Singing each part will also reinforce the legato and tone quality desired, he adds. It is almost essential to sing the long, eight-bar line that is the work's first theme.

Don't be afraid of nuance in this Andante expressivo. The bridge at measure 39-40, for example, is an apt place for a slight retard. Measures 13-16 cry out for a change in dynamics. ("Soft the first time, louder the second—or whichever way the pianist likes them," says Anievas.) Each harmonic change should be underscored without, of course, jarring the sense of a phrase (e.g., measures 18-19 or 28-29).

Control is certainly called for "within this very small framework," says Anievas, and the sensitive player will learn to seek out the small details that highlight Mendelssohn's craft. Note, for example, the slight variants in the accompaniment each time the theme returns; the similarity of idea in the accompaniment in measures 29 and 72; the close, fuguelike entries of the theme on the tonic and dominant in measures 77 and 81.

Agustin Anievas

"It's like a daisy," Anievas says of the song. "A small flower that looks very pretty but simple—until you pick it and see how intricately it's constructed."

As for pedaling, he says, "Learn to syncopate the pedal: depressing it immediately after, not on, each beat." In the song's coda, Anievas recommends pedaling very slightly (lifting dampers until they just barely touch strings). He uses only one pedal for the seven A's in measures 88-90 to achieve a portamento effect, and again at the song's close.

Photo by Gideon Lewin

190

SONG WITHOUT WORDS
Op. 19 No. 2

FELIX MENDELSSOHN
(1809-1847)

ORGAN TECHNIQUE & STYLE

Turning From Piano

EVERY PIANIST

by *George D. Nixon*

It seems that many pianists hesitate to enrich their musical experiences by including organ as an instrument of musical performance. In talking with them, we find that they give various reasons for this. One reason, they say, is that they do not like the organ as well as they like piano. Another is that they feel that learning to operate the foot pedals and all those other "gadgets" is an obstacle that would be almost impossible to overcome.

May we suggest that one should put aside any bias one has for or against the piano or the organ, as they are not competitors nor mutually exclusive. Each instrument has its own uniqueness and each has an important musical role to play. The piano is essentially a percussive instrument with the sound produced by a hammer striking a string. The pipe organ is a wind instrument with the sound produced by air passing through a pipe. The modern electric organ imitates the pipe organ through the miracle of electronics. The fact that they use similar keyboards does not make the piano and organ competitors.

The pianist should think of the transition to organ as an expansion of one's musical horizons—an opportunity to add variety to one's musical experiences. The pipe organ or the modern electric organ present an opportunity for a great variety of musical effects. When the new electric synthesizer is added to the organ, the number of possible effects becomes almost infinite.

There are certain physical advantages that the organ has over the piano. The new transistorized electric organs can be smaller and lighter in weight than the piano. Almost all electric organs have a jack outlet so you canplug in earphones. The earphones permit one to play the organ without disturbing others.

Now that you have been convinced you should make the transition to organ, "What", you may ask, "are the similarities and what are the differences you will encounter in making that transition?"

Of course, both the piano and organ use the same type of keyboard, and they use the same musical notation, although organ music may have an additional staff for the bass pedal notation. The musical theory is the same for both instruments; however, a more thorough knowledge and application of theory may be required if the pianist is not well grounded in this area. Much of the literature for the piano and organ is the same, that is to say there is much overlapping of the literature, with each instrument having some literature exclusive of the other.

Some of the differences one will encounter include one or more additional keyboard manuals. There is no reason to be intimidated by the multi-manualed instrument. Since one has only two hands, only two manuals can be used at any one time. The advantage of having more than two manuals is so the voicing can be set up in advance and therefore voicing can be changed quickly. The principal problems multi-manuals present concern coordination and balance.

Perhaps the most intimidating difference is the pedal board. To the pianist, this may seem to be the principal roadblock. Please be assured that the legs and feet are no more difficult to train and control than the arms and hands. It is true that the pianist has not had this training, so in this one area, we must start at the beginning. Raphael Mendez, once billed as the world's greatest trumpet player, is quoted as having said that

To Organ:
IS AN ORGANIST

when he started on the trumpet, his teacher assigned him the scale of C# Major for his first lesson. Mendez said that he didn't know that was one of the most difficult scales on the trumpet, so the others came very easily. This writer believes that the pedals should be learned first by the pianist who is learning to play the organ. This idea will be referred to again later in this article. In reference to pedals, one should also be aware that a spinet organ will have only one octave of bass pedals while a console model will have at least two octaves of pedals.

Another difference that will be encountered is the type of touch used. Since the piano is a percussive instrument, it is necessary to learn to strike the keys. Since the organ is a wind instrument, the keys must be depressed rather than struck. An analogy of the difference is a manual typewriter versus the electric typewriter. Since the organ is thought to be an imitator of the human voice, the attack and release of the keys to produce phrasing become somewhat of a different problem than on the piano. This idea carries over into fingering patterns. It often is necessary to do "finger sub-stitution" to avoid releasing a sound too soon.

Registration or voicing is another difference to be learned. This is an area that sometimes intimidates the pianist. They are concerned about "how do you ever learn to push down the right buttons (stops)?" Many are surprised to learn that after one becomes familiar with the function of each stop, the performer determines which stops are to be used depending upon which sounds he or she likes best. There is a great deal to be learned about registration, but it is not difficult to learn.

Finally, another added difference one will encounter is the use of the expression pedal. This is the "foot-feed" that is operated by the right foot. Its sole function is to control dynamics (loud-soft). Some of the larger consoles will have two expression pedals side by side. One operates the tibias and flutes—the other the reeds and strings. A control switch will permit one pedal to control all. Learning to operate the expression pedal will be quite simple for the pianist, since its subtleties have to do with phrasing with which the well trained pianist is familiar.

After reading this far, the pianist may ask "How am I going to be able to make this transition?"

The answer is that the best way is to find a good organ teacher—preferably one who also plays the piano. This teacher will be able to guide you smoothly through any problems you may encounter.

The other way, of course, is to train or teach yourself with the assistance of the many organ method books that are on the market. May we suggest that you resist trying to play the piano on the organ—that is, resist avoiding the transition problems. Attack those problems—one at a time. Also, may we suggest that you not underestimate the amount of study and practice needed. To do so will result in your becoming discouraged. It is much better to be surprised at how little time it takes than to be discouraged by how much time it takes.

To teach yourself, acquire one or more method books and master each lesson progressively. It is the writer's suggestion that you learn the pedals first. There is a method called the *NEW ORGAN COURSE/"Feet First": Books I, II, David Carr Glover.* (Charles Hansen, Distributor, 1860 Broadway, New York, New

Continued on page 220

195

the STUDIO ORGAN

by

Ruth Price Farrar

"MEMORY YOU CAN TRUST"

Many organ hobbyists would like to play for friends, family or clubs without using music but are afraid to try without a security blanket — the printed music. WHY? Perhaps years ago they tried and failed, were embarrassed and gave up. Most performers find if they utilize ALL their learning capacity, their assets, they become more secure.

Let's take a look at our learning assets, those that almost everyone possesses. Let's see if we can make them work for us. We have a mind, eyes, ears, hands and feet — put another way: Intellect, Sight, Hearing, Touch — yet another way: Analysis, Visual, Aural, Tactile. Whatever the name, you can learn to make them work for you — then you will feel secure.

ANALYSIS: Pull the composition apart, break it into little pieces, see how it is put together. It's like poetry. There is a theme, secondary themes and rhythm. For this lesson we are using a very short, simple folk dance. From this you will learn the concept of analysis and memory. You can use the same procedure to memorize any composition.

---

1. Look at the key signature. F#, Key of G. Play the G scale and the primary chords (G, C, D7).

2. Look at the time signature. 6/8 — the pulse unit is the dotted quarter, giving 2 strong beats to a measure rather than six 8th notes like a boat song or lullaby. Play the chord progression G, C, D7, G with a strong dotted quarter beat. Repeat, adding chord roots in the pedal. Repeat from memory.

3. Notice that the 8-measure piece is divided into four 2-measure phrases. This is form analysis.

4. Analyze the melodic patterns. Phrase 1 and 3 are exactly alike, both in pitch and time. Phrases 2 and 4 are the same time pattern but different in pitch.

5. Plan your fingering. All *like* note patterns should be fingered alike. Decide NOW what your fingering will be and stick with it.

6. You now have the chord (harmony) pattern, melodic pattern, time pattern and finger pattern. Think and memorize in patterns. PLAY phrase 1 melody (2 measures). As you play sing intervals, then sing time, SLOW TEMPO. Play twice. Close book and play again. You can't? OK open the book and this time really SEE which way the notes move and how far, really FEEL your fingers as they play, really HEAR the melody and chord progression. Close book and try again. You did it! Add the chords and pedal by ear if you can. DON'T go beyond phrase one until you play it freely, with good swing and expression.

If you are having a problem you may be working too fast or under tension. Slow down, take it easy. Let your motor memory catch up with your tonal memory.

7. When you have cinched this 1st little phrase rest assured you can soon tackle anything you want to memorize — just break the biggest piece into little fragments and settle in on it. Approach with analytical procedure. Next step is phrase 2, done in exactly the same way. Both end with a question. As you are studying the individual parts, keep at phrase one, then add 2nd phrase. Play these freely before moving on.

8. Proceed phrase by phrase until you become so musically involved while playing from memory that you forget to forget. If in a longer piece, you begin to hesitate as you approach phrase 5, 6, or 7, hold back, move slower. Going forward too soon can defeat your purpose. There'll be a day when you can memorize a page or more a day.

Be sure to select very easy music for your first efforts. Remember the old saying: "You must creep before you walk." And maybe you can think back to your first poem in school — a four line ditty — not a ten minute speech.

Take one step at a time. Work at memory a few minutes EVERY day, not an hour once a week. As you play in your own music room make believe there are friends all around you — simulate a public performance — it's not too much different from the real thing.

DONNYBROOK FAIR
(An Irish Jig Tune)

Arranged by
Ruth Price Farrar

DONNYBROOK FAIR
(An Irish Jig Tune)

Arranged by
Ruth Price Farrar

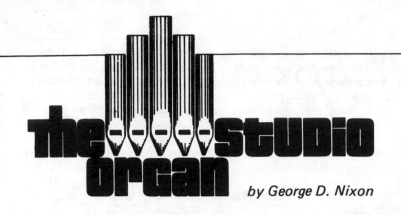

the studio organ

by George D. Nixon

Understanding Electronic Organ Registration

Many students of the electronic organ ask which are the best stops to use on a particular piece of music. The answer to the question is a very simple one. The answer is — "the ones you like best." We have also noticed that many students of the electronic organ who play quite well on their own instrument are mystified about which stops to use on an organ different from their own. This seems to be particularly true when changing from a drawbar type organ to a tab type organ, or visa versa. This indicates that, in many instances, these people have very little understanding concerning the stops of either instrument.

In this article, we hope to clear up some of this confusion and provide the understanding that will enable one to register any organ with just a little experimentation.

The principal difference between an artist and a technician is that the artist is capable of making tasteful decisions in areas in which the sciences can not prove him/her to be right or wrong. Choosing the stops or the registration on the organ for a particular musical selection is one of those artistic areas. Registration markings on a piece of music are one organist's idea of what they should be, artistic or not. This is not to say that there is not a scientific basis on which to base these decisions. To the contrary, there is a need to understand the basic physics of the organ if one is to be in a position to make tasteful decisions in registration.

To understand the stops of an electronic organ, we must have some knowledge of the pipe organ and how it functions. Since the basic premise of the electronic organ is to imitate the pipe organ, much of the terminology originates with the pipe organ. The principal difference between the two instruments is the method used to produce their sounds. The pipe organ produces sound by passing air through a pipe or whistle. The sounds of an electronic organ are produced by electronic oscillators or generators which are tuned to operate at specific audio frequencies. The design and control of these tone oscillators or generators enable the technician to make the electronic organ imitate the sounds of a pipe organ.

In the pipe organ, the length of the pipe determines the pitch (highness or lowness) of a sound. The timbre or character of the sound is determined by the diameter of the pipe, whether it is a stopped or open pipe, and by the materials from which the pipe is constructed.

Basically, there are only two types of pipes in a pipe organ: the flues and the reeds. The flues are the pipes that have a mouthpiece at one end. When the air passes over this mouthpiece, the air begins to vibrate and set up sound waves whose length or pitch are in proportion to the length of the pipe. The reeds have similar pipes except at one end is a brass reed which vibrates and sets up sound waves whose length or pitch are determined by the length of the pipe, but because of the brass reed, have a different timbre or character than the flues.

In addition to getting a variety of timbres by varying the diameter and shape of the pipe, a flue pipe may be made to sound mellower and softer by stopping the end of the pipe. Stopping it also makes it sound an octave lower than an open pipe of the same length. Thus the terminology, "stopped diapason", "stopped flute," etc.

So we may understand what is meant by 16' (sixteen foot), 8', 5 1/3', 4', etc., a graphic illustration is included (*see opposite page*) to help explain the physics of sound, and how it applies to the pipe organ.

The laws of harmonic overtones are graphically shown on the left side of the illustration. When a tone is sounded, in this case by a 16 foot pipe, the fundamental sound, in this case the C two octaves below middle C, predominates. However, the 16 foot sound wave also breaks up into less dominant fractionated waves called overtones. One has to have a well trained ear to hear and identify even the most dominant ones. The extent to which some of the fractionated waves or overtones are more dominant than others will determine the timbre or characteristics of the tone. For example, in a diapason pipe, the 1st overtone (8') will be secondary in intensity only to the fundamental (16') and each succeeding overtone is a little less intense. However, in the reed family, the 4th, 5th, and 6th overtones are the most intense, etc.

In other words, as shown in I. Illustration, the column of air not only produces sound waves 16' long, the fundamental or dominant sound, but also less dominating waves 1/2 of 16', 1/3 of 16', 1/4 of 16', 1/5 of 16', 1/6 of 16', 1/7 of 16', 1/8 of 16', etc. It is interesting to note that each time the wave is shortened by 1/2, it raises the pitch one octave, thus: 1/2 of 16' = 8', 1/2 of 8' = 4', 1/2 of 4' = 2', 1/2 of 2' = 1'. This helps us to understand why the stops on most organs are 16', 8', 4', 2', and 1'. These are known as the consonant stops; the fractional stops are known as dissonant stops. If your organ is limited to the consonant stops, you will have a very limited possibility for developing a variety of mixed sound because the consonant stops only reinforce each other and do not permit enough variety of overtones. This is why many of the more expensive organs will include stops such as 5 1/3', 2 2/3', 1 3/5', 1 1/3', and perhaps others.

If we think of each type of pipe, i.e., diapason, flute, string, and reed, as being primary colors, different lengths of those pipes will produce different shades of the same color. To carry the color analogy further, we not only have the length of the pipe, but the type of pipe to consider. On many organs, the flue pipe stop tabs are often color coded white. The flues include the diapasons, flutes and tibias. The string stop tabs are often coded yellow, although they are flue pipes with a variation in shape or material of construction. The reed pipe tabs are often color coded red and include the reed and brass instruments of the orchestra. If we may use these color codes in our color analogy, the whites can shade from purest white to all shades of off-white, the yellows from deep yellow to light yellow and the reds from darkest red to lightest pink. It is up to the organ artist to mix these colors in a way that makes for the best musical effect for that particular piece of music.

Most organists use the 8' flue stops as their primary sound and think of using all other stops to blend with this to produce the effect they desire. They know that they may add any number of flue stops and get a pleasing sound. They know that stops with a fraction should not be used alone, but only when mixed with whole numbers. They know that the reed and string stops may be used individually as solos and as mixtures with flues, but often produce very harsh sounds when used in groups of reeds or strings alone.

Although it is unlikely that any two organs will produce exactly the same

I. ILLUSTRATION OF HARMONICS AND OVERTONES RELATED TO THE ORGAN

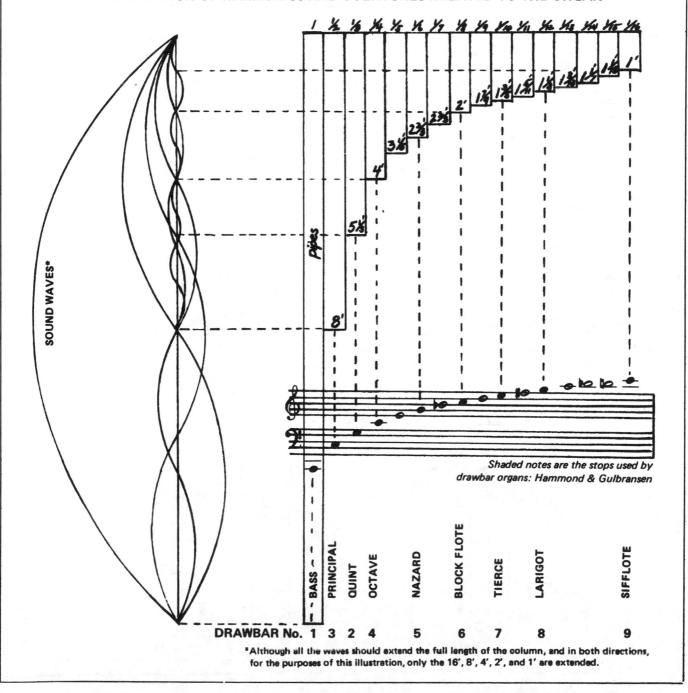

Shaded notes are the stops used by drawbar organs: Hammond & Gulbransen

*Although all the waves should extend the full length of the column, and in both directions, for the purposes of this illustration, only the 16', 8', 4', 2', and 1' are extended.

Continued on next page

sound for any given stop, it is important for the organist to be familiar with the sound of each stop by name, so when one plays different organs, he/she will know about what to expect from that instrument for registration. However, it is always well to check registration before a public performance as you may wish to make some adjustments.

Up to this point, we have not mentioned the "mixture" stops. Nearly all organs have what are variously called mixtures, pre-sets, or pistons. These vary greatly from one organ to another, but they are really stops which combine two or more stops in one. For example, a piston or pre-set tab might combine 16', 8', and 4' flutes, so if you want that combination, you would need to operate only the one piston or tab. There is usually no way of knowing what these combinations are except through experimentation.

Aside from getting the right blend of sound, there are the very important considerations of dynamics, balance, and contrast which may be somewhat controlled by registration.

The dynamics are usually built into the presets of a "tab" organ, but the drawbar organs have this problem to consider. A solo violin, for example, would sound much softer than a solo trumpet. This can be controlled on drawbars by how far they are extended.

The farther the drawbar is extended, the more intense the sound.

One may also use the stops to determine the balance between the manuals and the pedals. It must be decided whether one should dominate or whether they should blend evenly. Some of the more expensive instruments have special controls for balance. This permits the organist to use any desired stops and then acquire balance with the balance controls.

Contrast is another quality that may be controlled by stops. For example, if one manual is playing a solo part, it is usually desirable to have the accompaniment in a contrasting and subdued voice. Contrast in music is also obtained with the stops by changing them frequently. Some teachers advise changing for contrast every 8 or 16 measure phrase — others advise changing when starting a new section of the selection, i.e., A B A, etc. The greatest musical asset of the organ is its variety of musical sound. This asset should be utilized to its fullest as long as it is consistent with good musical taste.

The following graphic illustration (II) is intended to aid drawbar organists to translate drawbars to tabs and to help tab organists to translate to drawbars.

It is necessary to know (it is not marked on the drawbars) that the drawbars are flutes. The first one is 16'

(brown), number 2 is 5 1/3' (brown), number 3 is 8' (white), number 4 is 4' (white), number 5 is 2 2/3' (black), number 6 is 2' (white), number 7 is 1 3/5' (black), number 8 is 1 1/3' (black) and number 9 is 1' (white). On the spinet organ, the lower manual drawbars omit the 16' and the 5 1/3', but include an 8th drawbar of harmonics higher than 1'.

As an example of translation, if a drawbar organist had a registration of 00 7654 321 (see diapason family in II. Illustration), on a tab organ, you might start with a 8' diapason. Realizing that no two organs produce identical sounds, this might only be the starting point as you might wish to add additional diapasons or flutes to get the desired sound.

It is a practical idea for all organists to memorize these basic drawbar patterns (II. Illustration; Diapason Family, Flute Family, String Family, and Reed Family) to help with registration as they move from one organ to another. This will give one the basic knowledge needed to reduce trial and error time.

Another aid in understanding stops and registration is the following glossary of stops. Since the modern pipe organ had much of its development in Germany and France, much of the terminology is in their languages. Although this is not a complete list, it is quite comprehensive.

II. ILLUSTRATION OF BASIC DRAWBAR PATTERNS

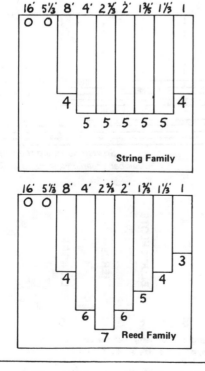

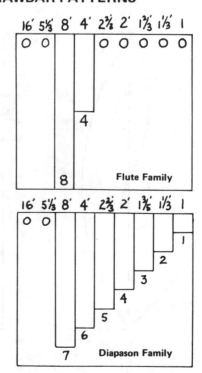

GLOSSARY OF PIPE ORGAN STOPS

Pipe Organ Stop	Definition	Electronic Organ	Drawbar
Aeoline 8	Harp-like	Harp or harpsichord or violin	00 5141 100
Clarinet 8	Clarinet	Clarinet or 8', 2 2/3' Flutes or Tibias	00 7462 420
Clarion 4	High reed	4' Clarinet or Oboe or Saxophone or Flute	00 0555 452
Cornet V	Mello trumpet	8' Cornet or Trumpet or Horn	00 6867 531
Concert Flute 8	Strong flute	8', 4' Flute or Tibia	00 4511 000
Diapason 8	Principal flue	8' Diapason or Flute	00 3412 210
Double Trumpet 16	Low trumpet	16' Trumpet or cornet or Horn or Tuba	36 6420 000
English Horn	Alto double reed	8' English Horn, Bassoon or Oboe	00 3744 320
Dulciana 8	Bassoon, low double reed	8' Bassoon or English Horn or Oboe	08 7500 000
Fifteenth 2	Interval of a 15th above the fundamental 8'	2' Flute or Tibia or Piccolo	00 0002 223
Flageolet 2	Piccolo	2' Flute or Tibia	00 0004 112
Flute d'Amour	Piccolo	4' Flute or Tibia	00 0501 000
Flute Triangulaire 4	Light flute	4' Flute or Tibia	00 0503 010
French Horn 8	Mellow tenor, brass	8' Horn or Trombone or Trumpet	00 7531 000
Gedecht 16	Stopped pipe, soft, mellow tone	16' Bourdon or Diapason	32 2000 000
Geigen Diapason 8	Violin Diapason	8' Violin or string or Viola or Diapason	00 4743 221
Gemshorn 8	French Horn	8' Horn or Trombone or Trumpet	00 3511 110
Grosse Flute 8	Grand flute	8', 4' Flute or Tibia	00 8723 100
Heckelphone 8	Tenor double reed	Bassoon, English Horn or Oboe	00 6776 400
Hohl Flute 8	Open Flute	8' Flute or Tibia	00 5311 000
Melodia 8	Reed	8' Reed or Clarinet or Saxophone or Oboe	00 5200 000
Mixture IV	Four stops combined	4', 2 2/3', 2', 1' Flute	00 0564 123
Nazard 2 2/3	Flute 2 2/3	2 2/3' Flute or Tibia	00 0040 030
Oboe 8	Double reed	8' Oboe or Clarinet	00 4764 210
Octave 4	Flute 4'	4' Flute or Piccolo	00 0525 342
Octave Geigen 4	High string	4' String or Violin	00 0414 231
Open Diapason 8	Principal Diapason	8' Diapason or Flute or Tibia	00 5311 000
Orchestral Flute	High Flute	4', 2' Flute or Tibia	00 0805 000
Principal 4	Diapason 4'	4', 2' Flute or Tibia	00 0415 112
Salicional 8	Reed	8' Clarinet or Oboe or Saxophone	00 2433 222
Super Octave 2	Diapason 2'	2' Flute or Piccolo	00 0545 452
Tierce 1 3/5	Flute 1 3/5	1 3/5' Flute or Tibia	00 0000 500
Traverse Flute 4	Open Flute	4' Flute or Tibia or Piccolo	00 0601 010
Tromba 8	Trumpet	8' Trumpet or Cornet or Horn	00 6868 642
Trumpet 8	Brass Horn	8' Trumpet or Cornet or Horn or Reed	00 6867 531
Unda Maris 8	Flat, wavering sound	Calliope	00 3421 000
Viol Da Gamba 8	Cello	8' Cello or String or Violin	00 2423 221
Voix Celeste	Heavenly voice	4' Vox or Reed or Violin	00 2434 432
Vox Humana 8	Human voice	8' Vox or String or Reed	00 3453 542

REGISTRATION FOR CONTEMPORARY ORGAN STYLES

PART I

by Debbie Culbertson

As I began to write, I hoped that I would have enough to say to fill an entire column on registration. The more I wrote, the more I thought of, so we have "Registration, Part I" and "Registration, Part II." These days, it's stylish to have a sequel anyway.

CONDUCT

Do you play the violin? How about the trombone? Drums? String Bass? If you play the organ, you can answer "yes" to the above questions, and probably many more, depending on the capabilities of your particular instrument. You should consider yourself the conductor of an orchestra, deciding which instruments will play and when. You have an advantage over the real conductor, though, because you also play each part yourself, interpreting it any way you feel.

ORCHESTRATE

Learning to think of yourself as an orchestra will make your playing more interesting and exciting for you and for your listeners, and it is probably the easiest phase of organ playing. I guarantee it's more fun than practicing your scales. Simple single-note melodies are very effective when you treat them as instrumental solos. Many people are under the impression that several stops or tabs must be on all the time. Using a single tab is not only simpler, the voice is more recognizable. Usually when several instruments are combined, it is much harder to identify the individual voices. A tasteful cross of "solo" melodies and more complex combinations of voices will give your music the variety it needs.

VIBRATO

Use of "effect" controls, such as vibrato, sustain or tremolo, can play a big part in making your solo voices sound more authentic. Many instruments use vibrato, which is a slight waver in pitch. A trombone player moves his slide to create vibrato. A clarinet player moves his lips. A violinist moves his finger against the string. Many times the instrumentalist hits the note, introducing the vibrato just slightly afterward. If you have a "delayed" vibrato feature, you can create the same effect.

Sustain would not be used for most instruments; the possible exceptions being the piano, harpsichord, vibraphone, etc. Remember, we're talking about AUTHENTIC instrument sounds. There is no reason for not using sustain to create a particular effect.

SPEAKERS

The rotating speaker is found on many organs today and each manufacturer seems to have a different name for it. It creates a variance in volume, as opposed to the variance in pitch created by vibrato. In order to sound authentic, usually the rotating speaker would be off. Picture the clarinet player on a turning pedestal as he plays. You'll not only make him dizzy, he won't sound like he's supposed to. For solo voices, it's best to use the main or stationary speakers, while many *combinations* sound best when used with the rotating speaker.

PHRASING

Try to develop a mental picture of the instrument and player you are imitating. Remember that in most cases he has a specific "range" that he must play within. For instance, you wouldn't hear the trombone playing the highest notes of your keyboard. Nor would the flute play the lowest notes you have available. Also keep in mind that all wind instrument players have to breathe. There are proper places to breathe; it's called phrasing. Normally it's every eight measures, sometimes every four measures. Some melodies are marked for phrasing with the curved lines above the treble clef. Each phrase is a musical sentence, with time to "breathe" between. If you keep this in mind, it will help your phrasing technique as well as putting you one step closer to sounding "authentic."

ENJOY

In "REGISTRATION FOR CONTEMPORARY ORGAN STYLES, PART II" we'll talk about accompaniment, special features and when to change registrations. It's not really very complicated, and after awhile it almost becomes second nature. Your playing will be much more relaxing for you when some of these "hurdles" are overcome. In the meantime, no matter how good or bad you think you sound, the most important thing is that you *enjoy* your music.

REGISTRATION FOR CONTEMPORARY ORGAN STYLES

PART II

by Debbie Culbertson

Once you decide on a registration for the upper keyboard, you'll need to consider the accompaniment. Try to choose something that is a contrast to your upper keyboard setting. For instance, if you are using a "reed" voice such as a clarinet, try to use a different type of voice, such as a string for the accompaniment. Using the same basic sounds on both keyboards makes it very difficult to discern which hand is doing what and many times notes are completely lost.

Most organs don't offer a great deal of choice for the pedals. Usually just 16' and 8' stops. If you are weak on pedals, for practice purposes try using just the 8' stop. It's much easier for the ear to hear than the 16', so you will be more able to tell when you hit a bad note and correct it. Once you are confident of the notes, use whatever sounds best to you. For a string bass effect the 8' is best.

The orchestra doesn't use the same instruments all the way through a particular song, and neither should you. There are proper places to make changes, and too many changes can be more disastrous than none at all. If you use an introduction, it's nice to use something other than what you plan to use when the melody begins. Another spot is at the beginning of the "bridge." At the end of the bridge you could go back to your original instrument. For the ending, try using the same registration that you used for the introduction. It brings everything "full cycle" and tells your listeners that you are ready for their applause. (Unless your listeners happen to be asleep.)

There are a couple of very easy ways to sound different without having to touch a single control. Drop your right hand to the lower manual. Those of you with spinet organs will have to be careful that you don't run out of notes for the melody. The bridge is a good place to use this tactic. When you get back to the original melody, or "A" section, bring your right hand back to the upper keyboard and play the melody an octave higher. It will sound different and you haven't had to work very hard. Don't forget the "effect" controls: sustain, vibrato, etc. Your registration changes don't have to blast you over the head; they can be subtle and effective too.

The automatic rhythm unit can be a big help, if used correctly. It will improve your timing and force you to "push on." That is, unless you're one of those people who turn on the rhythm and then ignore it until it's time to turn it off. If you find that you absolutely cannot keep up with the automatic drummer, it's probably best to leave it off. I hope you don't give up too easily, though. Sometimes it takes a fair amount of time to become comfortable with this sophisticated metronome.

Some organs have a synchronized start switch so that the rhythm begins when you touch the lower keyboard or pedals. This allows you to play "pickup" notes on the upper keyboard and still bring the rhythm in on the downbeat. It's a great feature and if your instrument has it, I hope that you are making use of it. Another convenience found on some organs is a rhythm on/off control on the expression pedal. This allows you to turn the rhythm off and on without taking your hands from the keyboard. Back to "REGISTRATION...PART I" and the key word "authenticity," think about a real drummer. In a lot of cases, he doesn't play all the way through a song. He might sit out during the first chorus and then begin. Or he might stop for a short time in strategic places. And he usually ends with everyone else. Sometimes that is a problem when you have to hit the last note and turn the rhythm unit off at the same time. The foot switch can be a very handy device. As with the synchro start, if you have this feature, make use of it. Keep in mind that not all songs require rhythm and that some unlikely ones sound great with rhythm. It's trial and error, but you will have a lot of fun trying new beats.

It is very difficult to set rules for registration, since a good deal depends on the individual's taste and his knowledge about his particular instrument. The worst mistake you can make is to find one setting that you like and never change it. Explore your instrument and don't be afraid of sounding "wrong." Remember, you're the conductor and as long as you can find the power switch for your "orchestra," you are in control.

————HAPPY CONDUCTING!————

ORGAN STUDIO

DEBBIE'S SONG: REGISTRATIONS AND STYLES

by Debbie Culbertson

We have talked about general registrations and rules, but sometimes it helps to have someone tell you *exactly* which buttons to push. So, I have written this song as an exercise in registrations. Changing registrations can change the style or mood of any song—here are four "styles" with playing hints as well as registrations.

Latin Style

I composed "Debbie's Song" in this style, so I will use it first. The flute is a commonly used solo instrument for latin styles, so we will use a flute 8' with vibrato (delay vibrato if available). The "Leslie" or tremolo should be off. We will use the flute 8' and spice it up with a horn 8' on the lower. It is best not to set both keyboards with exactly the same sounds, because you won't be able to distinguish one manual from the other. Use an 8' voice for the pedal (string bass if available). The bossa nova rhythm will add the final "latin" touch.

For variety, the bridge (letter B) can be played on the lower manual. For console organs, play the melody where written. Spinets will have to play the bridge one octave lower so as not to run out of keys. The melody will run into your left hand chords, spinet owners, so you might want to leave the melody on the upper keyboard. The melody at letter C is on the upper manual. The notes in parentheses are optional. Use them in the styles that you feel are appropriate. Personally, I would use them in the latin style.

workshop

Heads up at letter C! We have changed keys, so don't forget F sharp. No rhythm is given for the left hand or pedals, because it varies with each style. With the latin style, try sustaining the left hand and playing pedals on beats *one, three* and *four.* Play the root on *one* and the fifth on *three* and *four.*

Be creative! Think up your own introduction and ending. Just as the appetizer and the dessert make a meal complete, the introduction and ending are essential to making your song ''whole''.

Ballad Style

The ballad style allows you to take liberties with the rhythm and tempo. I have found the trombone to be an effective solo instrument. Try playing the melody one octave higher than written (on some organs the tone is better in this range). Use a flute 8' and cello 8' on the lower keyboard for contrast. The pedal should be a 16' voice. If you have an automatic arpeggio, this might be a good time to put it to use. Automatic rhythm is not needed in the ballad style.

At the bridge (letter B) try using a piano for the melody (played where written) and back to trombones at letter C. If you feel up to it, try playing three or four note chords in the right hand—you'll have your own trombone chorus.

Continued on next page

Swing Style

This style requires a little different "feel". Grace notes can be used sparingly. Just play the note one half step below the melody note and slide up.

The pedals can make or break a good swing style. A walking bass will add lots of rhythm. In order to spotlight the bass, try playing the left hand chords on just the first beat of each measure and resting for the remainder, except where the chord changes *during* a measure. Here's an example of the left hand and pedal:

Now let's get to the registration. A good "jazz organ" sound is flutes 16', 8' and 5 1/3', with a percussive attack. The lower keyboard is not really spotlighted so a simple flute 8' will do. Use an 8' bass voice (string bass if available) with very little sustain. The "Leslie" or tremolo should be at a slow setting, but don't be afraid to speed it up and slow it down during the song for effect. The bridge (letter B) could be played one octave higher for variety. Play where written at letter C. Set your automatic rhythm on swing, and SWING!

Theater Style

We're going to use a "full organ" sound for this style. Everyone has a little different idea of what a full organ sounds like, but here is what I think. For the upper, try using all of your "even" flutes (16, 8, 4, 2) and 1' and add another 16' voice to that. I prefer a 16' violin, but a saxophone or trombone makes a nice sound also. I use a fair amount of vibrato. For the

lower, try using a flute 8' and cello 8'. The pedal should be a 16' voice. Use the "Leslie" or tremolo on a fast speed affecting only the flutes, if that is possible on your organ. No automatic rhythm is needed.

If you're brave, use a block chord style (right hand full chords, melody always on top; left hand on upper playing a single note melody). The right hand would be played one octave higher than written. The pedals can be sustained.

At the bridge try using a flute 4' and oboe 8' on the upper. Play a single note melody one octave lower than written with the left hand on the lower keyboard. At letter C resume the block chord style. Grace notes and glissandos are appropriate if performed smoothly.

You should now see how much influence your registrations have on "Debbie's Song" or any song you play at the organ!

Now go back to your favorite songs and experiment more freely with registrations and registration changes. Or, do what I did. Write your own song!

Flutes and Nuts (Without the Nuts)

MORE ON BASIC REGISTRATION

by Debbie Culbertson

Most organs use the flutes as a foundation of tone. In fact, some organs use only flutes. They give us the rich sound that can be immediately identified as organ music. The flute sound is not really an orchestra voice, but it will always be associated with the organ and organ music, so you should be able to utilize this sound effectively.

Each tab usually gives you the name of the voice and a number. The number is the "footage,"

such as flute 16'. These numbers or footages date back to early pipe organ days. The footage was the actual length of the pipe needed to create that sound. Turn on a flute 8' and play middle C. You are hearing the "fundamental" tone, or the same tone you would hear if you played middle C on the piano. Turn off the flute 8' and turn on the flute 16'. Now you are hearing the note one octave below the note you are holding down.

206

Turn off the flute 16' and turn on the flute 4'. Now you are hearing the note one octave above the note you hold down. Flute 2' will produce the note two octaves above the note you play. Go back to a simple flute 8', hold down middle C and add the 16', 4', 2' and 1' slowly so that you can hear each additional octave. If all five footages are used, you are actually hearing five notes at once, aren't you? This is one reason for the "rich" sound we associate with the organ.

There are other footages also. They contain fractions and are called "partials". If you were to use flute 5 1/3' alone, the note you hear is actually an interval of a fifth higher than the note you play on the keyboard. For example, play middle C. The note you hear will be G. Flute 2 2/3' will give you the note an octave and a fifth above the note you play. Flute 1 3/5' will give you the note two octaves and a third above the note you hold down. Flute 1 1/3' will be the note two octaves and a fifth above the one you play.

The order of footages is usually 16, 8, 5 1/3, 4, 2 2/3, 2, 1 3/5, 1 1/3 and 1. Some drawbar organs do not label the footages, but with one exception, they are the same.

For a clarinet:
Flute 8', 2 2/3' and 1 3/5' 008080 800

For a bell-like sound:
Flute 8' and 1' with sustain 008000 008

For a music box sound:
Flute 4' with sustain 00 0800 000

For a whistle:
Flute 4' with slight vibrato 00 0800 000

For a vibraphone:
Flute 8' with sustain and vibrato (delayed if available) 00 8000 000

Other generally good flute combinations:

Flute 16' and 4' 80 0800 000
Flute 16', 8' and 1' 80 8000 008
Flute 16' and 1' 80 0000 008
Flute 16' and 2' 80 0008 000
Flute 8' and 4' 00 8800 000
Flute 8' and 2' 00 8008 000
Flute 8', 4', 2' and 1' 00 8808 008
Flute 8', 4' and 1 1/3' 00 8800 080

If the registration called for flute 16', 8' and 4', the drawbars would look like this: 808800000. Although you won't always want to use each footage at full volume, for the suggested flute registrations that follow, I have used full volume for ease. You are welcome to adjust these volumes to please your own ear.

The jazz sound has always been an important feature on the organ. Here are several possibilities:

Flute 16', 8' and 5 1/3' with percussive attack 88 80000 000
Flute 16' and 1 1/3' 80 0000 080
Flute 16', 2 2/3' and 1 1/3' 80 0080 080
Flute 16', 2 2/3', 1 3/5' and 1 1/3' 80 0080 880
Flute 16', 8', 2 2/3' and 1 1/3' 80 8080 080
Flute 16', 1 3/5', 1 1/3' and 1' 80 0000 888

These are by no means the only combinations acceptable. You should be willing to explore on your own. When you find a combination that you don't want to forget, WRITE IT DOWN! Keep a pad of paper and pencil at the organ to record your discoveries. It is very frustrating when you can't remember a particularly nice registration.

The rotating speaker makes a big difference in the effectiveness of many flute combinations. For a jazz sound, the rotating speaker should be used, switching back and forth from slow to fast for effect. If you are unsure about using the rotating speaker and when to switch from slow to fast, listen to any good jazz organist.

For the clarinet, bells, music box, whistle and vibraphone, the rotating speaker should be stationary or off. The other suggested registrations can be used with the rotating speaker on either a fast or slow speed, depending on the song and your own personal taste.

Now take a cup of almonds . . .

DRAWBAR REGISTRATION

by Francine Linhart

Have you ever purchased organ music, only to find that the suggested registration didn't work on your instrument at home? This article will try to clear up some of the confusion surrounding registration and provide the information necessary to adapt different registrations to your instrument at home.

Although there are many brands of organ, there are two basic styles. The first group of organs is 'drawbar' organs. These instruments have bars that pull in and out. The companies that manufacture them include Gulbransen, Hammond, and Kawaii. The second group has tabs that move up and down. These instruments include Baldwin, Conn, Kimball, Thomas, Wurlitzer, and Yamaha.

In this article we will deal with the drawbar organs, starting with an explanation of how they work. . . .so you'll be able to adapt a registration, or sit down at a different instrument and be able to find sounds you like.

How Do Drawbars Work?

Drawbars move in and out, and the distance a drawbar is pulled out determines the volume of that particular tab. When a drawbar is pushed completely in, the volume is off.

On some drawbar organs, the bars are colored. The first white drawbar in the group plays at an 8' pitch. The rest of the drawbars provide harmonics or 'overtones', or in some cases, sub-octaves. (The illustration includes 9 bars, some organs may have more.)

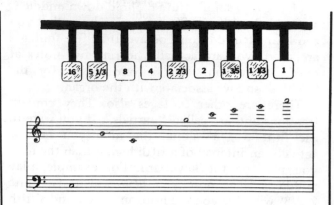

Basically, the white drawbars represent *fundamental* tones. When you play a drawbar organ with the first white drawbar on alone, and then add additional white bars, you can hear the addition of the same note an octave higher.

The black drawbars represent the dissonant harmonics. Although the word *dissonance* conjures up images of clashing, or unresolved sounds, use of these drawbars does not necessarily produce an unmusical sound. In fact, many instruments in the orchestra (strings, horns, reed instruments) owe much of their distinct sound to the presence of these harmonics.

It should be pointed out that you don't want to overuse the black drawbars. If a black drawbar is to be featured, it's a good idea to also use the two white drawbars on either side. Use of too many black bars may cause the music to sound out of key. Of course, a lot of the technique of registration is based on personal opinion, and to truly understand these instruments, you must experiment and find out what sounds best to your ear.

Orchestration

The families of the orchestra can quickly be set up on a drawbar organ by remembering shapes. The illustrations offered below are general. Try one, then make small variations, and listen to the sounds.

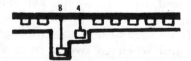

FLUTE
Flutes represent one of the simplest sounds. This registration basically features the third and fourth bar.

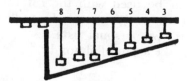

DIAPASON
The diapason sound is characterized by a strong fundamental and second harmonic, with weak upper harmonics.

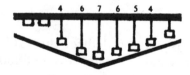

REED
Notice how this has a triangle shape with the fifth bar the most prominent.

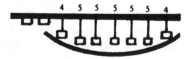

STRING
To produce a string sound, pull out the bars in a 'bow' shape.

Adapting Registrations

If a piece of music recommends a 008 808 008 registration, what would you do? If you don't own a drawbar instrument, look at the first diagram in this article. The first and second bars would not be pulled out, but the third, fourth, sixth, and ninth would. The pulled out bars would correspond to an 8', 4', 2', and 1' flute. Easy, isn't it!

Let's try a more difficult registration, 006 777 776. If you studied our charts, you'd see that this resembles the 'string' diagram, so you'd probably want to register full strings.

These are very general ideas for registration. However, they will get you, or your students, started. The best way to create music, of course, is to create your own sounds. . . .the sounds that you like the best.

The Organ—The Orchestra

MORE ON BASIC REGISTRATION

by Francine Linhart

If you've recently had the opportunity to attend an organ program or listen to an organ record, chances are you've heard the organ sound like everything from an automobile horn to a xylophone. In fact, today's instruments recently inspired a clinician from a major company to say "the only thing that could take the place of an organ is an *entire orchestra!*"

Now that's a strong statement to make, but one that many players feel is absolutely true. One thing to keep in mind is that a performer in an orchestra only has one instrument to play, while an organist has hundreds of sounds to choose from. So every time an organist sits down at a console, there is a decision to be made . . . how to register the organ?

As a starting point, remember that there are three basic sounds that an organ can produce:

BASIC ORGAN SOUND—By using flutes, tibias, and diapasons in various combinations, the player can recreate the sound of the old theatre pipe organ, the cathedral organ, and full lush flutes. This category is the most popular, and many people purchase an organ just for this particular sound. In addition, most of today's organs also offer . . .

ORCHESTRAL SOUNDS—With today's technology, organs can sound like a harpsichord playing a Bach fugue or a horn player in Jimmy Dorsey's band. In fact, some of the sounds are so realistic that you can almost hear the horn player taking a breath between notes.

NOVELTY EFFECTS—The newer organs also offer sounds that have never appeared in an orchestra or in more traditional organs. These sounds include the 'funny', 'wah attack', 'string ensemble' and the 'human voice' tabs. Many of these sounds are heard in contemporary music. When a popular group creates certain sounds or effects, these sounds sooner or later find their way into today's organ.

When a performer sits down to play, the *very first* question he or she has to ask is, "how do I want the piece to sound?"

If a musician is playing a hymn or show tune number, it would be wise to choose a registration from the 'basic organ sound' group. On the other hand, if the piece were the "Clarinet Polka" or the "Hawaiian Wedding Song", the organist would use a setting from the second group. And if we were to play a disco number, chances are the registration would come from the third 'novelty effects' group. Thus, the character of the piece combined with the player's own personal taste will quickly determine a general registration.

ANIMATION—Let's take the process one step further and discuss what needs to be done after you've chosen one of the three categories. If you decide to play a full organ sound, putting down all the flute tabs will *not* guarantee you the sound you desire. In addition to using the flutes, you will need to change or 'animate' the sound.

What is *animation*? When a violinist adds vibrato to a note, he's *animating* the sound. When two flutists perform together, and there's a slight "celeste" to their music, there is *animation*.

Every single organ on the market today has the capacity to animate its sound. There are several types of animation, and they include:

VIBRATO—Vibrato is a slight wavering in pitch. For example, Middle A on an organ or piano vibrates at 440 pulses per second. Vibrato causes the pulses to increase and decrease in frequency, so that Middle A might go from 443 to 437 pulses per second.

This effect is used most frequently with solo instruments, particularly the strings and horns. Most people agree that a tone in which vibrato occurs is more pleasing than one that remains constant . . . it seems to be richer and more satisfying.

The general rule to remember is that every time you use a solo orchestra sound, such as flute, strings, or brass, use vibrato. Adjust the amount of vibrato to suit the instrument. A fragile, light sound, like the flute, will need only a little vibrato. A more brusque instrument like the saxophone will require a deeper vibrato.

Continued on next page

CELESTE—This is a relatively new effect, and may be labeled as *celeste, orchestral presence, symphonic chorus,* or *singing strings.* This tab will slightly detune the registration, creating a shimmery, full, lush sound.

How does it work? When two violin players are playing the same melody, how do you know there are two players? Why is it that you don't even have to see the players, yet you know there is more than one? Many times while performing, they aren't perfectly in tune with each other, and the slight 'out-of-tune sound', the "celeste", tells the listener there are two separate instruments. On the organ, use the celeste controls when you want lush theatrical or full organ sounds.

TREMOLO—Have you ever stood at a train crossing and noticed the change in pitch that occurred when the train sped by? As the train approached the crossing, the sound it made was higher than normal, and as it pulled away, the pitch became lower. This same phenomenon occurs when the listener is moving and the sound source is stationary.

The principle noted above is called the "Doppler Effect," and was named in 1842. Today's modern organs have incorporated Doppler's theory and use it all the time. This effect goes by many names, including tremolo, Leslie, Spectra Tone, Rotary, Spacious Sound and many others. Most organs except for the smallest models have the effect, and here's how it works:

The sound comes from a stationary speaker. A baffle rotating above the speaker compresses and expands the sound wave, creating the characteristic "Doppler Effect."

There are slight variations on this process. With modern technology, some model organs are able to reproduce this sound electronically, with no moving parts. Some organs actually have the entire speaker spinning.

One more point: most organs have two speeds of tremolo — fast and slow. The fast tremolo is good with up-tempo music. The slow speed tremolo is suited for ballads and liturgical type music.

No one ever said that playing a musical instrument was easy. As everyone knows, it requires a bit of practice every so often. But we're all fortunate to have chosen an instrument that gives us the versatility to sound like anything in the orchestra. If we wake up and it's foggy and damp, we can play a bassoon; but if we feel in a light mood, we can try a flute solo. The important point to remember is that today's organs give us a full range of expressive possibilities — we can choose a mood, a sound, and then modify it however we wish. Ready, orchestra? ♩

organ studio

Be A Pedal Pusher

by Debbie Culbertson

Some artists are known for great finger dexterity; some are known for their showmanship. Some bring to mind a particular style, fancy clothes, or a sense of humor. Then there's me. I find I am best known for my feet. Not the way most women prefer to be remembered. . . .

Of course, I'm not speaking of my designer shoes, but my pedal work. My first confrontation with a *real* bass line (not the usual organ root-fifth) occurred while listening to a Henry Mancini recording and realizing that if I wanted to play that arrangement, I would have to do *his* bass line—with my *feet,* of all things!

It takes some time to build up the muscles in the legs, and some people experience a cramp or two. There are two very important ingredients in good foot work: the physical ability, and mentally knowing what pedals to push. Both are extremely important.

PHYSICAL ABILITY

You must be willing to make a few mistakes —and admit them. Some people leave the pedal volume so soft that the pedals are barely heard. Mistakes cannot be corrected if you can't hear them. Practice with the volume a bit louder than necessary to accentuate the bass. When you hear a "clinker", try not to look down—let your ear tell you if you are too high or too low. After some practice this "ear training" will become second nature.

Be sure that your bench is placed correctly each time you sit down to play. Also make sure that you are sitting in the same spot each time. (I have a "worn" spot on my bench). Your foot learns the position for each pedal, and if you sit in a slightly different spot, your foot will be confused.

Use your ankle as a pivot to strike the pedal— don't use your whole leg. Use the inside of your foot on the low pedals, gradually moving to the outside of your foot for the higher notes. For spinet owners—you can easily play all thirteen pedals with the left foot. For console owners—you should easily reach the higher D with the left foot, but be prepared to play higher than that with the left foot and lower than that with the right foot. Many times the decision of "which foot" is made by the steps and jumps—not the note itself. You must also decide whether to use the heel or the toe. It is much like fingering—you must find the most convenient way to play the passage smoothly.

The first time you take your right foot off of the expression pedal, you might feel as if you will nose—dive into the upper keyboard. You should learn to balance without the help of the expression pedal.

Here is a familiar bass line from a popular song. The markings designate which foot, and heel or toe. ⊔ means heel and ∧ means toe. If the marking is below the note, use the left foot. If the marking is above the note, use the right foot.

Continued on page 220

by Ruth Price Farrar

YOUR FEET CAN PLAY

Since pedals seem to be a problem for many, we thought you would welcome a few pedal studies. Those of you who have played the piano for years seem to have the most trouble. Your left hand tries to take over the entire accompaniment. Your feet wonder if they will ever catch up. Your eyes find themselves seeing just two staves instead of three.

The first glance at music to be played with the feet often causes alarm. This is a psychological alarm — not at all real. If you have reasonably good coordination, if you can walk with a nice rhythmic stride, you can teach your feet to do pedal solos — this is, if you want to do pedal solos.

Books, articles, lecturers, teachers can tell you how to do something but the learning is up to the learner. You turn ON the switch. Only You can turn it off. Don't blame anyone else if your feet don't do what you want them to. It is all up to you. Be patient with your feet. Go slow. Be accurate in pitch and time. What's the rush? By working slowly and accurately you will learn MORE, faster. Don't despair. Don't stick to those two over-used pedals, the root and 5th of the chord symbol. That kind of Oom Pah bass is OK to "run" through a piece to see if you like it well

enough to put forth the effort and thought to learn the printed arrangement. Remember most arrangers and composers are full time musicians and they probably know a little bit more about putting it all together than the novice.

You can buy many books that help you with pedal technique. Most of them have considerable merit but only you can determine if you are progressing or just treading a mill. I find it time-saving to make pedal studies from the compositions I am trying to learn. Our study today is just that— pedals only until they play automatically, then the whole thing.

Make a mental note of the importance of TIME, of good rhythmic flow — it's the life blood. Letter-playing without regard for time values is not only a waste of precious time, but also a hindrance to progress. Develop the habit of seeing pitch AND time at one glance and training your muscles to react instantly. This good habit will benefit you the rest of your music days. Likewise, the bad habits you take the time to create will haunt you.

This pedal exercise has a nice rhythmic flow. It can be used many times, as is, or with modifications. These 16 measures are exactly like the 3 stave arrangement that follows.

I would like to have you practice the pedal part, while reading the complete piece, then you will be aware of how all parts will synchronize. Some students have difficulty isolating one part, but it is a skill that can be developed and it pays dividends. READ IT ALL but play only 1 part. As you progress with this discipline you will be able to hum the melody as you play the accompaniment.

Here is the whole piece. The melody is written as simply as possible so you can think just how the foot and left hand work together. Do pedals and left hand until very smooth and rhythmic, then add the melody. If you are making mistakes SLOW DOWN, but keep a good rhythmic flow whatever the speed. It's not the speed that creates life — it's each beat steadily pushing into the next one, the accent.

YOUR FEET CAN PLAY

PEDALS!
PEDALS!
PEDALS!

by Ruth Price Farrar

Many people, including organ students, are awe-struck by the "foot work" of organists like E. Power Biggs, Virgil Fox, Joyce Jones, and other performing artists. Sometimes it seems they deliberately choose music that has more pedal notes per minute so they can musically say "Did you ever see anything like it"? But I believe if you talked with any artist about "foot work," he would agree with Bach when he said: "There is nothing remarkable about it. All one has to do is hit the right notes at the right time, the instrument plays itself."

"An over simplified statement," you say. Yes! But there is definitely much truth in it. Learn to play the right notes — in the right time AND keep consistently working at it. Each day you add more pedal technical patterns to your musical storehouse until your foot work matches your manual technique. Learn to put it all together — in your mind — in your ears — in your motor memory. Move to new patterns as fast as you can but be sure you have physically and mentally mastered each pattern before moving on. GO SLOW — BE ACCURATE — gradually speed up.

You will want to buy a book to help you with your pedal technique, something that will help you progress steadily and easily, and as fast as you can. There are many pedal technique books on the market. I will list a few that should be readily obtainable at any music store. If you study several of these books you may find conflicting statements, and each author will tell you "It must be this way." Give several different books a fair trial, then decide which works best for you, and stick with it. Clarence Dickinson in his THE TECHNIQUE AND ART OF ORGAN PLAYING, published by H.W. Gray, says "put your knees together" . . . "Do not forget that your knees must ALWAYS be held together" . . . over and over he states that. I have a friend who studied with Dickinson and he said his teacher never once mentioned to keep his knees together . . . but he did stress "Flexible ankle." Dickinson's book often mentions "flexible ankle." He said "ankle action corresponds to the wrist movement in manual technique."

Another large book worth hours of study is METHOD OF ORGAN PLAYING by Harold Gleason, published by Appleton-Century-Crofts. Yet another is SCHOOL OF ORGAN PLAYING, Op. 31, by Edward Shippen Barnes, Boston Music Company. His chapter on pedals is not long but it says a lot. By the way he also advocates "knees together." Flor Peeters wrote a course of three or four books, ARS ORGANI, published in Paris by Schott Freres, sold in the USA by C.F. Peters. Peeters wrote a little gem for the serious organ student called simply "THE LITTLE ORGAN BOOK", published by McLaughlin and Reilly. The text is minimal. Not much for pedals alone, but his practice tips help you to make pedal exercises out of pieces. If you want to be a church organist this is your book.

John Stainer wrote a book way back when, titled THE ORGAN. Original title, don't you think? Hallett adapted this good book to our modern day, topping it off with very light classics instead of Bach and Franck, yet it is basically solid.

All of these books are expensive, so if you can borrow them or form a club library and buy several, you can look over several without costing a fortune.

Now for a few books exclusively for pedal. The most recent that I have reviewed is PEDAL MASTERY by Dr. Joyce Jones, published by Bradley. She gives a quick survey of methods and approaches, shows notation for 13-, 25- and 32-note pedalboards. There are 70 pages of down-to-earth technique.

An older PEDAL MASTERY book by Rowland W. Dunham was published by Presser. This says much in its 40 pages. There are excerpts from the masterworks but no complete pieces. The text is very adaptable to self-study.

A recent course of study for the very beginner is published by Belwin/Mills, authored by David Carr Glover and Phyllis Gunter. It is THE CONTEMPORARY ORGAN COURSE . . . comes in five levels including a PRIMER level, each level consisting of STUDENT, THEORY, TECHNIC, and REPERTOIRE books. Could probably be used for self-study.

Now that you have a fair list of books to beg, borrow or buy you might like a couple of beginning two-foot pedal studies to start you off.

This mark ∧ below the note means left toe and above the note means right toe. In the following pattern the right foot repeats a tone while the left foot moves. Be sure to play very rhythmically.

Play as written for 13 pedal organ, extend another octave for console models. Try other rhythm patterns — ♩. ♪♩. ♪ or ♪♩ ♪♩ ♩. Practice this until you feel you have complete muscular control and freedom of movement. Demand ACCURACY of yourself. Whether you plan to be a one-foot or a two-foot organist, it is well to master alternate toe technique, crossing feet and heel-toe. You will find even the strictly "pop" organist uses his right foot for the expression pedal and to play intricate pedal parts.

Here is another exercise. The left foot repeats the note while the right foot moves.

organ studio

Let's Do Something About Those Ho-Hum, Hum-Drum Pedals

by Bill Horn

Do you remember when you finally got the right and left hand and pedals together? My gosh, wasn't that great? Such co-ordination! A "C" pedal with a "C" chord, a "G" pedal with a "G" chord, etc. That was some accomplishment, wasn't it?

Next was learning rhythm or pedal-chord, pedal-chord; that is, a pedal on the 1st count, a chord on the 2nd count, a pedal on the third count, and a chord on the 4th count (see example). For those who have never seen what this rhythm looks like in notation, here it is:

This is an example of what a person who has been taught correctly would be reading. However, many *so-called* qualified teachers do this pedal pattern by showing PCPC (pedal, chord, pedal, chord) for 4/4 rhythm or PCC (pedal, chord, chord) for 3/4 rhythm. It is usually taught as a verbal lesson, as opposed to a well-laid-out and prepared lesson so that you can visually see and hear what the rhythm is supposed to be.

Well, I hope you have progressed at least to that stage. Next is pedal, chord, pedal, chord, with alternating pedal. What? Alternating pedals? Are you crazy? I can just about get PCPC together. Say that out loud. Sounds weird, doesn't it? PCPC! PCPC! Or for those who want to be really different, how about PIC-PIC, PIC-PIC?

Enough jest! Alternating pedals is when you use the root of the chord on the first count on the pedal; the shown chord on the second count in the left hand or accompaniment manual as it is properly termed; the third count is what we call the alternating pedal; and then the shown chord on the fourth count on the accompaniment manual. (The alternating pedal for any given chord in the music is based on the 5th tone of the given chord's scales.)

For example, the fifth tone in the "C" scale is "G". So when you play in 4/4 rhythm, the pedal, chord, pedal, chord rhythm, the two pedals in the measure are going to be C and G on the first and third count respectively (see example).

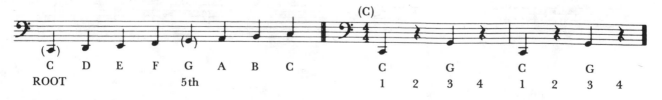

216

If you move to a "G" chord, and want to play alternating pedals on the first and third counts, you must use the "G" scale as your guide and find out what the fifth tone of the "G" is. If you know your scales, you will have already picked out the tone "D" as the alternating pedal for a "G" chord (see example).

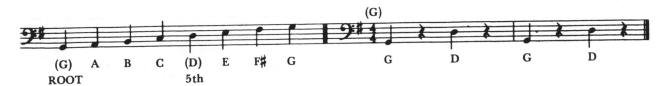

When this is shown in music as a complete pattern, pedal, chord, pedal, chord, with alternating pedals, it will look like this in 4/4 rhythm:

Key of "C"

Key of "G"

If you have been struggling with the pedals, be not dismayed! In the next few articles, I will try to clear up some misconceptions about pedal playing and will try to help you realize what your mistakes have been and show you how to correct those mistakes. Just remember that if you want to play alternating pedals and have not done so before you can find the alternating pedal by finding the fifth tone in the scale of the given chord. If you have not been taught good scale training, get yourself a scale book of which there are many on the market. In your major scales, find the fifth tone and you should begin to help your pedal playing sound better!

Here are two suggestions for pedal technique books that you might find helpful. I use them in my teaching program, and even though they are classically oriented, the material presented in them is invaluable.

1. *Joyce Jones (Pedal Mastery) for the Organ.* There are two editions: one for Spinet and one for full pedalboard. This is a Richard Bradley publications book.

2. *An Organ Instruction Book for the Organ and the Hammond Organ,* by J. F. Alderfer and Charles R. Cronham. This is a J. Fischer and Bros. publication.

organ studio

Be An Arranger

by Francine Linhart

Francine Linhart became a performing organist as a child, and has given concerts all over the world, including television and radio. A former concert artist for Wurlitzer organs, Francine is now Manager of Marketing for all Yamaha Keyboard educational programs.

Have you ever listened to an organist play a tune through 3 or 4 times, and each time play in a different style? Did you ever wonder how he or she learned those different styles? Basically, such players have a catalogue of musical ideas tucked away in their memory, and as they sit down to play they automatically retrieve those special ideas. Do you remember learning to write? In the beginning, it was a slow process, based on painstaking practice exercises. Now, we all take writing for granted. When we write something, we just do it automatically.

It's the same thing with music. To be successful as an arranger you need to build a storehouse of ideas. When you like a "special sound" in an arrangement, memorize it and apply it in another tune. If you find it can't remember all those sounds, keep a book of staff paper by your organ and write your ideas down. You can refer to them when you need some inspiration.

To demonstrate what we mean, let's take the tune "Make Someone Happy" and arrange it in several styles. We'll be working from a piano/vocal score (because that's the way the majority of music is written) but we will demonstrate specific arranging techniques for the organ.

Here's the score:

As you can see, it's a three staff arrangement, written with a lead line for the singer and an accompaniment for the piano.

The easiest way to "arrange" this tune is to use the vocal line and the chord symbols, and play it like a regular "lead-line" solo. Just a note for those of you new to organ playing. . . most professional organists using chord symbols try to stay between the F below middle C and the G above.

Musical examples used by permission of Chappell Music Co., Inc.

Let's get on to the "arranging". Some people think, especially if they've played piano before, that adding the extra notes from the piano score will make a special arrangement. Many times, that's the *worst* thing to do! In an example like "Make Someone Happy", incorporating the extra notes of the piano score will make the performer sound like a pianist trying to play the organ. Remember, organists play with a smooth, legato sound, and rather than play the "exact" piano arrangement, you must adapt it to the organ.

To get that same effect, transfer the rhythm pattern and the chords to the left hand.

SWING (FOXTROT)

Look back at the original score and notice how the accompaniment pattern makes up a nice "counter melody". Apply the counter-melody to the chords in the previous example and it will sound like this:

SWING WITH COUNTER-MELODY

In example one, the original piano score featured a rhythm chord pattern played in the right hand.

So far, the melody has been accompanied in a "swing" or foxtrot style. The original piano score suggested that particular style. However, "Make Someone Happy" would also sound good as a *beguine, rhumba* or even a *jazz rock* piece. In these examples, notice how the "counter-melody" can be added:

BEGUINE

BEGUINE WITH COUNTER-MELODY

JAZZ ROCK

RHUMBA

organ studio

"BLOCK" HARMONY

The last two styles to be demonstrated are *block harmony* and *open harmony*. In either style, both hands should be played on one manual. With *block harmony,* the right hand adds chords below the melody, and the left hand repeats the melody an octave lower.

"OPEN" HARMONY

Open harmony is similar to *block,* for the performer chords with the right hand, but omits the middle note, playing it an octave lower in the left hand. By omitting the middle note, a hollow or "open" sound is created . . . hence the name *open harmony.*

Of course, these are suggestions. However, if you play through these ideas and try applying them to other tunes, you become an arranger. The ability to play any tune in several styles is a skill that *can* be mastered, and if you have a desire to do so nothing can stop you. Start now with these ideas, collect a few of your own, and in a short time, your friends will wonder how *you* do it.

Every Pianist is an Organist — *continued from p.195*

York 10023.) This is an excellent method for learning the pedals first. It coordinates the pedals with one hand at a time.

Some other good methods with which the writer is acquainted are listed below: *From Piano To Organ, Books I, II, III, IV; Arthur Wildman;* (Belwin Mills, Melville, N.Y. 11746). As the name implies, this series is designed for the transition process. It covers learning the pedals, manual coordination, organ touch, fingering and pedal substitution, the expression pedal, registration, etc., as well as sufficient examples applied to the literature. *BELWIN ORGAN LIBRARY FOR ALL ORGANS,* "*Pedal Play*"; "*Manual Play*"; "*Organ-Piano Play*" (piano accompaniment to the other books); "*Method Play*"; "*Theory Play*"; "*Chords and Keys*"; *Levels I thru VI*; (Belwin Mills, Melville, New York 11746.) This is a very comprehensive course with many of the titles having various levels from I through VI. This series has the distinct advantage of permitting one to concentrate on various phases of organ playing and at the same time providing the opportunity to select each phase at a level of difficulty consistent with the individual's needs.

It is hoped that this article will encourage more piano players to add the organ to their musical experiences. If you are contemplating purchasing an organ, please refer to the article "So You're Thinking of Buying an Electric Organ".

Be a Pedal Pusher — *continued from p.211*

MENTAL ABILITY

It is difficult to find published organ arrangements with strong bass lines, so you are often left to your own devices. The best thing to do is *listen*. Zero in on the bass player and try to analyze what he is doing. Recordings are best, because you can listen over and over until it sinks in. I have learned the most from recordings by Henry Mancini and Percy Faith. Although you can't always exactly duplicate the bass part because of its range or difficulty, you can pick up enough ideas to go ahead on your own.

As in many aspects of musicanship, one of the most important ingredients is confidence. Don't worry about your bass line being "wrong". Relax and listen. If it sounds good to you and you are enjoying yourself, what more can there be?

Being known for one's feet is interesting. My favorite remark was made by a young man who told me that I "would make a great snake stomper". Oh well. . .

From its earliest beginnings, the organ has been considered to be a "serious" musical instrument and it is still considered so today. We are using the term serious to mean that it is an instrument to be studied under a competent teacher over a period of years with the purpose of mastering the instrument with the goal of being capable of artistically performing the total literature available for the instrument.

When we speak of the organ as being a fun instrument, we are referring to the idea that the present day electric organ makes it possible for the person who has not previously played a keyboard instrument to take a much shorter and less strenuous route to producing sounds which are satisfying and fun for the performer.

Two words of caution regarding the fun approach. First, the fun approach should generally be limited to adults; and secondly, the fun approach should be thought of as an enjoyable, *progressive* method of learning to play that will have limits of performance which are somewhat more restrictive than those of the serious method.

This fun approach, even with its limitations, provides a wonderful opportunity for the adult who did not learn to play a keyboard instrument when a child. Most adults find it extremely difficult to develop the eye-muscle coordination to master the techniques needed to be a serious keyboard student. However, the adult's mental maturity enables them to quite successfully use a thoughtful, logical approach to learning.

Although children, even very young children, can learn quite rapidly with the fun approach, it may be unfair to them to pre-set limits by not exposing them to the serious approach. The eye-muscle coordination comes to them quite naturally and they are also more patient and have more years in which to learn.

The fun approach should include a planned, *progressive* method. By progressive, we refer to the idea that the performer should start with easy material and progress gradually to more difficult material. The principal reason for this is so one may avoid developing bad habits of technique that become very difficult to break. These bad habits can limit one to a very low level of performance. This statement should not be interpreted to mean that one should not use the automatic features that are available, or that to use such features is "cheating". On the contrary, proper and progressive use of such features becomes a part of a progressive method which makes learning fun. By using one of the several good fun methods which are published, one seldom practices the

organ, because one is always playing the organ — even on the first day.

Regardless of whether you choose the fun approach or the serious approach, there is no equal substitute for a

good teacher. A teacher can give the student the individual guidance needed to make the maximum progress in the shortest amount of time.

However, if a good teacher is not available to you, you may wish to purchase a series of lessons that are published on cassette tapes. Many of the newer organs have built-in cassette tape player-recorders, but this is not necessary. Any cassette tape player may be used. Included with the tapes, which have verbal instructions as well as playing demonstrations, are written instructions and music. By using such tapes, you can progress at your own rate, you may repeat lessons as you desire and you not only receive instruction, but hear it as it should be performed.

There are several of these taped organ courses available, but as an example of what one may expect, the Wurlitzer Home Entertainment Organ Course, The Wurlitzer Company, DeKalb, Illinois, 60115, has 127 assignments which include six cassette tapes, an 80-page instruction book and seven books of music (127 musical selections). This packet of materials retails at about $150.

Most of the major organ manufacturers publish progressive method books and there are many methods books published which were written by organ teachers. Several different approaches to learning to play are available. Perhaps

the greatest variation in approach is in methods of learning to read musical notation. Some use color, some use numbers, some use letters and various symbols, some use regular musical notation in large print, and most use a combination of two or more of these. In selecting a method book, there are two very important factors. The method chosen should be easy enough so the novice can play a melody with accompaniment during the first hour, and it should progress easily and naturally to regular musical notation and realistic keyboard techniques. If the method chosen meets these two criteria, the student never "practices" the organ because even on the first day, he is playing the organ and having fun.

One of the better fun methods is the *Thomas Color-Glo Plus* published by the Thomas Organ Company through Glaser Publications, Inc., 916 19th Avenue South, Nashville, Tennessee. It comes in five volumes and uses a combination of the color approach along with letters, graphics and regular large print musical notation. This method will have you reading and playing well known songs in the first hour. It also is a progressive method which leads you easily to regular musical notation and good fundamental techniques.

Those who prefer a little more intellectual approach may like the *New Hammond Organ Course — Hammond Touch* published exclusively for the Hammond Organ Company, Sole Distributor — Learning Unlimited, Division of Hal Leonard/Pointer Publications, 6525 Bluemound Road, Milwaukee, Wisconsin, 53213. This method contains two volumes and 56 selections in sheet music form. It takes a more direct approach using graphics and regular music notation which includes the grand staff and basic techniques from the first lesson.

Another fine fun method, perhaps a compromise between the two methods mentioned above, is the *Yamaha Electone Organ Course Family Fun Box* published by Hal Leonard Publishing Corp., Milwaukee, Wisconsin, 53213. This consists of one volume and 45 songs in sheet music form. It uses graphics and regular musical notation but delays the bass staff to the seventh lesson. Each new idea is well explained in detail and the progression is gradual and logical.

Regardless of whether you approach the organ as a serious student or as a fun student, you will have many hours of musical satisfaction and enjoyment. It is an instrument that has so many possibilities that it can serve whatever musical purpose you wish it to serve.

THE SIXTH FINGER

by Ruth Price Farrar

Organists often find themselves in a situation that seemingly calls for more fingers than they have. It has been said that Bach used his thumb as a sixth finger. I have seen no detailed information on just how he used his thumbs to add those needed fingers but I have found the thumb to be a most useful resource in working out a problem passage — single or double note passages or chord progressions.

You have probably been using your thumb in a situation like this, especially those of you who began your study of organ playing with the chord system:

It is easy to anchor your 5th finger on G, to drop your third finger on B then slide your thumb from E to F. In the next example you will anchor your 5th finger on D, drop the 3rd on F# and slide the thumb to C. Maybe it was so easy and natural to slide the thumb that you were not aware that you were using the thumb as a 6th finger.

How have you managed a chord progression like the following 3 examples for the right hand?

You had no problem sliding your thumb from C to B in the progression C chord to G7. But did you hesitate to move the thumb from G to F# or D to C# in the G to D7 and D to A7 progressions? Perhaps you thought you shouldn't use your thumb on a black key? If it seems a little awkward try moving your hand forward into the black keys so you don't have to twist your wrist to get that short thumb up on a black key. Master this little movement of playing so your fingers are well into the black keys and you will play in all the keys with much more ease.

I can hear some of you say "So I've been doing that since the year one, why is it such a big deal now?" It is true that many teachers and some books will gently guide you into this thumb moving habit. On the other hand I have many transfer students who have been taught "NEVER use the thumb on a black key". When I tell them about Bach's 6th finger and show them how easy it works, they are elated. With the sixth finger they are able to work out many problem spots by recycling the thumb.

The examples cited are only a few spots where the thumb doubles for another finger. Let's look at a double note passage for the right hand:

Use 3rd, 4th and 5th fingers on the upper notes and play all the lower notes with your thumb. Now try the same passage with a fingering that might appear in printed music:

These finger patterns are a bit more intricate and therefore more difficult to remember. Substituting the 2nd finger for the thumb on the G# is more difficult than sliding the thumb from G# to G and it makes little difference in the sound.

Fingering a series of parallel 6ths is an ideal place to use that agile thumb. Try these 6ths with your left hand:

Your thumb slides along on all the upper notes, while the 5th, 4th and 3rd fingers provide the smooth legato needed in this passage.

If you are playing the soprano and alto parts of a song with your right hand you will find that the 6th finger can do the alto part with ease while the 5th, 4th, 3rd and even the 2nd fingers are playing the soprano part. Try these few measures with your right hand — listen! it sounds so smooth.

Always listen carefully as you play, not just to the tones that are sounding at any given moment, but to the sequence of sounds, how they move from the beginning of the phrase to the end. Decide what you want to hear then teach your fingers how to produce the sounds your ear is demanding. But don't torture your fingers, doing all sorts of acrobatics. And don't overwork your brain trying to remember all sorts of intricate finger patterns when maybe a simple solution is right there in that thumb — the sixth finger.

organ studio

"I Want To Sound Like An Organist!"

by Jeane Huls

Jeane Huls is an organ instructor in Arlington, Texas, and author of the Play For Pleasure *series of organ and piano courses.*

Today's organs are among the most popular musical instruments. Why? Because anyone at almost any age can easily learn to make beautiful music, and the manufacturers are making organs that are so easy to play. But, you still need to learn the techniques to get the sound you're looking for. One can always tell when a *piano player* sits down to play the organ — he or she sounds like a piano player playing an organ. The way an organist approaches the keyboard makes the difference. On the piano there is a sustain pedal for sustaining notes. On the organ there is no such thing. It is up to us, as organists, to "glue" our fingers to the keyboard, and literally *claw* the keys. An organ sustain tab is not enough.

In this article we're going to go after this *organist* sound. The musical term for what we're after is LEGATO. First, spread your right hand out over at least seven keys, and use every finger in playing the melody. We are all used to using 1-3-5, but we need 2 and 4, as well, to achieve the sound we're looking for. Move smoothly from one note to the next, connecting each note.

Now, on to the left hand. Here is where the real trick lies. As you change chords, try to hold at least one note down — the common note. Or, in a rhythmic pattern, hold one note down. You can sound bouncy and jazzy just the same, but that one sustained note will keep the smooth organ sound going.

Generally, music for beginners is not written with tied notes, and many beginners don't observe half and whole notes as they should because they are too busy trying to find the right notes. Connecting chords is the real secret to smoothness, and this can easily be accomplished by playing chords within a seven-note range, from F to E on either side of Middle C. *All chords can be played in this range.* The only problem you may have if you are not used to playing within such a range is in coordinating which finger to lift up and which to put down. Believe me, in time it will "gel" and you will find your chords changing smoothly without you stopping to think about it.

Look at these examples, and *play* them, thinking about tying the notes together. This is particularly important when playing the old oom-pah-oom-pah rhythm, to keep the smooth sound.

So now we have two things to think about as we try to sound like organists: the Legato sound, and playing within that range of 7 notes. I'm not saying you will always play chords in that particular range, but that thinking in terms of those seven notes will make it easier to sustain the common tones as you change chords.

Remember that these are tips to help you get started. I think that once you hear yourself mastering these "organ" sounds, you'll be encouraged to try new things.

Written like this:

Count   1   2   3   4

Play like this:

1   2   3   4

Written like this:

1   2   3

Play like this:

1   2   3

organ studio

Legato–Through Finger Substitution

by David H. Hegarty

David Hegarty is a Theatre Organist, Church Organist and Choral Director, Professor of Music at High School and College levels, composer and arranger, and Music Editor for the Lorenz Publishing Company.

This is a matter that is dealt with in a systematic and comprehensive way by students of the classical organ (who, incidentally, are generally prepared by a certain proficiency at the piano before endeavoring to conquer the added intricacies of organ technique). The *legato* approach is no less important to the student of popular music (who may be getting his initial keyboard experience at the organ rather than the piano), if he aspires to play smoothly and with a professional sound. Ironically, this skill is frequently given little or no attention by the amateur "pop" organist.

Many people instinctively play single-line melodies legato, but neglect to listen critically to the smoothness of the accompanying chordal passages. This subtle (or not-so-subtle) lack of continuity instantly sets apart the amateur from the professional. There is no reason why an organ student, even in the earliest stages of keyboard experience, cannot play smoothly and cleanly, especially if he has the benefit of a teacher who places emphasis in this area. Bear in mind that "legato" is only one of the touches used in organ playing and is often not a consideration when playing in a rhythmic style.

If you have not given this much thought, check yourself by going to the organ and playing a familiar progression of chords with the left hand, such as you would use to accompany a quiet ballad. If, in moving from chord to chord, there are any observable gaps in the continuity, READ ON!

Among the many aspects of organ technique that distinguish it from that of the piano is the necessity of connecting the notes together smoothly, without perceptible breaks or overlapping. This characteristic touch is known as *legato*. Since the organist cannot rely on a damper pedal, which can mask a multitude of sins on the piano, it is important to develop a special facility with regard to the fingering that is often overlooked by the beginning organist, or by the pianist who is attempting to adapt his pianistic skills to the organ.

First, it is important to become comfortable with the art of finger substitution—changing fingers on the same key without releasing it so as to prepare the position of the hand for the notes that follow.

Try the following parallel thirds with the fingering indicated—each hand alone, then together:

Now attempt the same exercise with an alternate set of fingerings:

Ex. 2

Sixths require somewhat more stretching of the
hand—an apparent inconvenience that is essential
to achieve the desired results:

Ex. 3

Triads moving from inversion to inversion may
also be played totally legato using the following
substitutions: (Again, these are best practiced with
each hand separately before attempting to put
them together.)

Ex. 4

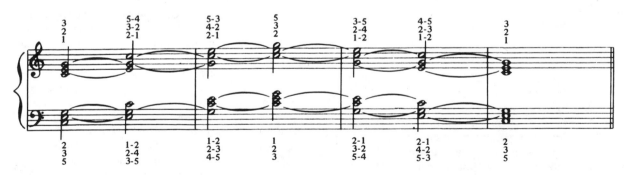

If you are able to play these exercises correctly
and accurately with little or no effort, you are probably an organist who already plays musically and
sensitively where legato is concerned.

However, if the fingerings seem awkward, your
playing would undoubtedly benefit from diligent
practice until finger substitution of this type is
achieved without much conscious attention. Only
then will you be able to apply these principles to
the actual musical situations in which they are
needed.

PLAYING FOR CHURCH

by Ruth Price Farrar

If you are a pianist-turned-organist and sometimes attend church, your chance of being asked to play a service is almost 99%. Somehow most people think that if you play piano you can automatically play the organ as if a magic wand had waved over you at your first organ lesson. We all know it is not magic that makes us play the organ — it's just plain fun-work.

Here are a few hints that might help you prepare for service playing. I say "prepare" because you should not wait to be asked, then madly dash to get ready. Be a good Boy- or Girl Scout — "Be Prepared." By careful planning and diligently doing your homework you will enjoy playing for church and you will be of real service to the congregation.

Since it is impossible to slant these hints to the needs of any specific religion or denomination, I will give you general concepts to follow. Then you can adapt the ideas to your own needs. There are books written as guidelines for many different religions. The church library or clergy will probably have a copy. Usually the church will gladly loan books to a person seeking information about their church music, as there never seems to be a surplus of church musicians.

Here are a few basic ideas that you can personalize and enlarge to suit your needs. They are applicable, of course, to other areas of performance, not just limited to service playing.

You must learn to play through the entire hymn, and/or other service music without hesitating or stopping — without making the least break in time. Keep the rhythmic flow moving smoothly. THIS IS AN ABSOLUTE. Imagine playing a few measures up to speed, (often the first 4 or 8 measures are fairly easy — the third phrase or section is most often the catchy one) then slowing down to get over the rough places, then picking it up for the repetition, then slowing down for the final cadence. What's your congregation doing all this time — wondering what you're going to do next? You can't stop, like some of my first-graders, and say, "Wait," while you back up and start over. THE MELODY MUST KEEP GOING, WITHOUT INTERRUPTION. And of course, the phrasing must be conducive to good interpretation; you breathe where the singers are supposed to breathe (breathe by lifting your hand to stop the tone at the breath places.)

You should be a fairly good sight-reader. This is a skill that takes a long time to develop. If you are not a good sight-reader be sure to get the hymn numbers well in advance and practice, practice, practice until you play them with ease and assurance. There are many good books and articles written on sight-reading, so why not start allotting a special time each day for sight-reading.

If you are new at organ playing a strange organ may cause you concern. To ease that strain try to make arrangements to practice on the organ well in advance of THE day. Even if you are an "old hand" at service playing, it is well to have a few moments alone at the organ to get acquainted. I had one experience, after I had played weddings, funerals and church services for about 40 years, that reinforced my thoughts on pre-play time. I was to play a funeral at an air base chapel. I called and was told they had a Hammond C3. I had it made (so I thought). I had played Hammond almost since they first hit the market, a C3 in church for several years, owned a B3 at home. Why drive all the way to the air base? Fortunately I arrived a few mintues before service time. I depressed E on the upper manual and D on the lower manual, expecting to have a nice quiet churchly sound. It was awful! How thankful I was for the empty chapel. I tried each pre-set and discovered some well-intentioned soul had been playing with the nine little screws inside and had re-set all the presets. Thank goodness for the A# and B controls for the Drawbars, and for my basic knowledge of tone mixtures. That was the last time I neglected to arrange for a get-acquainted rehearsal.

If possible, attend a service while the regular organist is still playing to learn the favorite way of singing the hymns and responses. Observe how the organist leads, or lacks leadership. You can observe the little idiosyncrasies of the clergy and the choir director (that could help you through some real rough spots). These eleventh hour emergency jobs are the toughest. You have a new congregation, new minister, new service, new hymns. Don't ever take one of those until you are seasoned and calloused. It is my guess that most people, including ministers, think there is no work connected with service playing. You (the organist) are filled with unfathomable knowledge and skill and all you have to do is open the door and out pours all that beautiful music. "It looks so easy when you play." Ah, yes! I wonder if the people who think and say just that have ever tried what they demand of you. Worst of all: "You seem to have so much fun playing, it would be a crime to offer you a living wage for your services."

Don't let that last paragraph turn you off. It's not all bad. Recounting some of the discouraging experiences might help you to better preparation so you can avoid problems. It's really a nice experience to feel yourself carrying a whole congregation in the singing of great hymns and creating an atmosphere of worship and meditation with your service music.

PLAYING THE HYMNS

by Ruth Price Farrar

The hymns that are in most hymnals were not written for the organ (nor for any keyboard). They were written for four part singing — soprano, alto, tenor and bass. Some times you will find it difficult to play the two bass clef notes with your left hand because they are more than an octave apart. See example.

In this case you can pick up the tenor note with the right hand because the top three voices are within an octave. In example (b) you cannot reach the top three voices so you move the bass note up one octave. This retains the harmony and brings the notes within a hand span.

If you are a pianist turned organist and are afraid to use the pedals in public you may play the hymn as written in the hymnbook, using the above helps when necessary. Play both hands on the same manual — all voices are of equal importance and should blend like a choral group sings. Use a good basic registration without vibrato (unless your congregation demands it).

Here is the 1st phrase of a hymn tune written in 1609 by Melchior Vulpius. Play on one manual, no pedals. Firm, steady, vigorous beat.

The next example is the first 2 phrases, the pedal duplicating the bass singer's part. Tie all common tones in the inner voices (tenor and alto). NEVER tie melody notes. Tie bass notes if you want a particularly smooth, legato effect, unless the tied note falls on a natural accent (a down beat). If you want a real snappy accompaniment, like a processional march, don't tie any notes. This is also a good way to make the congregation keep up their tempo, sometimes they lag behind and drag out the time — snap up the pedals and they'll come out of it.

The next example shows you a more professional way of playing hymns. (But don't be afraid to try the easier ways until you gain confidence.) Your eyes have to learn to read only the tenor for the left hand, and the bass for the feet. If your left hand has been programmed to play both notes of the bass clef you must re-program it to play only 1 note. Your eyes and left hand are your problem, not your feet. Here is the entire hymn.

The pedals can be played as written above on the spinet. On a console model play the pedal notes same pitch as bass would sing. You will need both feet on pedals to play legato. If you find it difficult to read only the tenor note for your left hand you will benefit greatly and progress more rapidly if you take the time to write a three staff arrangement. Maybe you aren't the speediest writer in the

Continued on page 234

MAKE MUSIC MEANINGFUL

by Ruth Price Farrar

Whatever you play, wherever you play, play with musical *meaning*. Ask yourself — does it swing along with a steady pulse? Are the recurring strong and weak beats where they should be? Is there enough elasticity in the rhythmic pattern to avoid that drone, dull oom pah oom pah? Does the melody flow along smoothly, breathing in the right places? Are the dynamics effective?

If the answer to any of the above questions is negative you are not doing enough to make your music meaningful. Music must communicate. If you feel you are not doing your best and you would like to do something about it, I would suggest that you sit back and take a good objective look (listen) at your musical product so you can diagnose the problem and then prescribe the remedy. You are asking how you can diagnose your own playing problems — how can you listen to yourself — either objectively or subjectively.

Make a tape recording of your playing. Then sit back and listen objectively, as if you didn't know the performer. Watch the music as you listen and mark the spots that sound like just notes — not meaningful music.

Since rhythmic pulse is as vital to music as the heartbeat is to living, that would be the best place to begin to criticize your playing. Once you get your time (duration of notes) and meter (arrangement of beats into patterns) under control, you will be on your way to making your music more meaningful.

There are many church players who neglect exact timing and phrase-wise patterns, so let's take a well-known hymn tune for a specific study of the general concepts of time — the life of music. "Onward Christian Soldiers" is a good piece to start with for two reasons: 1) It was written by a man who had a terrific sense of rhythm; and 2) it is one of those hymns that is often played without the decided march beat that was intended.

Organists seem to have an aversion to giving a whole note its full four beats, and you will notice that measures 4, 8, 12, 16 and 20 have a whole note for the melody. I'll grant that it is a bit dull to sit there on a chord counting out 4 beats — but what else can you do? Just exactly what you would do if you were playing a "pop" piece. When the melody sits still, do something with the left hand or the pedal. I like to keep the pedal marching as you will notice in the arrangement I have made. If you do not have a good pedal technique you could play the pedal notes (or a similar series of four quarter notes) with the left hand. Then you can use the arrangement as a pedal study.

Maybe you would like to know more about the composer, Arthur Sullivan. He is the same Sullivan who wrote the music for so many operettas with Gilbert, the librettist. Sullivan's father was a bandmaster and teacher of band instruments. He very early recognized the talent of his young son. The boy received training in music as well as academic subjects and at the age of 12 was accepted at the Chapel Royal as a chorister. The following year, 1855, his first anthem was published. Sullivan said of his training at the choir school: "The constant and kindly interest taken in my progress have been in no small manner influencial in making me what I am." In 1856,

age 14, he won the Mendelssohn scholarship at the Royal Academy of Music. Two years later he was sent to Leipzig to study under the same scholarship fund.

In Leipzig he became thoroughly steeped in German tradition but he never lost his individuality — that ability to inject life and spark into his compositions with his rhythmic innovations. This seemingly bottomless well of rhythmic patterns made the Gilbert and Sullivan Operettas instant successes. It was not unusual for a new opera to run 6 or 7 hundred consecutive nights — or to run in two theaters at the same time.

But Sullivan wasn't just a composer. He was a conductor of a symphony. He was a noted organist. He not only composed the orchestral scores for the operettas, he also wrote for all instruments and all styles of music. He edited a collection of hymns for the Society for the Promotion of Christian Knowledge. He wrote a number of original hymn tunes — one of them was "Onward Christian Soldiers" — 1872. Good music is almost timeless. Maybe that is why so many adults play the organ — music has roots and lends stability. Music is timeless but it is also a forward-moving medium of expression.

With melody, rhythm, harmony, dynamics and form at our fingers (and foot) we can make music communicate. Music can be MEANINGFUL.

Onward, Christian Soldiers

arr. Ruth Price Farrar

ARTHUR SULLIVAN

organ studio

Ending with a Flair— Harmonic Alterations and Chord Cycles

by David Kopp

Dave is an arranger as well as the official organist for the New York Cosmos *and New Jersey* Rockets *soccer teams, performing at the Brendan Byrne Meadowlands stadium in East Rutherford, N.J.*

One of the biggest factors in successfully achieving a "professional sound" in organ a rangements is that all-important *ending*. A good ending is important for one simple reason: It is the very end. Musically, nothing follows it. The right ending should leave the listener with a pleasant feeling of satisfaction in having heard the song, much in the same way as a fine dessert satisfies the diner after a meal. The good ending should complement and never supplement an arrangement.

The intent of this workshop is to provide you with a few "patterns" for developing good "complementary" endings based on some fundamental concepts of harmonic theory.

All popular music revolves around a tonal key center. Some songs are written in C, others in G, F, A flat, etc. In all but a few cases the song ends with that chord which names the particular key center of the song. We call this chord the tonic chord.

In any particular key center there are eight scale tones (not including the accidentals [sharps and flats] which occur in the melody).

Each of these single scale tones can be expanded into a major or minor chord with all its variations (diminished, augmented, sixth, seventh, major seventh, ninth, etc.). When we refer to these scale tones as "chords" we use roman numerals. (Roman capitals are used for major, and lowercase for minor.)

	I	i	iii	IV	V	vi	vii°	I (or VIII)
Key of C:	C	Dm	Em	F	G	Am	Bdim	C
Key of G:	G	Am	Bm	C	D	Em	F#dim	G
Key of E♭:	E♭	Fm	Gm	A♭	B♭	Cm	Ddim	E♭

Ninety-nine percent of all pop tunes revolve around one particular chord pattern which musicians call the I - V7 - I cycle of chords. This simply means that if a song is in the key of C, most of the chords will be C(I) and $G^7(V^7)$, and that they will occur most often in the $C - G^7 - C$ cycle.

Endings are constructed entirely of chord cycles. Look at the endings of these two songs ———
The first is in the key of E♭ and the second is in the key of G. Notice the last two chords in each one.

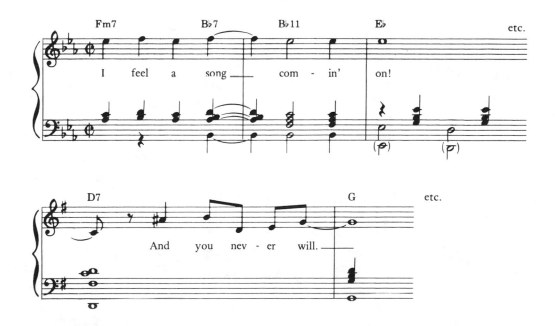

Once again, we have the V^7 - I cycle. Go through some of your own music and try to find an exception to this "ending" pattern. You are going to have to look pretty hard!

As the final resolution per se, there is nothing wrong with the V^7 - I cycle. That is the way Western music operates and that is what we want to hear. When it comes to "added" endings, however, many organists just repeat the V^7 to I pattern.

(Added Ending)

True, there's nothing wrong with this ending, but after a while it begins to sound very worn out. Instead of a complement to the arrangement, the ending becomes merely a supplement—something tacked on just for the sake of tacking it on. Here are two alternate chord cycle endings that work very well as "dessert." With the numerical chord theory they can be applied easily to any song in any key.

I. The flatted sixth/cycles—

In this case our song ends on the tonic chord (the I chord). We'll use the key of C as an example. Instead of using the V^7 to I pattern try this instead:

Here's the pattern expressed numerically.
I - ♭VI ^{6} - ♭II^6 - ♭V^6 - I^6

If the song were in the key of G the chords would be:
G - E♭^{6} - A♭^{6} - D♭^{6} - G^6

The numerical theory will provide the correct chords in any key and it will provide the same effect as long as you follow the pattern above.

II. Chromatic ascent of major triads—

Here's another pattern that's relatively easy to master. Once again our song ends on a I chord. (We will use the key of C.)

Expressed numerically it looks like this:

♭II - II - ♭III - III - IV - ♭V - Imaj 9

This pattern makes for a very interesting and unusual ending for slow ballads as well as up-tempo tunes.

These are just two alternatives to the V^7 - I ending pattern. Be careful not to overuse these in your arrangement of pop tunes. Try to work out your own chord pattern and then express it in numerical notation. Experiment! See what "new" and "pleasing" sequences you can develop.

organ studio

Teaching The Adult Organ Student

by Mark Laub

Mark Laub is one of the most prolific arrangers of organ music in the country today, as well as a great favorite of teachers and students of the organ by virtue of his hundreds of publications and arrangements. He appeared as solo organist with Fred Waring and his Pennsylvanians at an official reception for Queen Elizabeth at the White House, and he has scored a number of television shows.

In my teaching experience, I have found the average adult organ student to be a composite of these "types":

1. A person of middle age who will tell me "I've always wanted to play . . . I love music."
2. Intelligent, curious, enthusiastic, determined.
3. Nervous - especially at the prospect of playing for others, either the teacher or the class.
4. Self-critical - "I'm too old . . . clumsy . . . dumb. . .", etc.
5. Eager, and most anxious to learn and progress to the highest level of performance possible.

With that last point in mind, the unspoken question on the lips of the adult organ student is, usually, what level of attainment *is* possible? Realistically.

In this article I'd like to share my observations on teaching the adult student, in the hopes that these observations will be helpful to teacher and student alike.

The total personality plays an important part in the ability to learn and perform music. I have found that beneath much of the trepidation of the adult student is the fear of failure, the feeling that being unable to play after X number of lessons is a form of defeat, an affront to the Ego. After all, many students are successful doctors, lawyers, business people, etc., and "failure", (in their opin-

ion) is difficult to accept. At this point, I explain that reading and playing music is a form of mental conditioning to which they have not been previously exposed. It involves reflex and coordinated movements that one acquires gradually, through systematic, daily practice. Turn that maturity of the student to his own advantage! Explain that the mind is quicker than the (reluctant) fingers; they must be taught to work together.

Now, can this organ student be taught anything past "Somewhere My Love" and "Alley Cat" using a conventional program of keyboard instruction, ultimately eliminating 60% of the automated gimmicks presently reinforcing his or her repertoire? Yes! Very much so. We begin during the initial interview, when the student complains of the sameness and monotony of what he plays. How about frequent registration changes? That helps a little. The reason for this monotony is the imbalance between the minimal or limited input from the student (simplified melodies and chords) and the maximum output of the organ, with its sophisticated automation. My initial approach here would be to develop reading skills in *both clefs*. Many "secrets" of the professionals can be unravelled by the ability to *interpret* their arrangements! Another approach is to teach basics in theory and harmony.

Let's look at a typical "game plan":

Continued on next page

Upper Manual: Start with note and melody interpretation; treble clef, five lines, four spaces. Point out the long-range advantage of reading notes conventionally, rather than using "crutches." (Sometimes it's necessary to work with two lines, two spaces, and Middle C as a start).

Build confidence by teaching what the student most easily retains and remembers. Other fundamentals, such as note values, time signatures, etc., follow. Where registration is concerned, have the student play and replay a melody, using a different solo tab each time.

Lower Manual: It comes as quite a revelation to many students that a melody can be played here with the *left hand!* Chord accompaniment, if used, can be played on the upper manual with the *right hand!* I begin with a limited range in the Bass clef, from Middle C to fourth line F. We play a melody in this range, then expand it later. Then, the origin

and function of chords is presented, followed by inversions and their part in chord progressions.

Pedals: I explain bass lines, and the function of the pedals in complementing rhythms.

Rhythms: I ensure that the student can play and count in accurate time without automated assistance. The interplay of pedal and left hand requires the independence of each, and takes some time and practice to establish. Once this is accomplished, *then* the automatic rhythms can be introduced as embellishment, and also as restraint from deviations in tempo.

There is, obviously, a great deal more to all this than space allows. Using this game plan, I have found great satisfaction in teaching the adult organist. As for these adults, their maturity and determination make them excellent students. Given the knowledge and instruction they deserve and need, they become *excellent* organists! ♩

Playing the Hymns — continued from p.227

world, but it will save you much time at the console. You will also play more accurately because your eye is seeing exactly what you will play. Remember you learn the mistakes just as easily as you learn the right notes. So take time to be accurate. Speed will come.

Some hymns are definitely dominated by the harmony, the melody may be bland without the chord foundation. Other hymns lend themselves to a special solo treatment. Set your swell (upper manual) for a lovely solo voice and the great (lower manual) for a soft accompaniment. Use two chord tones in the left hand, the root of each chord in the pedal and play the melody on the Swell. Tie all the common tones in accompaniment for a smooth legato effect. Do not tie a pedal note into a down beat. You may use chord symbols if you don't read bass clef. This next example is a solo arrangement of the same 17th-century hymn.

Practice a new hymn each day, using various styles of playing. Write out the more difficult ones on three staff.

GO SLOW at first if the music is difficult. On the easier music set a singable tempo and keep the melody moving in exact time. Do not allow yourself to form the bad habit of stopping if you make a mistake.

Do not underestimate the value of good hymn playing. If your pre-service music is beautiful, well and good. But if you fall down on a hymn, you really disrupt the service. The main purpose of music is to unify the service as well as to teach. You can cover the "bloopers" you make in your solo music (to a degree) but a time error when accompanying shows up like a splash of red paint in a blue sky. Don't spoil your landscape when thorough preparation could have made a perfect picture. ♩

SPECIAL FEATURES

BASIC ELEMENTS OF POPULAR PIANO

by Raphael Crystal

As a popular pianist you may sometimes play by ear, sometimes from a lead sheet, sometimes from sheet music that needs a great deal of changing, and sometimes from music that is perfectly playable as it is. In all of these situations you will want to be aware of some of the principles of popular piano arrangement. By this we mean how the pianist uses his or her two hands to supply the fundamental elements of popular music — melody, harmony, a rhythmic background, and a strong bass line.

The simplest form of piano arrangement consists of a melody played by the right hand, accompanied by sustained block chords in the left. This is the form in which most people "pick out" a tune by ear, and it is also the form in which many songwriters invent their tunes. It is sometimes used in popular piano for introductions, ad lib sections, or when a rhythmically relaxed feeling is called for.

A more rhythmic effect can be achieved by repeating the chords on every beat. Here the accompaniment starts to have a rhythm of its own, what we have referred to as the "rhythmic background." This kind of arrangement is used to create a very regular, even pulse. (We should point out that the best range for block chords is from an octave below middle C to a fifth above it. Below this chords must be spaced more widely, to avoid a muddy sound.)

In most popular music the need for a more nuanced rhythmic background, a more clearly defined bass line, and a wider use of the keyboard dictates the employment of more complicated arrangements. The most basic of these is the "stride" piano style. Here the left hand plays bass notes on the downbeats and chords on the upbeats, to accompany a melody in the right hand.

This kind of arrangement is very useful in ballads, where the pattern of bass and chord alternation can be varied to create many rhythmic nuances. Notice that now the right hand part includes octaves and chords which "thicken" the melodic line. In the third bar the right hand part splits into two "voices," as a single note and then a chord are held through several notes of the melody.

The stride technique functions just as well in 3/4 time, and is used for blues, jazz standards, in fact almost anything in a moderate tempo. It can be endlessly varied and elaborated, but it always consists of three basic elements: melody, chords and bass notes, with the last two combining to create a rhythmic background.

At faster tempos the upbeat chords may move into the right hand. This is the usual technique for playing "untempo" show tunes. Now the left hand is free to add another voice: a sustained melody in the middle register, often called a "thumb line" for obvious reasons.

Complicated patterns of bass and chord alternation are also best dealt with by putting the chords into the right hand. Latin rhythms such as Bossa Nova are a good case in point.

In rock and rock-influenced music the bass line is particularly important and often needs to have a more sustained but accented quality. (Here the influence of the electric bass is evident.) Often the left hand plays only a bass line. In the right hand the main notes of the melody serve as the top notes of chords. Notice that during the long notes in the melody, in bars two and four, we have added a lower voice in the right hand, playing upbeat chords. These upbeats are often absent in rock sheet music, but you may want to add them to keep the rhythm moving.

Continued on next page

Our next example is in disco style. Notice the very active bass part — it provides most of the rhythmic energy, and is prominent as a melodic line. Here, too, upbeat chords appear in the right hand, but in this style they occur on the eighth note rather than on the quarter note.

Ex. 8

The moving bass line of the previous example brings up the subject of another kind of piano arrangement, in which the left hand plays broken chords, supplying in a single line the bass notes, harmony, and rhythmic background. This kind of accompaniment is often used for ballads. Notice how the left hand motion fills in the duration of the long notes in the melody. In this style it is customary to hold down the pedal through the notes of each broken chord.

Ex. 9

A more modern version of the broken chord accompaniment is often used in folk or folk/rock songs, somewhat in imitation of an acoustic guitar. Here the eighth note flow is continuous, and the bass line is brought out by sustaining the first left hand note in each bar.

Ex. 10

In the category of broken chord patterns we should probably include the venerable boogie-woogie bass line, which is still very useful for many contemporary rock and rhythm and blues songs. This pattern is usually played with a 12/8, or "swing eights," feeling.

Ex. 11

Continued on page 253

238

An excerpt from Chopin's *Etude in F, No. 10.*

From the A section of the G minor *Ballade.*

Advice for Pianists
From Byron Janis

In talking to Byron Janis about the technical problems pianists face, the logical place to begin seemed to be the question of what Vladmir Horowitz had focused on with him. "He thought I should know more about the capabilities of the instrument, tonewise, colorwise. This is terribly important in music," says Janis who, when giving occasional master classes at universities around the country, finds that the lack of beautiful, multi-colored playing disturbs him most.

"It's like being a painter with a palette . . . otherwise the sound is monotone. Even now as I get older, I become more and more interested in the music of the piano, its many layers and dimensions. Here's an instrument with eighty-eight keys, an instrument that accompanies itself, is capable of all kinds of polyphony."

Tone color being one of the most important attributes of a good pianist, Janis stresses the use of the wrists in relation to it and to its corollary, beautiful phrasing. "Of course, no two pianists in the world have the same hand positions. Horowitz plays in a kind of extraordinary low wrist fashion. It didn't work for me.

"But we must have a varied arsenal of motions. Chopin said the use of the wrist in phrasing must be like the breath of a singer. That's important. Using a locked wrist, for instance, won't give you a fluid sound." To illustrate, Janis plays parts of the Chopin *Etude in F major*, Op. 10. Many pianists exaggerate the fingers' role in the scale and arpeggio figurations here, he says. They don't use the wrist to propell the phrases along. Result: a locked, static effect.

Other pianists' problems? He mentions performers' tendencies to exaggerate dynamics—particularly a forte. "In the Chopin G minor *Ballade*, for example, the middle section that starts in A —well, it gets forte and then explodes into a beautiful theme marked double forte. The idea is misunderstood. Some people play everything double forte which is sheer banging. Obviously, it's the melody that must be loudest, with the rest kept down. Sometimes the score tells much more than you really see."

Must the score be followed to the letter, then? How much change is allowed? "The things you can change, or modify, are the tempo and the place where a crescendo starts," says Janis. "You can start it earlier or later. Sometimes you can make several crescendos within one marked in the score. But these things are only effective if you have a strong musical sense—if you are convinced that what you are doing is not an isolated moment. If it doesn't sound contrived."

I ask about Chopin's stunning notion that "each finger has its own job to do. Do not try to make them equal." Does Janis agree? What about the voice leadings in chordal passages, especially in Beethoven?

When you play a concerto with an orchestra you have only two choices. Either you ask them to play softer so your pianissimos can be heard. Or you increase your dynamics in relation to them.

"Chopin was saying that if you need to bring out the (weaker) fourth finger, then you must lessen the third finger." – L.V.

ACCOMPANYING SINGERS WITH THE PIANO

by Raphael Crystal

As a pop pianist you will often be asked to accompany singers. This is a specialized skill, requiring some very different techniques from solo playing. Naturally the precise form of the accompaniment will depend on the style of the song. But we will try to point out some general principles, drawing examples from various styles.

Let's begin at the beginning of a song. Some sort of introduction is always necessary, to give the singer the pitch. This is most simply accomplished with a "bell tone" which gives the first note, often enhanced by a chromatic grace note and octave doubling. This sounds especially well if the song begins on the fifth note of the scale, or dominant. (Ex. 1a). Slightly more elaborate is an arpeggio on the dominant seventh chord (e.g. a D7 chord if the song is in G). (Ex. 1b). Sometimes the singer can be guided to a particular opening note by approaching that note chromatically. Our next example is designed to bring the singer in on the note B. (Ex. 1c).

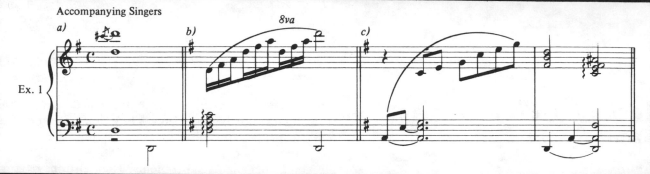

For more elaborate introductions four bars is a standard length, although you may want to double that at faster tempos. If the song is lively and begins in tempo, a chord progression which introduces the basic rhythm of the song can be effective. Notice that now the piano is setting the tempo as well as giving the pitch, so you must be sure just what tempo the singer wants. (Ex. 2)

In a lyrical song a more melodic introduction may be desired. Sometimes the first four bars of the tune can be used for this purpose. Our example shows another tried-and-true method: using the *last* four bars of the tune, provided with a suitable "turn-around" which leads the singer into the song. The E7-9 chord in the fourth bar has that function; presumably the song begins on an Am7 chord, with an E in the melody. (Ex. 3)

Once the singer enters, the pianist is faced with a crucial decision: whether or not to double the melody. In most pop sheet music the melody does appear in the right hand piano part, but this is often not an effective kind of accompaniment. It may result in covering up the singer, and it actually works against a good blend since it is almost impossible for the piano to duplicate the phrasing and dynamics of a sung melody.

Nevertheless it is often necessary to give the singer some assistance on the melody. One way to do this is by playing a sustained line in the right hand that touches on the main notes of the melody. Often you can derive this kind of line from a tune by eliminating the repeated notes, as well as any little detours, twists, and turns. If the melody can be reduced to a largely stepwise line this method will be especially effective. (Ex. 4)

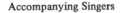

Even if the piano is playing a rhythmic accompaniment consisting of bass notes and chords, it is possible to suggest the melodic line with the top notes of the chords. Here some of the piano notes come after the singer hits them, but they still serve to confirm the singer and keep him or her on pitch. (Ex. 5)

Of course it is sometimes very desirable to double the melody — for instance, in particularly rhythmic passages, or for special emphasis. (In our last example the piano doubles the singer at the end of the third bar). It is often effective to do this an octave above the singer, or in octaves or block chords.

You may want to add countermelodies or background figures in the piano part. Sustained lines are useful because they don't get in the way of the singer. With more active figures it is best to move when the singer has a rest or held note. (We should warn against overdoing this technique however; you don't want to give the impression that the pianist is intent on filling in every nook and cranny).

Sometimes the singer may want to take part of a song "ad lib," or completely out of tempo. This is often done in the introduction, or as a means of varying the bridge the second time around. Here chords, broken chords or free arpeggios should be used. The pianist should avoid anything which suggests a definite rhythm, and follow the singer carefully. Again, it is best to move when the singer is holding a note. (Ex. 6)

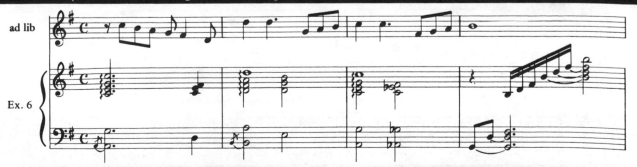

Continued on next page

Not to be confused with ad lib sections are passages where the singer handles the melody freely while the accompaniment remains in tempo. The first line of our example shows how a melody might appear in the sheet music, while the second line gives a possible free interpretation of it. Here it is vital for the pianist to have some idea of what the singer will do, in order to avoid being thrown off by the changes in the melody. (Ex. 7)

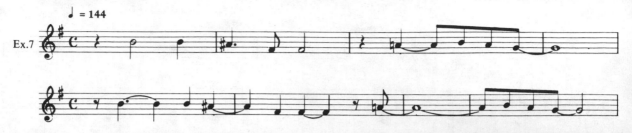

Somewhere in between the previous two examples are cases where the singer takes a passage somewhat freely and wants the pianist to follow. This can be especially difficult, and it is a good idea to mark the music with fermatas (⌢), cutoffs (//), and other indications ("ritard," "accel.," etc.) as you work out the interpretation of the song with the singer.

At some points in the song, possibly on a repeated chorus, it may be desirable to change the rhythm or tempo. It is important to know exactly where the change occurs and who initiates it. Often it is effective for the piano to introduce a new rhythmic feeling just as the singer hits the last note of a section or chorus. In this example the singer ends a chorus in ballad tempo while the piano introduces an upbeat, rock rhythm. (Notice that the piano also introduces a new key, by going to an E♭ chord, the dominant of A♭). (Ex. 8)

Sometimes the singer initiates the new tempo and/or rhythm. This is especially feasible after a cutoff. Here, in a passage which might occur toward the end of a song, the singer sets the tempo for a slower, strong beat with a swing eighths feel. (Ex. 9)

242

The pianist will sometimes be asked to change the key for all or part of a song. The technique of transposition is beyond the scope of this article, but we should point out that there are various levels of accomplishment in this area. Some people, by dint of much experience and practice, can transpose almost anything at sight. Others can transpose a song if they are already familiar with it. Some pianists like to write in the chord symbols for the new key; some like to take the music home and work out the transposition by themselves. Some pianists need to write out a lead sheet in the new key, while others will need to rewrite the entire piano part. All of these levels can be attained with practice, but it is important to know which category you presently belong to, so that you will know what is necessary for you when the question of transposition comes up.

The ending of a song requires special attention. It is necessary to decide how long the singer will hold the last note, and how that note will be approached. If the song seems to end too abruptly you may want to double the values of the closing notes. In our next example the top line shows the last four bars of a tune. Below that is an expanded version of the final two bars, suitable for the end of the last chorus. Notice that the last note is taken higher, and it is cut off by a "button" on the piano — which gives the note a very precise ending. (Ex. 10)

Accompanying Singers

Ex. 10

Rock and disco songs often end with a fade-out. This is usually not effective in live performance, so an ending must be constructed. In this example the first two bars represent the "repeat to fade" ending appearing in the sheet music. The additional bars would be invented by the singer and pianist. (Ex. 11)

Ex. 11

In performing a song the singer and pianist are partners, but to the audience the singer is always primary. The accompanist should respect and nurture this impression. Probably the most important thing for an accompanist to remember is: never drown out the singer. The accompaniment should be solid and supportive, but it should create the feeling that it is the singer who is making the song happen. To do this represents the accompanist's highest achievement.

Article and musical examples © 1979 by Raphael Crystal

finding the right music teacher

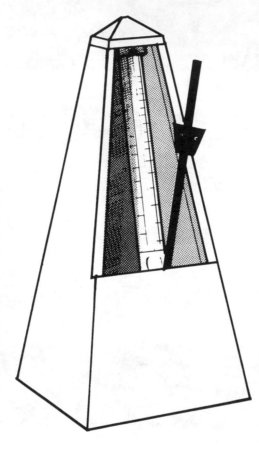

by Ed Shanaphy

The most important thing you will ever do with regard to your music, is getting a teacher. No matter if you are eight years old, or eighty, a beginner or an expert, whether your aspirations are for the concert stage or just your own living room, selecting the right teacher is most critical to your musical future.

How does one go about this very important business? If you live in a small town where there is only one teacher, your problem is solved. But those of you who have a choice should set up some basic criteria before you go shopping. During my years as a teacher of piano, I remember one mommy who had all prospective teachers for her little girl come to the house and play. Not only did I have to play music in my own repertoire, but I had to play requests! On top of that she opened her piano bench and selected pieces of considerable ambition and asked me to sight-read them. This lady wasn't going to buy any pig in a poke. After I was finished with this afternoon mini-concert, and the lady gave me her nod of approval, she disclosed that she had been going through this ritual for several months, and that I was the first teacher who could 1) play more than two pieces, 2) sight-read, and, 3) play by ear. I was absolutely shocked. And then I remembered all the piano teachers I had ever had as a youngster, starting at age six and going right through high-school, and I realized I had never heard any of them play save

one. She was my second teacher, and she played very well. And when her students' recitals were held, they played very well also.

Now I don't entirely agree with the methods that particular lady employed in selecting a teacher. I'm sure that it could turn out to be embarrassing for all parties concerned. However, her point was a valid one. She was making an investment and she wanted to be sure of her daughter's musical future. The girl, incidentally, was a marvelous pianist. As a matter of fact, the mother told me that she was superior to most of the teachers who dropped in for a go on her keyboard. Now if you are one of those people who don't have the chutzpah to do what this woman did,

and I don't blame you at all, there are other methods of arriving at the same conclusion. You can, for example, find out if and when your prospective teacher is having a student recital. Go hear for yourself what kind of product that teacher is turning out. Or ask some of his or her students what they think, and if *they* would play something for you. Ask if they started with that teacher from the very beginning.

Find out about the teacher's background. Where did he study? With whom? For how long? (I particularly love people who say they studied at Juilliard. Anyone can sign up for an extension course for a few weeks for one or two hours a week, pay their money, and attend, or perhaps not even attend, and bingo!, they can say they studied at Juilliard.) Is the teacher performing currently? In concert, at the church organ, in a supper club? Anywhere? Do you know anyone who has heard this person play?

The odds are that if your teacher plays well, he or she will be a better teacher. He can *show* you, for one thing. He can set an example for you, give you a goal to reach. There are exceptions, of course. When Jack Nicklaus needs a golf lesson, to whom does he go? Surely not someone who plays golf better than he does. No one plays golf as well as he does. But there are experts with a critical eye who can help Jack. The same is true with regard to music lessons. Especially with classical music. There are numerous teachers who never reach the concert stage, but know exactly how to produce a student who will.

In looking for a teacher, you must decide for yourself exactly what it is that you want to learn. Is it pops, jazz, classical? Do you want to be a concert pianist, a pianist for your own pleasure only, an accompanist for local groups? Or are you a trumpet player who wants keyboard theory to augment your instrument? Are you a composer who needs familiarity with the keyboard in order to compose more conveniently? The answers to these questions are for you to answer before you look for a teacher. The next step is to interview teachers and have them interview you. Tell them what you are after, and ask what kind of program and approach is best for your particular needs and goals.

Let's make you into a hypothetical new student. Your goals are: you would like to be able to play (someday in the not too distant future) the easy classics, nothing overly ambitious. You would also like to be able to play a moderately arranged piece of music on sight. You would enjoy playing some popular music by ear, to a certain degree. And you would like to improvise your own arrangements of songs. This would enable you to play for your own enjoyment, or, if you wished, to be the accompanist in the pit orchestra of your local community theatre. In other words, you have no burning desire to be a Van Cliburn, but you would like to put your pianistic abilities to good use. If and when your goals are broadened to the point where you might entertain the idea of being the pianist with the county symphony orchestra, you want to be sure that your early studies have provided a good foundation.

Okay. Now that we have established what you are after, what kind of a teacher do you need? Do you need the kind of a teacher who has you spend three months or more, God forbid, perfecting Edelweiss Glide, before going on to the next piece. Heavens no! If the teacher can adapt to your situation, and if the teacher recognizes that the Van Cliburns are few and far between, he will lay down a program which builds practical pianists, not concert stars; pianists who, after not too long a period, are capable of learning new pieces quickly, are playing by ear perhaps, and have a full understanding of what they are about. Learning one piece after the other almost by rote is

not good for anyone. You are after being a *musician*, not just a *pianist* who can play pieces. There's a world of difference there.

Your lessons should encompass:

1) **Learning new pieces for performance.** (Musical interpretation).

2) **A graded sight-reading program.**

3) **Music theory.** (Harmonic, rhythmic and melodic principles.)

4) **Technique.**

5) **Ear-training programs.**

Important: your lessons should be devoted to all of these programs. Your practice schedule should include them all *on a daily basis.* If this happens, you are going to develop quickly and thrill yourself with your accomplishments.

Talent? There are only two items mentioned above that require talent. The rest are learned functions which most of us are physically capable of accomplishing.

The two that require talent are 1) musical interpretation and 2) ear-training. Note: everyone can train his ear somewhat and accomplish a great deal. But some of us have greater natural ability than others. Musical interpretation is the commodity which separates a talented pianist from a genius. It's the one thing that elevates Artur Rubinstein above the rest of mankind.

So if you are not a poet at the piano, and if your ear isn't as trainable as you would like, do not abandon your instrument. The goals we have set up in our hypothetical *you* are still within reach.

When talking to a prospective teacher, therefore, find out what he or she plans with regard to those five points we listed. Be explicit as to what you want to accomplish. Most importantly, if you

are not progressing to the point where you feel awfully good about it, and you've been doing a fair amount of practice, question the teacher. "Why am I taking so long to learn this piece? What can we do to speed things up?" Use the "we" wisely. If you don't like the answers you are getting, look for another teacher. Try not to become friendly with your teacher to the point where you would find it difficult to part company. Maintain the student-teacher relationship. Keep it on a professional basis.

If you live where there are few teachers to choose from, then make do with what's available. But try to augment your lessons with as many books on the subject as you can get your hands on. There are many great books written on theory, sight-reading, ear-training, technical aspects, and musical interpretation. But do try to stay with a teacher. It will keep you at it, it will give you a critic, it will give you a weekly goal.

Enjoy it all. Producing music on pipes, or strings, or vocally, is one of the greatest gifts we have. It should never be a chore. The only time it becomes a chore is when it becomes too repetitive, ergo too boring. Avoid repetition. Keep moving on.

Someday, who knows, you may become a teacher yourself . . . and if you do you will forever have my deepest admiration. You may never become famous being a music teacher, but as Thomas More says in "A Man For All Seasons," *if you are a good teacher, you will know it, your students will know, and God will know. Not bad company that!*

"Go Practice...

You've just decided that little Johnnie is going to take music lessons. He seems to have talent. He can carry a tune, march in rhythm, tries to pick out tunes on the piano, any or all of these things. And you've come to believe that perhaps he has talent. That's a sound assumption. If he couldn't do any one of those activities mentioned, chances are that he may not have any natural music ability. On the other hand, he still may, and a good teacher could bring it out. Who was it who said

that we know everything on the day we are born, and day by day we un-learn it all?

For the sake of this article we will assume that at this very minute there lives in your house a small person who just happens to be a latent Isaac Stern, or Vladimir Horowitz, Alicia deLarrocha, Louis Armstrong. In short, you have a genius on your hands. Don't laugh. It could be. Think of this: suppose every mom and dad in the world for the last thousand years insisted that each of their children study music for two years. How many more Beethovens, Mozarts, Chopins, Chet Atkins',

Oscar Petersons, Jeff Becks, Bob Ralstons, would the world have? I tell you, there would be millions! Musical giants have lived and died without the world ever having discovered them, without their knowing it themselves. Many parents will disagree. They think they know their offspring better than anyone. They are convinced they have a musical idiot on their hands, because they them-

selves are musical idiots. Not so. Did Thomas Alva Edison's father ever invent anything? The truth is, parents don't know. They may have an idea, but they don't know for sure. My favorite quote on the subject was made by Igor Stravinsky, when he was asked if he ever heard a student whose work was so poor that he would discourage him from pursuing his music studies. Stravinsky, realizing that it was impossible even for him to make such a talent judgment, said that he "would rather encourage an idiot than discourage a genius."

For better or worse, you have adopted the Stravinsky theory, and are now going to encourage your little idiot. I hope, as much as you do, that he or she is a genius. The all-important purpose of this writing is that you, the parent, don't blow it if he or she is.

The operative word here is "encourage." The parental obligation, musically speaking, cannot end with shelling out the weekly payment for lessons, and the detached admonition "Go practice or else!" Your child's practice time cannot be a solo endeavor. Practicing is a lonely business. Most kids don't like to be

lonely. Not in the very beginning at least. Later, when they become more accomplished, their music will keep them company enough. Like everything else, they'll need you in the beginning.

Things You Should Do

Kids love organization. They are business people in disguise. What you must get them is a big book. Not one of those little assignment pads, but a big, important-looking book like a loose-leaf binder. This is the book where your child records his daily practice. Time spent on pieces, exercises, theory. Remarks about the pieces he's practicing. You should help him start the book, and review it with him every few days. The book should be shown to his teacher. The teacher can find it very helpful in seeing how much, or how little, was accomplished for the time spent. Also, the teacher can see by his remarks, what kinds of pieces he likes to play. Obviously, if the child writes down a short critique such as: "The Minuet In G is stinko!" . . . flanking minuets might be in order. Whatever can be done by the teacher to keep up the interest in the early going, should

VAN CLIBURN OR BUST

Practice:

or Else!"

by Ed Shanaphy

be done. You as parents should keep that in mind.

After his lesson, have him explain his new assignments to you immediately. Familiarize yourself with each weekly goal. If he didn't understand it, call the teacher. If the teacher doesn't like being called, run, do not walk, to a new teacher. (Very important: if you don't think there is much being accomplished after a few months, get another teacher. In the beginning, you must give your child the benefit of the doubt. If a teacher can tacitly keep taking your money when nothing much is happening in the way of progress, GET AN-OTHER TEACHER BE-FORE YOU CONDEMN THE STUDENT. Chances are that that teacher is doing unto others exactly as he or she is doing unto you. Teaching and teachers are subjects worthy of many separate treatises. Suffice it to say, if a teacher does not have student recitals, a teacher has nothing to show. Beware of that one kind of teacher. See "Finding The Right Teacher" in our August 1977 issue.

The teacher will usually dictate how much time should be spent on practice. In the beginning it will only be 15 minutes a day probably, slowly being increased as the year goes on. It is up to you to fix a regular practice time for daily practice, and see that it is adhered to. By way of getting your child to practice if the spirit is unwilling, you should avoid calling it "practice" "I haven't heard that trumpet today, and it was sounding good yesterday." "How about some piano music, my little professor?" Let him know that he is producing music each day, pleasant to listen to, not just practice. That you enjoy hearing the repeated exercises because you can hear the improvement with each repetition. *Lie, friends, lie!* Don't give your student Saturday off. Pick out the best time on Saturday, and make it a practice day. And on Sunday, tell him he doesn't have to practice if he doesn't want to. But when Sunday comes, ask him to play that new piece just once through.

Two last thoughts. A few times each week, sit down during the practice session and listen. Make comments. **Encourage.** If you are not a musician yourself, be amazed at "how you can make music from all those signs, notes and things." Or if you are

a musician, don't always be showing the child how, and thereby showing him up. Let him get it on his own, unless of course, he is having a particularly rough go. Better to say things like, "I don't remember being this good when I was your age!" In that way, he's thinking he's really better than you

are, or will be. And that's encouraging. Lastly, do your best to keep his practice time a quiet and uninterrupted one. No TV's, brothers, sisters. Without concentration, a practice session is useless. At any rate, when everyone else gets ushered out of the room, he'll get the idea that this is pretty important stuff.

Perhaps you are going to teach your child yourself. That's another whole problem. Hopefully, we'll be able to write about it soon. After we gain some experience. My son wants me to start giving him some formal lessons rather than the bits and pieces I now give him. I told him that I thought he might do better with an outside teacher because I might be too impatient these days. He said, "I don't mind. Anyway, who plays better than you do? Rubinstein maybe?"

That's my boy!

The Parent's Role

How To Practice
Part I

By Anatole Zemlinsky

"If I don't practice for one day," said the great Ignacy Paderewski (1860-1941), "I know it; if I don't practice for two days, the critics know it; if I don't practice for three days, the audience knows it." Everyone has to practice at some time, but few pianists know how to make the most of their practice sessions.

Often, practice boils down to a hit-and-miss routine of dreaded finger exercises, a quick dose of some uninspiring "studies," and the painstaking work of learning to keep up with the tick-tick-tick of that cruel machine—the metronome—as you pound out the notes of a piece you once loved and now wonder why. There are pianists who read the morning newspaper while going through the scales. Others look for quick "tricks" to shorten the ordeal.

But if the thrill is gone, the practice session is not doing its job. Actually, practicing can be *fun!* It can be a time of discovery and relaxation. When Wanda Landowska, the famous harpsichordist, said, "I never practice; I always play," she meant that she gave her all every time she sat down at the keyboard—and that those moments were always filled with musical rewards and pleasures!

Somehow, the idea that practicing should feel bad got started in the nineteenth century. Pianists were even encouraged to inflict pain on themselves as part of a "healthy" regimen. In Germany, there was the vise, constructed to stretch the fourth finger into obedient submission.

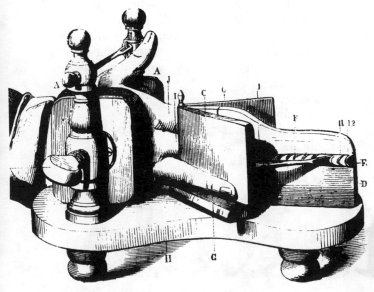

Die Hand in dem Chiroplast: Aeußere Seite.

In America, we had the Atkins Finger-Supporting Device, to hold the fingers in "correct position." Springs overhanging the rings on each finger forced the wearer to use extra strength when depressing the keys. It was, indeed, a very depressing device!

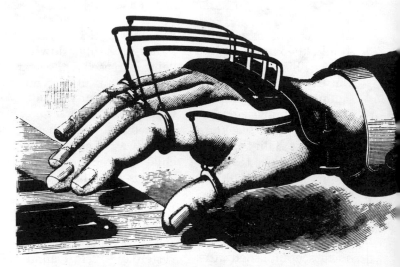

ATKINS' FINGER-SUPPORTING DEVICE.

Today, most experts encourage their students to find a "natural" way of moving. And that is one of the first rules of good practice: *nothing should be forced.* That is not to say that discipline is unimportant. But if the approach to each aspect of the practice session is one of openness and discovery rather than rigidity, so much more will be accomplished!

For example, exercises enable the muscles of the hand to "memorize" a sequence. This learned behavior is needed. But a pianist who places too much effort on this "acquired reaction," and not enough on bringing out spontaneous, instinctive actions, will find himself in a rut. That's one of the reasons it is sometimes important to practice with your eyes closed!

Another rule of good practice is to *look at things from as many different angles as possible.* A pianist who is asked to play these two figures against each other might have a hard time:

With the right analysis, though, the solution could be easy as pie:

Anatole Zemlinsky is a pianist and psychologist.

How To Practice
Part II

BY ANATOLE ZEMLINSKY

"As Fast As Possible!"

One of the rules of practicing we all hear over and over is "Be sure to practice slowly." Often the result of this is a feeling of inhibition, which leads to tedium. Picture yourself filled with excitement and yearning in setting out to learn a new piece. Suddenly a voice from the darkness whispers: "Don't touch those keys! Sit erect, play slowly, stay strictly in time, watch that fingering. . . ." and your smile is gone. I'm beginning to feel a cramp just talking about it.

The fact is, a certain amount of slow practice and attention to small scale detail is absolutely necessary. But there is something lacking in the approach so many of us have taken; we set out to make *music,* and end up playing what amounts to no more than a series of sterile exercises.

How can we overcome this problem? First of all, it's important to remember that music comes to life through shading, dynamics, differences in touch, the shapes of its phrases, the rhythmic vitality that is so much a part of the right tempo. These qualities are all missing in a slow, rigid "practice" version of a piece. They are just as essential as correct fingering, and they don't come across without careful work.

So, perhaps we should change that rule from "Be sure to practice slowly" to "Practice as fast as possible." But wait! This requires some further discussion. The slow part of practice helps teach the fingers where to go, and makes it much easier to learn the work. But in order to learn how to create music—how to make the piece sing—we must practice it at a tempo that will help reveal musical relationships and subleties of form. Pianists must have the opportunity to experiment with touch and phrasing while practicing—and there is little chance of boredom when so many exciting elements are introduced to the practice session.

Ideally, then, *both* ways of practicing should be used! First, we should practice slowly enough to learn the notes and fingerings. Then, we should "practice as fast as possible"; that is, as fast as we can without losing control of the basics we learned in slow practice.

Here's how this would work. Take a short part of the piece; you might choose a four- or eight-measure phrase. Practice it slowly. When you feel comfortable with the music, increase the tempo. *Don't* wait until you've practiced the entire work slowly. In this way, at each sitting you'll get to learn a little section, bring it up to tempo, and feel into what is needed to bring it to life.

At the next sitting, work on the next four or eight measures. When you have that section brought up to tempo, combine it with the first section. Now, you will begin to understand how the phrases relate to each other. You can introduce the idea of dynamic shading and decide which lines to bring out at a given moment. In fact, you will be making real, exciting music—even before you've learned the whole piece!

As you go on in this way, you will probably change your mind about how to play the work as new sections are added. This is part of the process of discovery and experimentation. Concert artists are always re-interpreting, because they think about these elements all the time.

So play as slowly as you need to; but as fast as you are able!

Anatole Zemlinsky is a pianist and psychologist.

Above: A caricature of Paderewski that appeared on the cover of the World's Fair edition of Puck *in 1893, in which he seems to be playing at super-human speed. The caption read: "A Peaceful Solution—at the next World's Fair Paderewski will play on all the pianos at once."*

POP Piano

by Raphael Crystal

As a popular pianist you will sometimes have to play from a lead sheet. You might be playing an original, as yet unpublished song, or you might be playing from a "fake book." In either case you will be faced with a melody line, chord symbols, and lyrics if there are any. You will have to translate these elements into a full-fledged piano part.

Suppose you were to encounter the following phrase on a lead sheet (we will not include lyrics in these examples):

Let us assume that you are accompanying a singer, or playing with a group where some other instrument will carry the melody. In such situations, the piano part can be quite simple. You can play chord roots in the left hand, and chords in the right. We can arrange these to create the rhythm of a typical "rock ballad" accompaniment:

If you are playing solo piano your task becomes more complicated. Now you must play the melody, as well as the bass line, chords, and rhythmic background. Let's apply this treatment to another lead sheet phrase:

Here the phrase suggests a "standard" tune (i.e. not rock or rock-influenced). We shall put the melody in the right hand, together with chords on the second and fourth beats. The left hand will play a bass line on the first and third beats, consisting of chord roots alternating with the fifths of the chords.

Article and musical examples © 1979 by Raphael Crystal

Sometimes, of course, you will want to play more than just a bass line in the left hand. This is especially desirable at slower tempos. In our next example the lead sheet phrase suggests a languid waltz. In the piano arrangement the left hand plays a root on the first beat of each bar, and then shares in a chord with the right hand on the second beat.

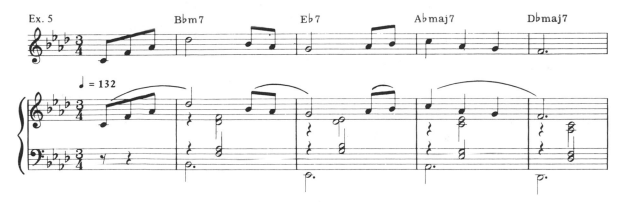

As you can see, you must understand the character of a tune to invent an appropriate accompaniment, especially when it comes to giving it the right rhythmic background. In fact, lead sheets are most useful when you have already heard the tune, and can bring into play your memories of it. Failing this you must make an educated guess about the style of the song. In the example below you would have to recognize the '' '50s rock-and-roll'' feeling. This suggests triplet chords in the right hand underneath the melody, and a left hand part that adds strong accents on the second and fourth beats:

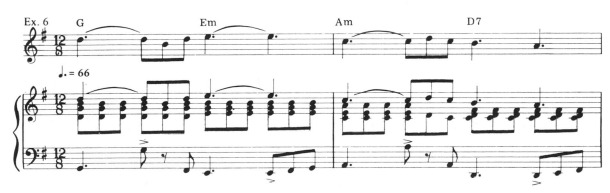

Certain problems often come up when you are playing from a fake book, which is a collection of lead sheets for a large number of popular songs. Fake books are made by photographing or copying the vocal lines and accompanying chord symbols from standard sheet music. Unfortunately these chord symbols are sometimes incomplete. Especially in older sheet music they sometimes only indicate what is played by the right hand; they do not take account of the bass. This can create a problem when ''inversions'' are called for (i.e. when a note of the chord other than the root should be played in the bass). In the following phrase, for example, it would be a mistake to use a bass line consisting only of chord roots:

The experienced musician will recognize a familiar formula here, which could be more fully expressed by writing the symbols as: F, F6/E♭, B♭/D, D 7, F/C, C+7, F7 (add 6). The inversions create a smooth, stepwise line in the bass. The F/C chord on the second beat of the third bar is a particularly important kind of inversion — a tonic chord with the fifth in the bass (called a I $\frac{6}{4}$ chord in harmonic analysis) used as part of a cadence. Actually it doesn't sound like a I chord at all; it simply prepares the V chord which follows. You should be suspicious of any tonic chord that comes right before a dominant at the end of a phrase, chances are the fifth should be in the bass.

Continued on next page

Ex. 8 ♩ = 108

The absence of bass notes in the chord symbols is especially misleading in the case of "slash chords." These are harmonies in which the right hand plays one chord over another note in the bass. (They are so called because, like inversions, they can be symbolized as "chord-slash-bass note.") In our next example you would be wise to be skeptical about the two bars of Dm7 followed immediately by a Cmaj7:

Ex. 9   Dm7   Cmaj7   Am7

The correct solution is shown below. The Dm7 is right for the first bar, but in the second bar there should be a G in the bass. Incidentally, this chord, which can be represented in Roman numerals as IIm7/V, is the most common slash chord. Whenever you see a IIm7 on a lead sheet that goes directly to a I, you should suspect that it is really a IIm7/V.

Ex. 10 ♩ = 138

If lead sheets often give too little harmonic information, they occasionally give too much. Sometimes large numbers of non-essential "passing chords" are present in the original sheet music, and these find their way into fake books to mystify future players. Our next example illustrates this phenomenon:

Ex. 11   G7 Db9 C9   Gb7-5 F6 F#m Bb9   E7   Db7   A7 Eb9   Dm(add9)

Given sufficient time you might be able to reconstruct the original arrangement and account for all of the chords, as in (a). But a simpler arrangement touching only on the main chords, such as (b), would be quite satisfactory and might even be preferable. The problem, of course, is to know which chords can safely be omitted. Often, as in this example, the chords on the strong beats are the important ones; but your ear must be your guide.

Ex. 12 ♩ = 132

a)

252

Ex. 13

b)

Once you have mastered the art of deciphering lead sheets you will be able to bring into play all the resources of your piano style. Remember that the lead sheet is a vocal line which you are transferring to the keyboard. Sometimes the tune will sound better on the piano played an octave higher, doubled in octaves, or thickened with chords. And you may want to invent "fills" for the long notes in the melody. All of these techniques are illustrated in our final example:

If you want to practice playing from lead sheets there is an excellent "teaching device" that you already have around the house. We are talking about the standard sheet music for any popular song. Simply cover up the piano part and improvise your part from the vocal line and chord symbols. Then compare your version with the printed keyboard arrangement. By doing this with a number of songs you will discover many of the ins and outs of lead sheet playing. You'll know you are on your way when you begin to prefer your arrangements to the printed versions!

Basic Elements of Popular Piano — *continued from p.238*

At certain points in a song a much simpler kind of arrangement may be used: both hands playing the same rhythm, in octaves or with chords.

Ex. 12

Of course this kind of unison arrangement will usually not persist for too long. Ordinarily, in fact, several different kinds of arrangement will be used during the course of a song. The trick is to go from one to another with fluidity, and at the right moment.

How can the pianist develop a feeling for keyboard arrangement? In part by playing through a lot of music in various styles, by listening to recordings or live performances, and — an avenue which is often neglected — by watching the hands of a pianist during performance. In all of these situations, try to analyze the arrangement. Where is the pianist putting the melody, and is it doubled or thickened? Where are block chords or broken chords used? How is the rhythmic background created? What kind of bass line is employed? All of these observations can then be brought into play when you experiment at the piano, in search of the right arrangement for a song.

JAZZ

And The Classics

by Stuart Isacoff

Of all the art forms that have sprung from the well of folk culture, jazz has met with perhaps the greatest derision. The great pianist Ignacy Paderewski called it "a terrible revenge by the culture of the Negroes on that of the whites." In the 1920s, the editor of *The Etude* linked jazz to America's crime rate. Russia's maxim Gorky described it in terms of "wild screaming, hissing, rattling, wailing, moaning, cackling." "Bestial cries are heard," he wrote. "Neighing horses, the squeal of a brass pig, crying jackasses, amorous quacks of a monstrous toad. . ." John Philip Sousa charged that " some of it makes you want to bite your grandmother."

Yet, since the turn of this century, composers have been delighting in the sound of jazz and writing pieces that celebrate its complex rhythms and colorful harmonies. Debussy and Stravinsky each produced several ragtimes. Milhaud, in *La Creation du monde*, gave us a classical Dixieland work.

Ravel was deeply influenced by our own George Gershwin, and Aaron Copland composed a *Jazz Concerto* and *Four Piano Blues*. Leonard Bernstein recently created a jazz-influenced piece for the 1981 Van Cliburn Piano Competition.

For some, the popular element must remain forever separate from serious music, but the two are not always so easily divided. After all, Satie played piano in a Montmartre bar; Brahms earned a living in taverns frequented by sailors; and Hindemith accompanied silent movies! Today, more than ever, it is impossible to make such black and white distinctions.

One of the most important features of jazz is its reliance on improvisation, and this was once a common element in the classical tradition too. "Whenever I play this concerto," said Mozart, referring to his *Piano Concerto in D Major* (K. 175), "I play whatever occurs to me at the moment." One of Mozart's contemporaries reported that his improvised performances were truly extraordinary. "If I dared to pray to the

Chic Corea

Billy Taylor

Almighty to grant me one more earthly joy," he wrote, "it would be that I might once again hear Mozart improvise."

Before Mozart's time, Baroque masters were equally adept at thrilling audiences with spontaneous variation and embellishment on fixed themes. Musicians were expected, as a matter of course, to be able to invent countermelodies and to improvise whole sections. Of course, florid embellishment had its critics in early times as well.

A most dramatic example is the colorful outburst reportedly let loose by composer Josquin des Prez upon hearing a singer ornament one of his pieces beyond recognition. "You ass," he exclaimed, "if I had wanted that many notes I would have written them in." In fact, both J.S. Bach and Mozart wrote ornaments into their works so that others would hesitate to change the written version.

Still, there is an exciting aspect to improvisational music, and it is what attracts most musicians to jazz. Verdi, who would, of course, have objected to any tampering with the notes on a page of his music, nevertheless summed up the matter nicely. "It may be a good thing to copy reality," he wrote, "but to invent reality is much, much better."

The rhythmic element in jazz is what critics have found most disturbing, but here, too, there are classical crossroads. Syncopation dates back to medieval times. The "jazz feel" can be compared to *notes inégales,* which was a technique used in French music during the time of Lully (1632–1687) up to the French Revolution (1789). In *notes inégales,* melodies that moved in steps were played unevenly in the same way that jazz phrases are today played with an uneven, accented list.

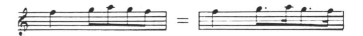

Just as composers in the classical tradition have turned at times to jazz, contemporary jazz artists are moving increasingly in the direction of classical music. We spoke about this recently with three outstanding jazz pianists: **Chic Corea, Roland Hanna,** and Billy Taylor.

"Jazz pianists like Bill Evans, Herbie Hancock, and even Art Tatum were all very much aware of classical music," says Chic Corea. "The harmonies they use in their improvisations are very sophisticated, and are a result of having assimilated the harmonic beauty of the nineteenth and twentieth centuries. Even an avant-garde composer like Stockhausen has had an influence on jazz. For a

Continued on next page

255

time I was looking at Stockhausen's piano music; I could see him thinking in terms of textures and weights instead of melodies, and that affected my own music.

"One composer who has remained of interest to me throughout the years is Bartók," he continues. "There are two things I love about him. One is that he found a way of writing music that makes it sound improvised, even though it is carefully architectured. The other is that he has such a clear definition of his musical universe. It is a special universe all its own."

Corea has a quality that seems essential in an improvisational artist. "As a student, I decided early on to be a blotter," he reports. "When I hear something I like, I want to be able to do it or understand it immediately. It doesn't even matter whether this will make me a better musician. I just love the process of being a blotter for all of the wonderful ways of making music." Chic Corea is at work on a chamber music piece to be performed by The Chamber Music Society of Lincoln Center at the New World Festival of the Arts next June in Miami.

Billy Taylor was a protégé of the legendary Art Tatum. "One of the things I learned from Tatum," he says, "is that you can learn great lessons from people who are not necessarily outstanding musicians. We used to go around and listen to pianists in after-hour places, and I would complain about the quality of some of the playing. Art would say about someone, 'He does some interesting things,' and I would respond, 'He's terrible!' Then Art would play back some of the devices he had heard during the course of the evening and I would be amazed."

Similarly, many great jazz artists take what they can from classical sources. "I was attracted to the impressionist harmonies of Debussy and Ravel," says Taylor, "and some of the things that Chopin seemed to suggest harmonically. Later I became more interested in the linear aspects of Bach's pieces. I also studied the Matthay system of touch for a better legato. Other pianists, like Teddy Wilson and Mel Powell, had also worked with this system."

Taylor is spending a good deal of time writing for orchestra now. "When I premiered my *Suite for Jazz Piano and Orchestra*, which was commissioned by Maurice Abravanel of the Utah Symphony," he remembers, "he programmed the work on one of his regular concerts, and the other two composers were Mahler and Bartók. There are many people who love Mahler, who love Beethoven and Brahms and Mozart, who also love the Modern Jazz Quartet and Dave Brubeck and Duke Ellington. One doesn't exclude the other."

Touches by Leonard Bernstein was composed for the Sixth Van Cliburn International Piano Competition at Fort Worth, Texas. It is a jazz-influenced work.

To my first love, the keyboard

TOUCHES
CHORALE, EIGHT VARIATIONS and CODA

LEONARD BERNSTEIN

"Let's take a look at Rachmaninoff's *Piano Concerto Number Three,*" says Roland Hanna. "There are all kinds of elements here that are similar to jazz. He begins with a melody.

"Then he develops it the way a jazz artist develops a tune. He improvises on the chords, while the melody appears in the orchesta.

Piano Concerto No. 3 (Rachmaninoff)
© by Editions Russe de Musique, Paris
Reprinted by permission.

"It is similar to what I do all the time: cadenza passages, changes in voicings, re-working of rhythmic ideas. Chopin is another good model for jazz pianists. He will play a certain melodic idea over and over, but with a slight change in the harmonies each time.

"Scriabin uses sevenths and ninths and elevenths in his harmonies, and these sounds form the basis for contemporary piano styles. He kept looking for new things to do.

"But when I study and analyze his music," says Hanna, "it doesn't become a part of me until I'm playing jazz. In performing I can begin to see what each of these composers meant, what each thought about. That's why I use this music. I don't want to copy what someone else has done. But it is important to be able to grab the elements from each musical tradition so that I can use them in my own way."

the Invention of
the
PIANO

In 1709, during the height of the Baroque, Bartolommeo Cristofori of Padua, a harpsichord player in the service of the Prince of Tuscany, produced an instrument he called the *Gravicembalo col piano e forte* — a harpsichord capable of playing softly or loudly. Since a harpsichord is only able to sound at one dynamic level, regardless of how lightly or heavily its keys are touched, this was a startling development. The new instrument's name eventually became shortened to pianoforte (soft-loud) and is known today as the piano. It was made possible by means of a tiny mechanical device called an *escapement* — a little invention that changed the course of music history!

The Harpsichord

The idea of combining a keyboard with a stringed instrument gained popularity in the mid-fourteenth century. One of the earliest attempts was called the *Schachbrett*. It was based on the *psaltery*, a primitive stringed instrument played with a quill (Schacht is Low German for quill). But by the 16th Century musicians were playing a complex instrument with long rows of strings plucked by plectrums (quills) attached to a keyboard; it was called a harpsichord.

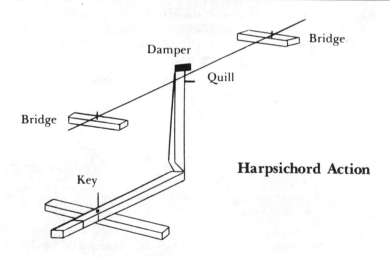

Harpsichord Action

Pushing the key raises a jack until the plectrum plucks the string. When the key is released, the plectrum moves back and away from the string, and a piece of felt or leather comes to rest on it to dampen the sound. But no matter how hard the key is struck, the sound level is always the same, since the string is simply being *plucked*.

258

The Clavichord

One ancient instrument in which the strings are struck, is the clavichord. By throwing a wooden or metal tangent against a taut string it sections off a portion of the string, which vibrates from the impact. One famous musician, Mattheson, recommended the clavichord for its "sensitive touch and pure style," against the harpsichord on which "too much clatter confuses the ear." But the clavichord cannot produce much volume, or sustain a tone for long. In fact, unless it is played in a small room with only a few people present, it can hardly be heard.

The Piano

Attempts to build a more responsive yet grander instrument in which the strings would be *struck* rather than plucked were foiled by a major problem: after a hammer hits a string it ends up resting against it, and thus dampens the vibration. Cristofori found a solution.

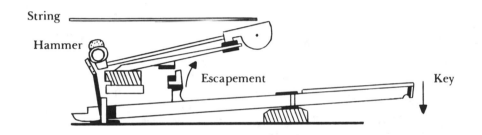

In between the key and the hammer he placed an intermediary — the escapement. The escapement helps throw the hammer up when the key is struck, but as it is raised it quickly moves out of the way, allowing the hammer to rebound off the string.

It took hundreds of years of further improvement before the modern piano came into being. But in this simple innovation the piano was born — and the world has never been the same. ♩

An early harpsichord.

PIANO TIPS FROM THE PROS

HOW NOT TO BUY A LEMON WHEN YOU'RE SHOPPING FOR A USED PIANO

— Katie Courtice Basquin

The time has come. You're doing just fine with the guitar chords, but a piano would make so much more sound. Or your daughter has been begging for a piano for months. Or you took lessons for a year or two as a kid, and it would be nice to pick it up again. For whatever reason, you're in the market for a piano.

However, you are not automatically ready to plunk down $1500-$2000, are you? That's the average price of a new name-brand spinet-style piano. A new grand will run $2500 more.

A professional musician will probably (grudgingly) pay $6000 or more for a six-foot Steinway or Baldwin or Knabe or Yamaha grand—but will also (legitimately) take an investment tax credit at income-tax time, and deduct depreciation on it yearly thereafter. Those of us who are pianists-for-fun aren't in that league at all.

So we find ourselves combing the classified ads, looking for the best used piano we can find. "Aeolian console from $750." "50-yr-old upright, excell. cond., negot." "Baby grand, beautifully finished, must see, $2900." Worse and worse.

I've lost count of the number of people who have asked me, "How can I select a really good second-hand piano?" Mind you, it is a mark of their desperation that they're asking *me* at all. I'm not a musician, barely play piano myself, and my only claim to competence in the field is that for some years now I've been married to concert pianist Peter Basquin. The real question they're asking is, How does *he* pick a piano?

His answer verges on the inscrutable: "You pick the one you like." That's not really much help, even if it is, in the last analysis, most of the truth. But figuring out what you like can be quite a chore.

Let's start with something simple— where are you going to put the piano, once you've got it? "An absolutely beautiful-sounding piano which is too big for the room will give you an awful clangorous reverberation," cautions

Herbert Rogers, another concert pianist who is frequently asked for advice in piano selection. Having toured both with the Philharmonic Piano Quartet and the Greenwich Quartet, he's made the acquaintance of literally hundreds of pianos all over the United States. Likewise, Peter comments that a piano which has a very respectable sound in a 10' x 12' recreation room will be whining and thin if placed in a 12' x 20' livingroom-with-cathedral-ceiling.

If you have the space and can afford it, *always* get a grand piano. The additional pleasure you will derive from the sound and from the physical action of playing on it will more than reward the extra expense. Furthermore, Erlo Wondracek, a well-known and highly respected piano-tuner working in New York and Connecticut, has found that a student with as little as three or four years of lessons will be dissatisfied with less. Peter adds that it's important for a learner to be rewarded by fine sound, and not frustrated by a balky instrument.

Although in some cases the strings of an upright will be as long as those in a small grand, the position of the sounding board within a room (especially coupled with the imprecision of the action in an upright) makes the grand superior. Remember, the sounding board of a grand piano (the bottom of the case) is always a leg's-length from the floor, while the sounding board of an upright (the back of the piano) is most often shoved flush against a wall.

If you'll be putting your piano in a small room, or have other reasons for not wanting to purchase a grand piano, continue to look for the biggest instrument possible. Prefer an upright to a console, a console to a spinet, and so forth. The sound of any piano is adversely affected by decreased size in two ways— a smaller sounding board, which reduces the amount and complexity of reverberation, and shorter bass strings. (A short, thickly-wound lower string has less reso-

nance and clarity than a longer and thinner one at the same pitch.)

But how big, finally, is too big? Musicians disagree, but as a very general rule of thumb: if the piano were to be expanded to a rectangle, its area should not exceed one-sixth of the floor space (and you'll probably be happier sticking closer to one-eighth). Keyboards are all about five feet wide, so a "five-foot grand" would have an "area" of 25 square feet and would go very comfortably in a room 14' x 14' or 12' x 16'.

Some thought should be given to the future use of the piano as well. Is it to be practiced on by a promising student? Make sure that it has three pedals, and that all of them work. The left one (the "soft" pedal) shifts the keys of a grand piano, or the hammers in an upright, slightly to one side, to diminish the volume. The center pedal on a grand piano sustains a note or chord through a number of notes played after it. It's called the "sostenuto pedal" and frequently malfunctions, so try it: Play a low note, and while holding down that key, depress the middle pedal. Now, keep the pedal down, release the note, and play some other notes, or a chord or two. You should still be able to hear the original note quite clearly.

Upright pianos may have a sostenuto pedal or either of two substitutes, a "fake" sostenuto pedal which is essentially a damper pedal for the left half of the keyboard, or a "rehearsal" pedal, similar to a soft pedal. Of course, some uprights have no middle pedal at all.

The right-hand pedal ("damper") on any piano suspends the dampers, so that all the notes reverberate. It should stop all sound cleanly when it's released.

Will you be doing a lot of sight-reading, or evening sings around the piano? Plan for light on the music rack, and when you do, remember that the tops of all pianos open to provide more sound, but opening yours may eliminate the surface on which you planned to put your lamp.

Now that you've done your general planning, and are looking at specific pianos, there are three "technical aspects" with which you must contend, of which the sounding board is the most controversial, the action (escapement) is the most aesthetically important, and the pin block potentially the most costly.

Literally every single part of a grand piano can be replaced or rebuilt, except the sounding board. Many people consider it "the heart" of a piano. It is made of specially seasoned and matched planks and glued together with maximum care. It should provide a smooth, even, blemish-free surface to vibrate with and amplify the sound of the struck strings.

Extremes of temperature and humidity are unhealthy for sounding boards (as for any good wood). A sounding board, even the very best, subjected to alternations of humid heat and dry cold —or worse, dry heat—typical of a centrally-heated house in a temperate coastal climate, is likely to crack after awhile.

Does a cracked sounding board forever ruin a piano's value? Not necessarily. Only if the crack is in such a position on the sounding board that it sets up an unwelcome vibration, or buzz, when certain notes are played, is it a substantive problem. The most likely location for such a buzz, according to my pianist husband, is in the octave below "middle C." Play a few notes in that range, rather loudly, as a test. On many pianos, you will never be able to hear that the sounding board is cracked. But it's easy to find out for sure. Open the lid of a grand piano (and does it have both long and short sticks for holding the lid open, by the way?), then lie down on the floor underneath the piano and look up. If you can see light through the sounding board, it's cracked. Similarly, look or feel for cracks in the backs of uprights, consoles or spinets. Depending on the importance of a cracked sounding board to the buyer or seller, it may or may not affect the price. Professional musicians tend to rely on their ears, not their eyes, in judging such things.

To the performer and the serious student, the piano's action assumes the greatest day-to-day importance. "Action" refers to the mechanical way in which the piano produces sound, and encompasses several concepts: the resistance which the finger feels when pressing down a key; the smoothness with which that key reacts with a series of levers to make its hammer strike a note; the rapidity with which the whole assemblage recoils and prepares for the next stroke. Pianists use words like "solid" or "smooth" or "even" when describing actions. "Every note should feel like every other note when you play a scale," says Peter. "And, as you play a scale, all the notes should strike with the same volume." Herbert puts it another way: "Your hand is used to a certain resistance, and you've got to have that in a piano . . . otherwise it's like telling jokes to an audience that won't laugh."

To test the action on a piano you're looking at, do as the pianists say, and play a scale all the way up and down the keyboard. To check the ability of the keys and hammers to "bounce back," try the melody of the *William Tell Overture* ("The Lone Ranger" themesong), or play a few rapid trills.

So far, you've checked and considered everything yourself. When it comes to the pin block, the felts on the hammers, and the condition of the strings, you might profit from professional advice. Pianists and tuners alike recommend paying the $15-$20 which would normally be charged by a tuner to check out a proposed purchase.

This little expense may avoid a big one later on. Replacing the pin block in a grand piano costs over $1000, plus shipping to the rebuilder or factory and back, and necessary attendant tunings. Replacing the felt on the hammers would probably run over $500. According to Erlo Wondracek, if the pins which hold the strings are not tight enough in the tuning block, the piano won't hold its tune. Only a professional technician with a proper set of tuning wrenches can properly assess that element of a piano.

Other points can be noted even before the tuner is called in for a look. On most grands you can study the hammers — do they have prominent grooves in the felt which have been pressed in by the strings? Is there less than ¼-inch of felt between the outside edge and the wood of the hammers at the top of the scale, and less than ¾-inch of felt at the bottom? For the health of your piano and your own aesthetic happiness, they will need some work. Are the strings rusted, especially near each end? You'll be replacing some of them soon.

All this information will not necessarily get you a "cheap" piano. Used Steinway grands, for example, are currently selling for $3000-$4000 in the New York area. "A used piano," says Herbert, "is acceptable if the action is solid, the piano's in generally good shape, and the parts are standardized with those of current manufacturers." Without standardized parts, he warns, "it would be like buying an Edsel."

To find a real bargain, he recommends auction sales, but warns that "a second-hand dealer may outbid you." Auctions are one of several ways in which second-hand piano-dealers obtain their wares. Others include placing advertisements to purchase old pianos and searching the classifieds. It is obvious that an individual pursuing the same route would save more money than one who bought a piano from a dealer.

Another, perhaps less obvious bargain-hunting techinque is to buy a used piano in May or June—the end of the school year, when Mommy and Daddy determine that Junior won't be continuing his lessons next fall. Several such decisions produce a temporary mini-glut on the market, which is generally absorbed the following September by the optimistic parents of other "Juniors." In between, it's a buyer's market.

The question of the finish of a piano's case has received little attention here, because frankly, it's not *musically* important. As far as most professional pianists are concerned, pianos come in ebony—period. Fancy mahogany, walnut, "antiqued" or Louis Quatorze cases add absolutely nothing to the sound of the instrument. Indeed, some musicians feel that the quality of sound is inversely proportional to the elaborateness of the case. "The better it looks," says Herbert, "the worse it sounds." Musicians and piano technicians consider a piano to be a musical instrument. If, in your opinion, it's simply a piece of furniture you're buying, you need only consult an interior designer.

Once you have found a good piano, there are several things you must do to keep it that way. We'll talk about that in our next article. Until then, happy hunting!

Katie Courtice Basquin lives in New York with her husband Peter, concert pianist. From the midwest, she learned her scales on an old Straube upright which was "uniformly and continually a half-tone flat." In addition to being very active in New York's music circles, she has been involved with publishing, writing and advertising ever since moving east. She has also been known to play a heart-rendering version of "Greensleeves" on her husband's Baldwin grand when he's on tour in the far west.

Play It Smart

Shopping for a used piano

by Mary Gail Rundell & Judy Hobbs

A used piano can be a treasured discovery or trouble discovered too late. How can you shop wisely? Bob Hunter, a Texas-based technician, suggests a helpful system. Start by deciding how much you can afford to spend. Allow about $200 of that for moving, minor repairs, and tuning. Then shop carefully.

As you visit rebuilders' shops and private homes, consider these points:

✔*How old is the piano?* Using the serial number and manufacturer's name, your technician can find out the age. The National Piano Manufacturers Association advises against buying a piano over 50 years old and suggests that the best buys are probably under 20 years old.

✔The older the piano, the more repairs it probably needs. An exception may be an older rebuilt piano. Some musicians even prefer rebuilt upright grands with their long strings and solid spruce soundboards.

✔*Look inside the piano.* Cracks in the pin block (where tops of strings are anchored) or bridge (across which lower ends of the strings stretch) can mean poor performance and expensive repairs. Loose tuning pins suggest that the piano won't hold its tune. Rusty strings may affect tone or break during tuning. String-cut hammers can often be filed into shape, but squared-off hammers must be replaced.

✔*Check the soundboard.* Fine-grained spruce is generally regarded as the best tone-producer. Lower-priced instruments sometimes use particle board or other woods. If the soundboard is cracked, it can often be satisfactorily repaired. However, a crack can also be a serious flaw, causing dead notes or buzzing.

✔*Strike every key.* Are the dampers functioning, or do the sounds seem to linger too long? Depress the damper (right) pedal and strike the keys again. Tones should be sustained longer now.

As you test the keys, note how they respond to your touch. Look at the keyboard. Key tops are easily replaced, but missing keys are difficult to duplicate. The keyboard should also appear level.

✔*Do you like the piano's tone?* Generally, a larger piano with its longer strings has a better tone than a smaller instrument. Tuning may improve the sound but it won't eliminate a hard, rough tone.

If your preliminary inspection reveals no major defects, obtain the name of the technician who regularly tuned the piano. Ask him about its maintenance. A piano that has been tuned at least once, and preferably twice, a year is more likely to stay in tune. If tuning is neglected for many years, the piano can lose its ability to hold standard pitch.

Once you narrow your selection to two instruments, enlist a technician to look at them with you. If you don't know a technician, ask a music dealer, school, church, or piano teacher to recommend one. The technician will probably charge $15 to $35 to estimate the needed repairs, but his expertise can prevent a serious blunder.

Add all anticipated additional costs to the seller's price. Compare this cost with the price of a similar-quality new piano. New spinets begin at about $1,000, while new consoles begin at about $1,200. For a smaller investment, you can often obtain the same or better quality in a used instrument.

Properly maintained, a used piano can appreciate in value. More important, it can bring you years of enjoyment. ♩

CARING FOR YOUR PIANO

by John H. Steinway

No owner of a fine automobile would dream of driving 50,000 miles without once checking the crank case oil or water level, or tuning up the motor. Yet, as unlikely as it may seem, some piano owners believe that their music-making machine of 12,000 parts is virtually indestructable and requires little or no attention.

The handcrafted piano is an aesthetic gift for both the eye and ear. As such, it should be given common-sense care like any piece of fine furniture; and it needs occasional adjustment like any fine instrument.

We at Steinway & Sons recommend at least three tunings a year — especially in those areas of the country with marked seasonal weather changes. In the winter, when the heat goes on at home, the air in rooms becomes dryer. Consequentially, the numerous different woods in a piano begin to dry and shrink infinitesimally at different rates. In the summer, the reverse happens.

A fine, handcrafted piano can normally withstand such changes to a large degree, yet it does require attention. Tuning is vital to counteract this process.

Ideally, a piano should be placed in a room so that it is least exposed to temperature and humidity changes. Which means that an inside wall is preferred to an exterior wall which is cooler (or warmer), and often filled with windows. In addition, the instrument should be positioned away from radiators and heating or air conditioning outlets. Pianos thrive and perform best in an environment whose temperature is between 72 and 75 degrees, with a relative humidity of between 45 and 50 percent. This is true in all climates.

The key is to avoid subjecting a piano to rapid changes of temperature or humidity. Sometimes such changes can occur without the knowledge of even the most caring piano owner. Some years ago a hospital purchased a Steinway grand for use in its doctor's lounge, a medium size room that was well maintained.

Temperature and humidity levels in the room were ideal, but no matter how many times it was adjusted, the instrument somehow failed to stay in tune. The mystery was finally solved by the building's maintenance supervisor. Since the room was not used at night, the heating system, on a separate thermostat, went off at 6:00 P.M., and then went on automatically the following morning. In the process, the room temperature and relative humidity plunged and rose in overnight cycles.

Pianos must be kept clean inside. The best procedure is to reverse a vacuum cleaner and put the hose on the outgo to blow lint and dust out. (Then you have to clean the room, of course, but it's the easiest and best way to keep the piano clean).

Additionally, vases, decorative art, clocks and other objects must be kept off the top of a piano! They will vibrate and most likely scar the finish. We were once presented with a piano that buzzed as well as hummed. The cause? Grandpa's ornately-framed picture bouncing on top, in time to the piano's vibration.

Nothing should rest atop your piano — except perhaps a light coat of dust. For exterior cleaning, a damp cloth is sufficient and will not harm the finish.

While ivory keys will naturally discolor with age, more recent models are constructed with plastic keys — these don't discolor and won't warp or crack like ivory. They are also very tough — impervious to most abuse (except perhaps an eight year old with a hammer).

Other piano maintenance includes voicing (balancing the sound across the keyboard). This should be done every two or three years, as should action regulating. These tasks are best done by an experienced piano technician, not a tuner.

By following the basic rules outlined here, you can be assured that your instrument will do its share to contribute to a lifetime of music enjoyment.

John Steinway is chairman of Steinway & Sons, a company that has made but one product since it was founded by his great-grandfather in New York City in 1853.

SO YOU'RE THINKING OF THINKING OF BUYING AN ELECTRIC ORGAN...

by George D. Nixon

The author, a musician who taught music for 25 years and who has had experience as a salesman, demonstrator and organist, answers the following questions:

* Can you learn to play the electric organ?
* Why should you learn to play the electric organ?
* How much should you spend?
* What brand should you buy?
* How should you shop?
* How can you get proper instruction?

A Buyer's Guide for the Neophyte

You can actually be playing a selection on a modern electric organ in a matter of minutes! Of course, how well you learn to play will depend on several factors:

1. The degree of interest or motivation you have.
2. The amount of time you spend playing the organ.
3. The amount of musical talent you possess; that is, your sense of pitch, your sense of rhythm, and your audio-pattern memory.
4. The amount and type of instruction you receive.
5. The quality and type of instrument on which you play.

The above factors have been listed in the order of their importance, but some degree of each is necessary in order to learn to play, even to a limited extent. Your degree of interest will be enhanced through the use of the automatic features and by the variety of sounds you are able to produce. Also, there is a wealth of instructional materials that make learning to read music fun and easy. Since these things will motivate your interest, this will help you qualify on the second factor: the amount of time you spend playing the organ. You will want to spend many of your leisure-time hours at the organ. Since you have headphones, you do not need to be concerned about disturbing others—even when playing late at night. The third factor, musical talent, is extremely important, but one can learn to play the organ even with a minimal amount of talent. If you can hum, sing or whistle a tune, you have a sense of pitch. If you can march, dance or clap your hands in time, you have a sense of rhythm, and if you can remember tunes, you have audio-pattern memory.

You will note that the quality and type of the instrument is listed last. This is not to say that this factor is not important, it is only the least important of the five very important factors. The quality and type of instrument needed will be discussed in detail later.

Also, we have omitted listing experience in playing other instruments as an important determining factor. This is because previous experience on another musical instrument will reduce the amount of time needed to learn to play the organ, but it will not be a factor in determining whether you can learn to play.

Every member of the family will want to play the organ—from grandpa and grandma, to the 3 or 4 year old child. The organ is an excellent instrument for young children. Their developing physical coordination creates a need for them to approach this learning process one step at a time. The automatic features not only provide for this, but also attract and hold their interest through the developing process. It is important for children to get a visual impression of music that a keyboard instrument presents, and since the various stops and other features of the organ eliminates the need to reach a large span of keys with the hands, it is more adaptable to small children than other keyboard instruments.

There are many reasons for learning to play the organ. Probably the most important reason is for your own entertainment. Learning to play the *modern organ* is really fun! The various automatic features will aid you in getting satisfying results. You will enjoy the many hours of creating your own beautiful sounds. Even as a beginner, when you can play only one or two simple selections, you will be able to make a variety of sounds and effects. Secondly, you will achieve a sense of ac-complishment. It is a thrill to realize that you have been able to produce the resultant sounds, and to know that you are the one who is in control of those sounds! You have achieved another degree of success with each milestone in your learning process.

Thirdly, everyone admires and envies someone who can perform and produce such beautiful sounds. You will have many hours of enjoyment playing for your friends.

And lastly, when you have become a really accomplished organist, you may find this is a pleasant way to earn extra money as a professional entertainer. There are many opportunities for those who are capable.

The amount of money you should spend for an electric organ depends upon several factors which are personal to you. As a general statement, one could say that you should buy the best instrument you can afford, consistent with the needs of you and your family.

It has been the experience of most people who purchase a quality organ or piano, that it becomes a part of that family's tradition for generations. These instruments do not quickly depreciate in value and those who have desired to sell their instrument have usually realized a good return on their original investment.

HOW MUCH SHOULD YOU SPEND?

The least expensive organs, at the present writing, sell for about $500; however, their qualities and features are so limited, it is recommended that one should

Continued on next page

What kind? What brand? How much should i spend?

expect to pay not less than $1000 in order to get minimum quality and features. The best organs range up to $10,000 and more, but one can get a very fine instrument for around $2,500. An instrument in this price range, with normal maintainence, should last one a lifetime. Spreading this cost over an adult lifetime would amount to less than $5 per month—not a lot of money considering the many rewards to the various members of the family. Minimum down payment required by many financing institutions at this time is 10% of the purchase price, and the balance plus interest may be spread over 36 months. It is the writer's opinion that more sound personal financing would be to make a down payment of one third or more of the purchase price. Your ability to make such a down payment might be a better criterion of whether you can afford an electric organ.

Most of the less expensive instruments will have certain basic components, such as:

> One keyboard, or manual, with 3½ to 4 octaves
>
> Bass pedals with one octave (12 or 13 keys)
>
> Two or three flute or tibia stops or "presets"
>
> A vibrato switch
>
> An expensive cabinet (plastic or pressed wood)
>
> A low wattage amplifier and solid state electronics
>
> An expression pedal
>
> One small speaker

Features?

266

Where can i find good instruction?

As you pay more for the instrument, you will get some or all of these additional features:

> One or two additional keyboards or manuals
>
> Additional stops and or presets for each of the manuals and pedals. These stops should include strings, woodwinds and brasses.
>
> Special effects stops such as piano, chimes, reverb, repeat, percussion, etc.
>
> Additional keys on the manuals or pedals. Five octaves on the two upper and two octaves on the pedal is usually maximum.
>
> One or more additional built-in speakers, usually Leslie or acoustic tremolo.
>
> A woofer and a tweeter in the main speakers.
>
> Separate voicing for each manual.
>
> Couplers, so voicing may be transferred from one manual to another and to the bass pedals.
>
> A built-in synthesizer
>
> Additional percussion effects
>
> Automatic drums
>
> Automatic accompaniment and bass
>
> Cassette recorder and player
>
> Crafted wood cabinet
>
> Additional amplifiers of high wattage
>
> Quality circuitry and electronics
>
> An arpeggiator

HOW MANY FEATURES DO YOU NEED?

Everyone needs as much quality as he can afford. For this reason, it is recommended that you do not buy the least expensive instrument. Not only do they have less features, but a great deal of the quality is sacrificed—particularly in the area of electronics. The organ you buy should have at least two manuals and an octave of pedals. This is fundamental to the learning process.

If it is necessary to sacrifice quality for a low price, it is suggested that the sacrifice be in the cabinet. This feature will least affect the performance and sound, although plastic portions of the cabinet may at times produce unpleasant vibration sounds, these can usually be easily eliminated.

Your individual needs will not only be determined by the amount of money you can afford to spend, but also by your musical taste and discrimination. Each of us has a standard of musical sound which is acceptable to us. Since your discrimination will become more sensitive with exposure, you should not purchase an instrument which violates your standard at the time of purchase.

If you have had very little or no experience at playing a keyboard instrument, or if there are members of your family who might play the organ who have had little or no experience, you should defintely include the automatic chord and bass, and the automatic drums. The cassette recorder-player is an important learning device, but you may have one which you can use—it does not need to be built into the organ.

As a minimum of instrumentation, it is recommended that there be 3 flute (or tibia) stops in the solo or upper manual—a 16', 8' and 4'. (The feet (') represent a comparison to the length of a pipe in a pipe organ —the longer the pipe, the lower the sound.) There should be a minimum of one 8' voice in the accompaniment manual, and one 16' voice in the bass. These last two may be any instrumentation that has a sound pleasing to you. I would prefer either a string or a tibia.

The advantage of having a third manual is that it enables one to set up a second instrumentation in advance, so it will not be necessary to change stops during a selection in order to get a different sound. These advantages can be partially offset by "preset" buttons or switches, and by couplers, features which are on some two manual organs.

One additional word concerning the automatic features. People often feel that using automatic features on the organ is "cheating". They seem to think that using those units is not really playing the organ, so they are deceiving themselves and others. This attitude is not substantiated. A very large percentage of our population has had one or more piano lessons, but because the piano is a difficult instrument to learn and takes many hours of painstaking practice just to play simple music, they became discouraged and quit before they learned to play. However, the automatic features of the modern organ, and the nature of the instrument, make it an ideal instrument for adults as well as for children. The automatic features make learning to play the organ an enjoyable experience, an experience that produces pleasing results right from the start. All organs can be played without the automatic features and when the time comes when one feels confident, he will gradually learn to play without them. They are not "cheaters".

WHAT BRAND?

When one is selecting an instrument, he should purchase a brand that has a good reputation for quality over a period of time. The same should be said for buying from a particular store. You will want to be reasonably certain that the store will be in business for at least as long as your warranty so you can obtain service. Some of the well known brands, listed alphabetically—not necessarily in order of quality or price—are: Allen, Baldwin, Conn, Gulbransen, Hammond, Kimball, Lowery, Rogers, Thomas, Wurlitzer, and Yamaha.

It is suggested that you hear demonstrations on at least six of these brands. Each brand will have many different models, but the mid-priced model will usually give you the basic sound for that brand. *Do not* submit to the pressure of the good salesman to buy before you see and hear the others. You are going to spend a considerable amount of money and it will pay you to be deliberate in making your choice. Many times, they will drastically reduce the price to get you to buy now rather than to consider another brand or store. Do not be tempted by this. If they will give you that price today, they will nearly always give it to you tomorrow. In no case will they sell at a loss.

It is the writer's suggestion that if you do not play the organ reasonably well, you should obtain the services of a capable, unbiased organist—not only to get his opinion, but to have him play the same selection on the two or three organs you are considering so you can get an equal comparison. Even if it costs a few dollars to hire such a person, it will be money well spent.

After you have become knowledgeable through shopping and listening to demonstrations, you may wish to consider buying a used organ. Some real bargains can often be found by consulting the ads in the newspaper. Quite often, for one reason or another, people are willing to sell a one or two year old organ for about ½ price. However, it is usually expected that one would pay cash on this kind of transaction. Again, I would suggest that you take an organist or an organ technician (repairman) with you to check the instrument.

Remember, there will probably be no warranty on this instrument and you probably will be expected to bear the expense of having it carted to your home.

When selecting a particular model, you should be aware that many retail dealers, upon request, will give you full price for your organ if you decide to get a more expensive model within a limited time. The time period varies from 90 days to one year. It is important that this provision be in your contract of purchase—not just a verbal agreement. Also, in your contract of purchase should be a warranty agreement which is not only backed by the factory, but also by the store. A minimum warranty would be five years on all parts and one year on labor and service.

GETTING PROPER INSTRUCTION

Nearly all of the various brands of organs have self-teaching instruction books. Most of them are quite good, but may vary considerably in their type of approach. In the writer's opinion, the best ones are those which make it the easiest to begin to play familiar tunes immediately. In the learning process, success is the most important element. Educators call this motivation. We should not be overly concerned, at first, with whether we are learning to "read" music. We should be concerned with whether we are learning to look at a printed page and "produce" music. Then in a step-by-step process, we can learn to read musical notation.

Of course, the best way to learn to play the organ is through a capable organ teacher. It is not always easy to find a good teacher, and they are often expensive. However, they can speed up your learning process and keep you from forming bad playing habits. Your organ store can usually provide you with a list of private teachers. Ask them for names of successful students of the teachers, then consult with those students before selecting your teacher.

Many organ stores provide free lessons when you purchase an organ. Some provide these lessons to any interested person regardless of whether they have purchased an instrument at that store. However, these are usually group lessons and are most often concerned with theory and registration, rather than with the techniques of playing the organ. Theory and registration are important elements of playing and this instruction is very valuable.

A very good substitute for the private teacher is the cassette taped lessons. These have been worked out in a step-by-step method and you have the advantage of being able to repeat lessons at your convenience until they are learned to your satisfaction. These tapes are relatively inexpensive (a two year course costs about $200) and many stores will give you the tapes as an inducement to purchase an organ from them.

Once you get involved with your new electric organ two things will happen for sure: you'll wonder what you did before you had one, and more often than not, you'll be late for dinner!

♩

ABOUT WRITING MUSIC

Some Personal Observations to Think About

by Ronald Herder

You are neither too young nor too old to compose music. If you think otherwise, get that fairytale out of your head.

A few geniuses began at age 3 and burned out in middle age. Giuseppe Verdi—composer of the operas *Aida, La Traviata,* and *Il Trovatore*—was still going strong at 87. Gustav Mahler—whose lengthy symphonies are now a cornerstone of the modern symphonic repertory—didn't start serious composing until he was 34. Some of the great pop, jazz, and rock music of our time has been written by musicians who consider the age of 25 as "over the hill."

Conclusion: Forget about age.

* * * *

What about music theory? Does it have anything to do with composing a piece of music?

Sounds come first. Theory books and systems tag along behind, explaining in words what you've already experienced by ear.

Composing is a "hot" creative act. Studying theory is a "cool" analytical act.

Theory explains what is going on in a piece of music. It shows us the machinery that makes the music tick. Training in theory helps sharpen our understanding, and helps the composer organize his or her musical materials.

Absorb theory for what it has to offer. But watch out for the trap of "rules." In the early stages of writing music, rules can be helpful disciplines to help focus our thinking. But given too much importance, rules become handcuffs; break them if you know what you're doing.

* * * *

Use your good ears to break through the endless blanket of sound that surrounds our lives.

Direct your hearing. Sharpen your perception. Isolate sounds. Listen, and make yourself aware of your sound-world.

* * * *

A painting, a statue, and a building have a certain kind of life. All of their parts exist at the same time. But music is like a movie or a stage play: it unrolls slowly, bit by bit. A movie begins, continues, and ends before your eyes. Music does the same for your ears. Your composition lives and breathes.

* * * *

Guidelines for Writing

How to start

Begin your sketches with a simple, basic idea: a sound you like, a group of pitches, an interesting harmony, an attractive rhythm pattern, an idea for lyrics, and so on.

Next step

Think out a number of possibilities for developing, expanding, exploiting, and contrasting your basic idea.

For example,

• A group of pitches can be played forward, backward, upsidedown, or with its order rearranged.

• You can keep the overall *shape* of a pitch group (the way it moves up and down), but change it by opening up or tightening the distance (interval) from one note to the next.

• The same pitch group can be varied by changing its speed, meter, or rhythm . . . or by changing its "color" through changes of instrumental register (high vs. low).

• A rhythmic idea, no matter how simple, can be stretched, tightened up, fragmented, or transformed into a repeated figure.

• A rhythmic idea can be applied to different pitch groups, or used to give movement to your favorite chord progression.

• A harmony can be intensified by adding "color" tones (7th, 9th, added 6th, suspended tones, etc.); or softened by subtracting chord tones; or given a refreshed sound by the way you voice the harmony on your instrument.

• Consider the kind of lyrics you have in mind, and their form. Will they convey a message, a feeling, or set a mood? Can they be in straightforward English prose, or must they be fit into a rhyme scheme to be effective? Is there a central word, phrase, or idea that you want to keep coming back to?

How to continue

Try to keep a relaxed attitude toward your piece, and an open mind about new ideas that almost always turn up while you're experimenting with your sketches. Above all, *don't lock yourself into one way of thinking.* After a certain point, a piece may have its own ideas about the way it should develop; don't try to force it into a cookie mold! Let it grow and breathe.

Problem-solving

1. If you can't get started, make a list of ways (write a memo to yourself) in which you can develop a simple, basic idea. Then begin experimenting.

2. If you get stuck, bored, frustrated, or run out of ideas, try to be more objective about your piece. Stop, think things out, and try to isolate your problem. Work out fresh combinations of pitches, chord progressions, rhythms, or words and phrases of your lyrics.

3. If your basic material seems dull, you may not be pushing experimentation to its limit. Unpromising material may yield good results if you stay loose and keep exploring the possibilities that are locked inside of it and still hidden.

4. If your piece is getting monotonous, redesign it with more variety: Does the melody keep hanging around the same pitches? Is a harmony too plain? Is your chord progression too old-fashioned, or too repetitive? Are the rhythms too square? Are the lyrics dull? Are the accompaniment figures lifeless?

5. If your music seems shapeless, or tends to wander aimlessly, try to reorganize your materials into clearly defined sections with definite character.

ABOUT WRITING MUSIC
continued

Then, perhaps, tie the sections together by threading a specific idea through all of them. Work for unity with variety so that discernable shapes hang together.

And finally . . .

Keep in mind that false starts, mistakes, misjudgments, hard work, and getting bogged down are all a natural part of the creative process. If you know that, you can ride out the rough sessions (the hair-tearing ones) and keep going. Few things match that joy of seeing the problems melt away, the ideas fall into place, and that moment when your music—done, copied out, titled, and signed—is alive, well, and out into the world on its own. ♩

* * * *

BUILDING A MELODY, PART 1
the composer's workshop

by *Ronald Herder*

BIRTH OF A MELODY

What we're now going to explore is the way melodies can be built from scratch by inventing, and then manipulating, a small group of pitches:

a 3-note sample

a 4-note sample

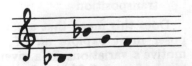

a 5-note sample

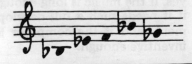

THE MELODIC MOTIVE

In each one of these samples, the small pitch-group forms the composer's "first melodic thought" — or what is traditionally labeled a *melodic motive.*

Each melodic motive is short and simple. Each one establishes the composer's basic melodic idea. Each one gives its tune its first memorable impact on the listener's ear.

CELLS

Each melodic motive is a rich, compact "cell" (a small organic unit) from which a new "organism" may develop. For the composer, that organism-to-be is the complete melody that will grow from small beginnings.

Exploitation of the motive (by repetition, development, or contrast) leads to the longer phrase. And the composer's response to that initial phrase (by repetition, development, or contrast) eventually leads to the building of an entire melody.

But how is this done? What's the next step?

THE BASIC SHAPE

Every melodic motive has a basic shape formed by the way its pitches rise or fall:

. . . a straight-line drop . . .

Continued on next page

269

... a straight-line rise ...

Prelude No. 6, Op. 28 (Chopin)

... an up-down curve ...

... a winding down-up curve ...

Invention No. 9 (Bach)

... and so on, through a gamut of designs.

As we will see in a moment, this sense of shape is fundamental to the growth of a melody: for shape has identity and elasticity — in short, something a composer can play with.

MANIPULATING THE MOTIVE

If we think of the motive as a basic "building block," and of shape as its most important feature, we are ready to explore ways to build a melody by manipulating the motive.

Here are a few typical devices:

1. TRANSPOSE THE MOTIVE

In this technique of melody-building, the motive is repeated, but starts on a new pitch. Shape is identical, and basic intervals (2nds, 5ths, etc.) are the same.

(a 4th higher)

Invention No. 9 (Bach)

m.1

m.2 (a 2nd higher)

2nd Piano Concerto (Rachmaninoff) (slow movement)

mm.28-29

mm.31-32 (a 3rd lower)

2. EXPAND THE MOTIVE'S INTERVALS

In this technique, the motive's shape remains the same, but some or all of its intervals are opened up: 3rds become 4ths (or larger), 5ths become 6ths (or larger), and so on.

Prelude No. 6 (Chopin)

---

3. CONTRACT THE MOTIVE'S INTERVALS

As before, the motive's shape remains the same, but some or all of the intervals are tightened up: 6ths become 5ths (or smaller), 4ths become 3rds (or smaller), and so on.

One inventive example of this technique will do for the time being: Cootie Williams' and Thelonious Monk's jazz classic *'Round Midnight*. Notice how the composers have combined the technique of interval-tightening with the technique of transposition:

m.1

m.3 (a 4th higher)

m.5 (a 7th higher)

COMBINATIONS

'Round Midnight introduces the writing approach of using two or more motivic manipulations at the same time:

- contraction + transposition
- expansion + transposition
- contraction + expansion
- contraction + expansion + transposition

Does this mean that a composer must explore *all* of a motive's variations in a given piece of music? Obviously not, if the piece is restricted to a thirty-two-bar tune; but possibly yes, if the music is long enough, if it needs such a full development, and if the composer is inventive enough.

Musical examples used by permission of Warner Bros., Inc.

In 'Round Midnight, Williams and Monk created a tightly-knit and expressive classic without going further than the variations shown above. But under different writing circumstances, the motive *might* have undergone any number of variations without disturbing its overall feeling or its basic shape — for example:

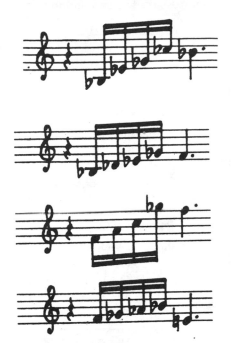

WE PASS THE BALL TO YOU

In the popular and classical literature, the melodic motive — that rich, compact cell of notes — is truly a generator that can drive an entire piece.

Although the manipulative techniques we've touched on are but a small part of the composer's craft (we'll leave the balance for future sessions), they are already grist for your mill as sight-reader, performer, or composer.

When you read, focus your attention on melodic shapes and the interplay of motives. You will play all the better for it, and with quicker perception of patterns and melodic construction.

When you perform, structure your interpretations, variations, and improvisation on the concepts of shape and design.

And when you compose, take your fair share of the writer's techniques without hesitation or limitation. The motives will be yours, but the craft belongs to all of us.   ▽

GETTING IT:
A Practical Approach to Composing

PART 2

—by Ronald Herder

Hollywood scene. Close-up: Beautiful wife (fresh hairdo) stirs in sleep. Hears distant sounds of piano. Opens eyes. 3 a.m. Smiles, throws off covers, rushes to hall overlooking lavish living room. (Piano up full, rich, lush.) Clutches railing, stares down, hand to parted lips. Cross-cut to: Beautiful husband-composer-pianist (stylishly rumpled hairdo) thunders over keyboard of 12-foot concert grand (freshly polished; no loose change on lid). Gorgeous melody. Eyes closed in creative ecstacy. Sound of full orchestra accompanying (hidden in giant kitchen?). Wife's face superimposed on music rack, streaming tears (face, not rack). She thinks (prerecorded voice-over): "Max! Max! Your concerto! You've found The Theme! All these months! Oh, Max!" Long shot, slow dissolve: Living room becomes full stage; Max's pajamas become full-tailed tux; piano now 20-foot concert grand (loose change not possible on polished full-tilted lid); lights up on 300-piece orchestra behind piano. Camera recedes: Packed concert hall, glistening chandeliers. Concerto, with The Theme blasting on both barrels, thunders to end. Audience wild. Wife cries in balcony (hairdo still OK): "Max! Your Theme! Your Music!" Max finishes; takes bow (hairdo stylishly rumpled). Fadeout. The End.

Familiar? You bet! So what's the movie all about? The movie is all about Max having Gotten It. Are you and I going to Get It that way? Don't hold your breath waiting. The Idea, The Theme, The Tune, The Big Melody can come this way, but in truth usually doesn't. For most of our writing lifetime, you and I stare at blank music paper . . . sketching, struggling, waiting, erasing, scratching out, going to the refrigerator . . . Where's the Big Tune? Where's The Idea? What if It never happens?

There's another way to Get It which is more of an approach or process than it is a "method." There's no question that it works. It's worked for me and for the composition students who work with me. It can begin to work for you because it allows you to focus on a single element of your music: *its melody.* Focusing on melody does not downgrade rhythm, harmony, texture, tempo, dynamics, lyrics, and so on — all the elements that will eventually play a part in your music. Consciously putting these aside during

Continued on next page

the melody-creating process allows you to fully experience, without distraction, what will become the beautifully organic growth of your tune, your theme, your Idea.

The process works, but I urge you to go about it patiently, and to read my guidelines patiently — and then to apply what you've read with loving care.

To prepare for a walk-through sample of this process, continue reading this at the piano (or with guitar in hand); take your time to absorb each step; and play all the examples.

Step 1: MAKE A SMALL PITCH GROUP.

Choose three pitches. These form your "pitch group" or "melodic motive." Sing them; play them; write them down. My model for this step — and every example that follows — is borrowed from a process actually carried out in a recent session with a beginning composer; they "belong" to her; I've added nothing to them. Sarah (change of name) picked  out the three-note motive — maj. 3rd up, maj. 2nd down — which we mark "O" (for "Original" example). Remember that we are thinking *pitch* only, not rhythm, meter, or tempo. This means that the quarter notes are meaningless.

Step 2: SHAPE.

 Above your motive, draw its shape: Shape is the contour or direction of the pitch group. This shape is a gentle curve; other pitch groups may have other shapes:

Step 3: EXPANSION.

Without changing the shape of the "Original," expand (enlarge) its intervals either partially or fully. Start on the same pitch as before. Sarah's first experiment (#1 below) was a partial expansion: the Original's opening maj. 3rd expands to a perf. 5th (G-D), while the second interval, a maj. 2nd, stays a maj. 2nd. But the next three examples are full expansions.

Step 4: CONTRACTION.

Without changing the shape of the Original, contract (reduce) its intervals either partially or fully. Start on the same pitch as before.

Obviously, a "tight" or small-interval Original reduces the number of possible contractions.

(Notice that a part of this process is to number all examples consecutively. This makes it easier to refer to them later.)

Step 5: TRANSPOSITION.

Without changing the shape of the Original, experiment with expansions and contractions that begin *on any new pitch.* Feel free to transpose examples you've already written; to write new transposed examples; to combine expansion and contraction in a new example. At this point, it's a good idea to keep examples somewhere within a comfortable (but not too limited) singing range; they'll be easier to hear and play. Sarah composed these five transpositions:

Step 6: INVERSION.

Reverse the Original shape:  Then experiment with inversions of your old examples, or create new ones that follow the inverted shape. Sarah's #14 is an exact inversion of "O"; #15 is an exact inversion of #13; #17 and #18 are new.

For your own use, other inverted shapes may look like this:

Step 7: RETROGRADE.

In "retrograde," a pitch group is played *backwards.* For example,

(I told Sarah to avoid a lot of writing by simply *playing* her examples in reverse. That's what she did.)

Step 8: FAVORITES.

It is perfectly natural to favor certain examples (and to actively dislike others). Check the ones you especially like. Here is Sarah's complete set, with her favorites checked off: